Lionel Cantú, Jr., was Assistant Professor of Sociology at the University of California, Santa Cruz, affiliated with the Department of Latin American/Latino Studies. He received his Ph.D. in sociology in 1999 from the University of California, Irvine. He was the recipient of numerous awards, including fellowships from the Social Science Research Council's Programs in Sexuality Research and International Migration and the University of California's Presidential Postdoctoral Fellowship. He coedited, with Eithne Luibhéid, Queer Migrations: Sexuality, U.S. Citizenship, and Border Crossings (2005). After his unexpected death in 2002, the GLBTI Resource Center at the University of California, Santa Cruz was renamed the Lionel Cantú Gay, Lesbian, Bisexual, Transgender, and Intersex Resource Center, in his honor. All author proceeds from this book will be donated to the Lionel Cantú Memorial Award to support graduate students in the social sciences at the University of California, Santa Cruz.

INTERSECTIONS
TRANSDISCIPLINARY PERSPECTIVES ON GENDERS AND SEXUALITIES
General Editors: Michael Kimmel and Suzanna Walters

The Sexuality of Migration

Border Crossings and Mexican Immigrant Men

Lionel Cantú, Jr.

*Edited by Nancy A. Naples
and Salvador Vidal-Ortiz*

NEW YORK UNIVERSITY PRESS
New York and London

NEW YORK UNIVERSITY PRESS
New York and London
www.nyupress.org

© 2009 by New York University

Library of Congress Cataloging-in-Publication Data
Cantú, Lionel, d. 2002.
The sexuality of migration : border crossings and Mexican immigrant men /
Lionel Cantú, Jr. ; edited by Nancy A. Naples and Salvador Vidal-Ortiz.
   p   cm.—(Intersections : transdisciplinary perspectives on genders and sexualities)
Includes bibliographical references and index.
ISBN-13: 978–0–8147–5848–9 (cl : alk. paper)
ISBN-10: 0–8147–5848–7 (cl : alk. paper)
ISBN-13: 978–0–8147–5849–6 (pb : alk. paper)
ISBN-10: 0–8147–5849–5 (pb : alk. paper)
   1. Mexican American gays—United States. 2. Gay immigrants—United States. 3. Gay
men—Mexico. I. Naples, Nancy A. II. Vidal-Ortiz, Salvador. III. Title.
HQ76.2.U5C37 2009
306.76′620896872073—dc22   2008038155

New York University Press books are printed on acid-free paper,
and their binding materials are chosen for strength and durability.
We strive to use environmentally responsible suppliers and materials
to the greatest extent possible in publishing our books.

Manufactured in the United States of America
c   10 9 8 7 6 5 4 3 2 1
p   10 9 8 7 6 5 4 3 2 1

This is dedicated to all those people who have believed in me and supported me throughout my graduate career. To my mother and father, Rosario and Lionel Cantú, my sisters Rose and Rachel and my brother Charles, and my grandmother Herlinda G. Reyes—I love you.

Lionel Cantú

Contents

Acknowledgments

In the research study that formed the basis for *The Sexuality of Migration*, Lionel Cantú thanks "the numerous individuals and organizations (the Lesbian and Gay Immigration Rights Task Force, Inc. [especially the Los Angeles chapter, Immigration Equality], the International Gay and Lesbian Human Rights Committee, the Los Angeles Gay and Lesbian Center, the Orange County Center, Immigration Equality, the Delhi Center, Bienestar, and The Wall-Las Memorias) who participated in this research project and shared with me their professional expertise, personal experiences, and insights. I owe a special thanks to the many men who shared their lives and thoughts with me.

I also want to acknowledge the numerous scholars who have, either directly or indirectly, informed or shaped my theoretical development, including Tomás Almaguer, Joseph Carrier, Stephen Murray, Pierrette Hondagneu-Sotelo, George Sanchez, and Ramon Torrecilha. I would like to express my gratitude to my dissertation committee members, David A. Smith, Raúl Fernández, and Rhona Berenstein, and chair, Nancy Naples—thank you for your support and faith in my scholarship.

In addition, my research was supported by the American Sociological Association's Minority Fellowship Program, the Social Science Research Council's (SSRC) International Migration Program Minority Summer Fellowship, the SSRC Sexuality Program's Dissertation Fellowship, a Dissertation Fellowship from the Ford Foundation, and a grant from the Center for Latinos in a Global Society at the University of California, Irvine (UCI).

I think it is also appropriate to acknowledge affirmative action programs that opened doors for me. Also, the programs in women's studies and Chicano/Latino studies deserve a special thanks.

Finally, I want to acknowledge the love and support of those dearest to me, including my family, members of the Dissertation Liberation Army (Chrisy Moutsatsos, Ester Hernández, Vivian Price, Clare Weber, Jose Alamillo, Jocelyn Pacleb, Karen Kendrick, and Chelsea Starr), Michelle

Madsen Camacho, Stella Ginez, Denise O'Leary, and two special men who put up with so much: Donald Gausman and Hernando Molinares. Thank you all."

For support of his work on chapter 5, Lionel expressed his "heartfelt thanks to the many colleagues who have shared their insights and critical commentary on this essay. These include John Borrego, Pedro and Shirley Castillo, Guillermo Delgado, Norma Klahn, Alexandra Stern, Salvador Vidal, and Carter Wilson. Special thanks to Jasbir Puar and anonymous reviewers for their detailed comments and suggestions."

For chapter 6, Lionel acknowledges "the comments and suggestions of the editors [of *Queer Families, Queer Politics: Challenging Culture and the State,* Mary Bernstein and Renate Reimann] and Nancy Naples."

For chapter 7, Lionel "is indebted to the comments of numerous readers, including the editor [Peter Nardi], an anonymous reader, Nancy Naples, Pierrette Hondagneu-Sotelo, Raul Fernández, David Valentine, and the illustrious members of the DLA [Dissertation Liberation Army]."

The editors acknowledge the following publishers for permission to reprint previously published chapters and articles or excerpts from these publications: "Well-Founded Fear: Political Asylum and the Boundaries of Sexual Identity in the U.S./Mexican Borderlands," in *Queer Migrations: Sexuality, U.S. Citizenship, and Border Crossings*, edited by Eithne Luibhéid and Lionel Cantú (Minneapolis: University of Minnesota Press, 2005); "*De Ambiente*: Queer Tourism and the Shifting Boundaries of Mexican Male Sexualities," *GLQ: A Journal of Lesbian and Gay Studies* 8(2002) 1:141–68 (Copyright 2002. Duke University Press. All rights reserved. Used by permission of the publisher.); "A Place Called Home: A Queer Political Economy of Mexican Immigrant Men's Family Experiences," pp. 112–36 in *Queer Families, Queer Politics: Challenging Culture and the State,* edited by Mary Bernstein and Renate Reimann (New York: Columbia University Press, 2001); "*Entre Hombres*/Between Men: Latino Masculinities and Homosexualities," pp. 224–46 in *Gay Masculinities*, edited by Peter Nardi (Thousand Oaks, CA: Sage Press, 2000).

The gathering, editing, and publication of Professor Cantú's scholarship was made possible with the support of the Social Science Research Council (SSRC) in a grant to the Lionel Cantú Working Group. Shortly after his death, a group of Professor Cantú's colleagues began to discuss the importance of publishing his research. The Working Group included University of California, Santa Cruz (UCSC) scholars Olga Nájera-Ramírez, associate professor of anthropology and codirector of the Chicano Latino Resource Center (CLRC); Patricia Zavella, professor of Latin American and Latino Studies and codirector of CLRC; Candace West, professor of sociology; Craig Reinarman, professor and chair of the sociology department; Alejandra Stern, currently assistant professor of OB/GYN and American Culture at the University of Michigan; Deborah Vargas, former UCSC graduate student, now assistant professor of Chicano/Latino Studies at UCI; sociology graduate student Sarita Gaytán; and his UCI faculty mentors, Dr. Ramon Torrecilha, executive vice-president for institutional advancement, Mills College, and Nancy Naples. The editors and the Working Group are grateful to the University of California, Santa Cruz, and to SSRC for supporting our efforts to make Lionel Cantú's work widely available to the academic community and beyond.

Our gratitude to Ilene Kalish, Suzanna Walters, and Michael Kimmel for their enthusiastic support of the project and their helpful editorial suggestions. Sarita Gaytan organized Lionel's files and assisted throughout the early stages of the editorial process. University of Connecticut sociology students Nikki McGary and Brianne Kennedy provided essential research assistance at the final stages of manuscript preparation. We would also like to acknowledge the valuable recommendations for revisions offered by Mary Bernstein, anonymous external reviewers, managing editor Despina Papazoglou Gimbel, copyeditor Emily Wright and indexer Martin Tulic. We are especially grateful to Gloria González-López for her insightful comments and to Eithne Luibhéid for her encouragement and her own efforts to ensure the legacy of Lionel Cantú's scholarship.

To Lionel's family, friends, students, and colleagues: we hope that this book will further ensure the legacy of Lionel's innovative scholarship and inspire others to carry forward his intersectional project.

Foreword

Lionel Cantú, Jr.

In 1992 several events transpired that would, although it was unsuspected at the time, have a profound effect on my research interests and intellectual development. First, in the summer of 1992, *Out/Look, National Lesbian and Gay Quarterly* featured an article entitled "Queen of Hearts: Dancing till Dawn in the Artichoke Capital of the World," by Carter Wilson, which described events that had transformed "Norma Jean's, a rundown Castroville bar and grill, into the hottest Latino gay nightspot between San Francisco and L.A." The story of gay Latino farm laborers and their drag shows in the "Artichoke Capital of the World" so fascinated me that I held onto the article, which planted an intellectual seed that eventually grew into this book.

Several months later, after having moved from San Antonio, Texas, to Irvine, California, to pursue my graduate education, I went out with a friend to an Orange County Latino gay bar. That night would forever be imprinted in my memory. All around were queer Latinos (and their admirers), and I felt as if I had been suddenly projected to some fantastic gay bar south of the border. All night long, same-sex couples danced to *quebraditas* (a fast-paced polka-like jig) with leather woven key chains that announced their home states dangling from their belt loops. And for the highlight of the evening sequined *"travesti"* lip-synched on stage to popular Latin ballads. I met people from all over Mexico and Central America and was astonished at the number of immigrants present. Since I am a gay Chicano, gay Latino bars and nightlife were not new to me, but I was used to the San Antonio scene, where the majority of patrons were Latino but not immigrants. This was a whole new world.

I mention this personal experience because, like Joan Scott (1992) and Patricia Hill Collins (1991), I believe that the experience and my social location as "an outsider within" has informed my theoretical development. The experience seemed to clash with the education and training I was receiving in international migration at the University of California, Irvine, and created a sort of maelstrom of questions for me to which, quite simply, the literature had very little if anything in the way of answers. I wondered what the lives of these immigrants must be like. Why had they been so invisible in the literature? Are their migration experiences the same as those of heterosexual immigrants? Why do they move to the United States? Where do they work? In sum: Does sexuality influence the lives and experiences of these immigrants? And, does it do so *only* for *these queer* immigrants? That is, does sexuality *only* influence the migratory processes and experiences of queer immigrants *or rather* is sexuality a dimension that shapes and organizes *all* migration? This study is an attempt to answer these questions, among others.

Irvine, CA

Editors' Preface

Nancy A. Naples and Salvador Vidal-Ortiz

The Sexuality of Migration: Border Crossings and Mexican Immigrant Men, by Lionel Cantú, presents an innovative study that highlights the intersection of immigration and sexuality, what Cantú terms a "queer political economy of migration." Until recently, researchers working on immigration and those working in the field of gay and lesbian studies rarely engaged with issues of relevance to the other. Cantú was one of the first to address this gap in the literature. He recognized a broader weakness in both literatures, namely, (1) political-economy-of-immigration approaches ignore how issues of identity are both shaped by the immigration experience and constitutive of it; and (2) scholars writing in gay and lesbian studies too often privilege the individual and cultural aspects of identity formation. *The Sexuality of Migration* shifts the standpoint on these interrelated phenomena to the experiences of "gay" immigrants from Mexico and, as a consequence, provides a reconceptualization of the relationship between economic and political processes and national and sexual identities.

Many scholars in the field have anxiously anticipated the publication of this book. Cantú, assistant professor of sociology at the University of California, Santa Cruz, had published several significant articles and chapters in the areas of immigration and sexuality studies before his untimely death, in May 2002. However, this book offers the most comprehensive explication of his innovative research findings.

Since 2002 there has been an exponential growth of research and published work on sexuality, migration, immigration, and their intersections. As we acknowledge these developments, especially in the interdisciplinarity of the work published over the last decade, Lionel Cantú's scholarship offers an important and timely contribution to this new field.

The research on which this book is based was a multimethod, interdisciplinary, and boundary-spanning study of Mexican men who migrated to the Los Angeles metropolitan area. Cantú's interdisciplinary training at the University of California, Irvine (1992–1999), and his subsequent postdoctoral fellowship at University of California, Davis (1999–2000), contributed to his unique ability to identify and analyze the complex forces and everyday experiences that shape the lives of "gay" migrants who have been neglected in prior research on migration.

As a consequence of working with Cantú from the start to the finish of his research for this book and having had the opportunity to discuss the changes he anticipated making to the book manuscript, Nancy Naples, as his dissertation advisor, was well positioned to oversee the completion of this writing project. Salvador Vidal-Ortiz, who as a graduate student at another university became a close intellectual comrade of his during Cantú's dissertating years and whose research in the area of queer and Latino studies dovetails well with his theoretical project, agreed to serve as coeditor.

The Editorial Process and Its Challenges

As editors, we were committed to retaining Cantú's voice and approach to the greatest possible extent. We come to reflect on his work from two different angles of vision. We both consider him a dear friend and an inspiration to us. He was a passionate intellectual and activist. As colleagues, we are dedicated to advancing conversations about his theoretical thinking and empirical work. As friends, we chose to work on this project as a way of remembering him. This process has not been easy. As coeditors, we valued the opportunity to reread his work and to discuss it with each other. Each reading and each discussion brought with it a new understanding of his project. We also experienced sadness for what more he could have contributed had he lived beyond his thirty-six years.

The project of editing and publishing this book took much more time than we both anticipated. Part of the long time frame can be accounted for by the unexpected turns life sometimes takes (more time than she would like to admit can be explained by the birth of Nancy's twin girls, and more time than he would like to admit by Salvador's completion of his Ph.D. and the start of a new job). But some of the time delay can be explained by the grief and loss we experienced each time we turned back to the unfinished manuscript. While not the authors of the material you are about to read, we spent countless hours editing the various articles, book chapters, and unpublished manuscripts in an effort to include as much of Cantú's scholarship as possible and to ensure that the book read as a seamless text.

We have incorporated Cantú's published chapters and articles with unpublished work. Publications that followed the 1999 dissertation offer Cantú's most current theoretical perspective and analysis of the data he gathered (additional articles were published in 2000, 2001, 2002, and 2005). We also had access to Cantú's computer files and looked at other versions of his work to ensure the inclusion of his most recent writing. Because we dealt with several sources, sometimes we found overlaps or repeated text, and we discussed, in every instance, which text to cut and which to retain in the final version of the manuscript. This meant careful cropping or weaving of arguments and conscious decisions about how to continue unfinished points and where it was necessary to provide editorial notes. At times, we wove some of the paragraphs and ideas together with a sentence or a small paragraph to provide clearer transitions from one chapter to the next.

We also updated some of the statistical and organizational information and offered clarifications at various points through the text. These additions are presented as editors' notes. The end result has been a single document that offers a comprehensive book that illustrates all of Cantú's writing that relates to his "border crossing" project. Our intervention throughout the text has been minimal, so as to keep, to the extent possible, Cantú's voice intact.

Our editors' introduction is designed to locate Cantú's work within more recent political changes and to provide a theoretical and political context for his research. In this introductory chapter, we outline the main contributions of Cantú's intellectual project and highlight the work of other scholars who have been in dialogue with him. This was, in our judgment, the best way to maintain Cantú's work as he conceptualized it, while at the same time providing enough context for readers not familiar with his thought until this book's publication. We also offer a concluding chapter that further outlines the contribution of his analysis in light of new scholarship in the fields of sexuality and immigration studies.

We include an afterword by his colleagues at the University of California, Irvine, who participated with him in a dissertation writing group. In it, they describe their intellectual and personal experiences working with him during the 1990s and the importance of his work.

Editors' Introduction

Nancy A. Naples and Salvador Vidal-Ortiz

The Sexuality of Migration examines the role that sexuality plays in processes of immigration and identity formation from the standpoint of Mexican male immigrants to the United States who have sex with men. Viewing the immigrant experience from the standpoint of the "gay" immigrant raises critical questions regarding sexual identity formation in a transcultural setting and the linkages among human sexuality, state institutions, and global economic processes. As Lionel Cantú argues in this book, the concept and identities of "gay" do not translate perfectly into Spanish and the corresponding worldviews of the Mexican immigrants that he interviewed. Therefore, although he uses the terms "gay," "men who have sex with men," "queer," and "homosexual," he does this with the awareness that the translation is imperfect. Cantú puts these terms in quotation marks or brackets to signify their complexity and to reflect this tension, a practice that also highlights his understanding that sexuality is shifting and, therefore, changes over time and across space.

Cantú utilized a multimethodological strategy that drew on ethnographic methods, participant observation, oral histories, and archival data to offer a new way to frame the construction of sexuality in a migratory context. The central argument of the book is that sexuality shapes and organizes processes of migration and modes of incorporation. In turn, the contextual and structural transitions that mark the migration experience impact the ways in which identities are formed and reinvented. As social constructs, the sexual identities of gay immigrants assume multiple and shifting meanings as influenced by structural variables, institutional policies, cultural influences, social relations, and the dynamics of migration. *The Sexuality of Migration* both contributes to studies of international migration and sexuality and proposes a new theoretical framework, a *queer political economy of migration*, for under-standing these dimensions.

Cantú's queer materialist theoretical approach sheds light on how migration and sexuality are mutually constitutive. This book contributes to a relatively new but growing literature that incorporates gender, race, and sexuality in analyses of migration.[1] At the time when Lionel began the research in the early 1990s, few scholars had explored the relation-ship between sexuality and migration.[2] *The Sexuality of Migration* offers an important contribution to the still scarce academic literature on the significance of sexuality as a key factor in motivations for, and expe-riences of, migration. In addition, Cantú's work breaks the presumed rigidity of the border by exploring the experiences of men who have sex with men both in Guadalajara and in Southern California, as well as of men who travel transnationally between these and other locales.

Cantú's long-term academic project involved explicating the discursive and material practice of pathologizing Mexican men's sexualities across many different institutional sites, including immigration policy, the fam-ily and community, and academia. *The Sexuality of Migration* provides a rich ethnographic analysis that adds to the important yet more gen-eral approach of texts like *Sexual Cultures and Migration in the Era of AIDS: Anthropological and Demographic Perspectives*, edited by Gilbert Herdt (1997). Although *The Sexuality of Migration* does not foreground health and HIV/AIDS, it does explore the relationship of sexuality and migration to HIV status. Cantú argues that it has been through HIV/AIDS prevention efforts that "gay Latino" organizing has taken place. By incorporating activities with nonprofit, sociocultural, and HIV-pre-vention community-based organizations as part of his mapping of the larger Southern California landscape for immigrant "gay Latino" men, Cantú shows not only the impact these nonprofits have had in the devel-opment of a "gay Latino" men's culture but also, more importantly, the culturally specific (and negative) readings of Latino homosexualities as risk factors for HIV infection.

Cantú saw his project as a transdisciplinary one and, in this regard, in chapter 1 he refers to Edward Soja's (1996) notion of Thirdspace, "a transdisciplinary project that examines the 'simultaneity and interwoven complexity of the social, the historical, and the spatial, their inseparabil-ity and interdependence'" (1996, 3). *The Sexuality of Migration* addresses gaps in various fields of study by simultaneously problematizing a fixed notion of sexual identity, exploring the complex factors that influence immigration and migration experiences, and challenging current analyses of "otherness" in liberal multicultural frameworks. While the field of immigration studies has a long history and has produced a large number of classic studies (see, for example, Piore 1979; Portes and Rumbaut 1990), few works have incorporated an intersectional approach and even fewer studies have included sexuality as a significant dimension of analysis.

The texts that do attend to sexuality often draw distinct lines between culture and political economy (for an example of this distinction with reference to Latina adolescent mothers, see Erickson 2001; for a different reading on African American culture see Seidman 2002). Cantú's approach calls this distinction into question and offers detailed ethnographic evidence to demonstrate the blurring of culture and political economy in the lives of gay Mexican men. As he explains in chapter 7, "not only do cultural arguments in the literature on gay Latino men serve to create a discourse of difference, but also such explanations mask the structural dimensions that shape gay Latino men's lives." Furthermore, *The Sexuality of Migration* offers a refreshing alternative to publications that stress sexual and gender difference based on oppositional notions of culture (that is, between the United States, or European cultures, and "Latin American" cultures) (Lancaster 1992; Murray 1995).

Cantú's queer materialist approach provided him with a methodological and analytic framework for exploring how "relations of ruling" (Smith 1987) are experienced and contested by Mexican immigrant men who have sex with men. Before he died, Cantú was in the process of deepening his analysis, gathering new data, and broadening his interdisciplinary framework with greater attention to cultural studies and queer theoretical innovations that had developed since he completed his dissertation in 1999. During the seven years that have passed since his untimely death, new scholarship has been published that affirms and, in some cases, builds on his intellectual contributions. Some significant political events and demographic shifts have also changed the environment that contours the lives of gay immigrants from Mexico. One of the purposes of this introduction is to foreground the theoretical influences that shaped Cantú's approach as well as to link his work to recent scholarship and contemporary debates over immigration and sexuality in order to illustrate the contributions of Cantú's work to this larger body of research. In this way, we first place his work within several interdisciplinary fields of study and the contemporary political context surrounding immigration of sexual minorities to the United States, and second, illustrate how his work has influenced the various fields of study referenced in the first part.

Changing Faces of the Political

The events of September 11, 2001, changed much of the discourse on race, ethnicity, immigration, and nationality, as well as religion, as did the U.S. and other allied forces' invasion of Iraq. While Arabs, Middle Easterners, Muslims, and South Asians have been a primary target for violence (Ahmad 2002), and discrimination has evolved to include religious beliefs and other cultural attributes, migrants from many other parts of the global South continue to experience racism and xenophobia that have intensified since 2001. As Vidal-Ortiz (2004) argues, these discriminatory practices enforce a White supremacist nation-building project as well as negatively impact the possibilities for coalitional work among the various people-of-color groups.

Mexicans have been historically viewed as among the least desirable of immigrants to the United States (Cornelius 2002; Gutiérrez 1995). From the violent U.S. acquisition of the Mexican territory of Texas in 1845, which included the stationing of troops at the mouth of the Rio Grande, to the current patrols placed along the U.S.–Mexico border, Mexicans who attempt to cross the border have been met with violence and fear. Those who do make the crossing, including many who have done so legally, face racism and discrimination as they establish homes and communities in the United States (see, for example, Naples 1994, 1996). The debates on the need for tougher immigration laws and the U.S. surveillance of the Mexican—U.S. border (including the Minute Men) have escalated in this post–9/11 era. Indeed, recent years have shown how the conservative U.S. society's focus on "the border" fuses the anti-immigrant sentiment along the U.S.–Mexico line with fear of presumed immigrant terrorists, successfully (and in a frightening way) solidifying notions of "Americanness."

The 2000 U.S. Census reported that there were 35.6 million Latinos living in the United States (U.S. Census Bureau 2001). This represented 12.6 percent of the population, a slightly smaller number than reported for African Americans, who comprised 12.7 percent of the population. By 2003, the number of Hispanics in the U.S. increased to 13.7 percent of the U.S. population surpassing African Americans to become the largest minority population (U.S. Census Bureau News 2004). The Hispanic population grew to 45.4 million and formed 15.1 percent of the U.S. population in 2007 (U.S. Census Bureau News 2008). The number of African Americans was estimated at 40.7 million. Contemporary discussions of Latinos numerically surpassing African Americans reveal the tensions within ethnoracial politics in the United States that serve as an important context for Cantú's research. Debates over immigration control are fueled by the political implications of these demographic trends. The impact of 9/11 has further fueled negative sentiments against migrants from many other parts of the world. These two sentiments come together in recent anti-immigrant publications and political rhetoric that affects racial minoritarian and immigrant communities' coalitional work in the United States and solidifies the national tendency to view foreign as dangerous. For example, Samuel P. Huntington (2004), author of *Who Are We? The Challenge to America's National Identity*, presents the idea of Mexicans as antagonistic to the American dream and as a danger to the Anglo-Saxon and Protestant soul of the country. In such a context, Cantú's analysis of the American social imaginary of the Mexican immigrant in relation to gender and sexuality offers a powerful framework for understanding contemporary anti-immigrant sentiments such as Huntington's (see, especially, chapter 2). His work also highlights the ways in which immigration policy regulates and stratifies citizenship through heteronormative and racist constructions of the acceptable citizens (see chapter 3).

Alongside the growth of anti-immigrant sentiment, we have seen a growing recognition of same-sex relationships through legalization of same-sex civil unions and marriage. Civil unions for same-sex couples are now legal in Connecticut, New Hampshire, New Jersey, and Vermont. Domestic partnerships are legal in California, Hawaii, Maine, and Oregon. As of this writing, same-sex couples can marry in Connecticut, Massachusetts, and New York State recognizes same-sex marriages performed in other states. In May 2008, the California Supreme Court, in a 4-3 ruling, overturned the state's ban on same-sex marriage (Dolan 2008). However, on November 7, 2008, California voters approved a ballot initiative designed to amend the State Constitution and limit marriage to heterosexual couples. Same-sex marriage advocates plan to appeal the new law based on both procedural and constitutional grounds. Many LGBT activists in states across the country, as well as national LGBT activists, have placed the struggle for relationship rights at the top of their agenda. Much of the work of some of the activists who served as informants for Cant''s research is now directed by the same-sex-marriage agenda, although not all same-sex organized communities are rallying behind this agenda.

On November 9, 2006, Mexico City's assembly passed a bill that gives legal recognition to same-sex civil unions, surprising many in the United States who believe that Mexican society is more traditional in terms of gender and sexuality than the United States and other so-called first world countries (Castillo 2006). Against the strong opposition of the Catholic Church and other conservative groups, Mexico City mayor Alejandro Encinas signed the bill into law. However, due to the Defense of Marriage Act, even if Mexico City approved same-sex marriage, same-sex couples would not be recognized as married for the purposes of immigration to the United States even if one member of the couple was a U.S. citizen. Immigration Equality, one of the organizations with which Cantú worked closely, is spearheading a campaign for the passage of the Uniting American Families Act, which would make it possible for U.S. citizens and legal residents in same-sex relationships with someone from another country to sponsor their partners for immigration to the United States.

Yet marriage and the related issue of adoption rights—and what they imply—are framed by a very limited notion of citizenship. The desire for marriage requires a minimal sense of entitlement that many immigrant communities do not have. Thus the political call for same-sex marriage and adoption rights, like other LGBT issues in the past, has its own set of exclusions. Even with the achievement of relationship rights at the state level, binational same-sex couples cannot use this as a basis for immigration by the non–U.S. citizen partner. The movement for same-sex marriage has also garnered intense backlash. States that did not already have Defense of Marriage laws that formally limit marriage to opposite-sex partners are passing similar laws. Conservative religious institutions are leading the charge. For example, in Massachusetts, the Catholic Church is seeking to prevent same-sex couples from adopting through Catholic adoption agencies (Wen and Phillips 2006).

During the last decade, we have also seen an increasing attack against "inside the closet" sexualities, including those of men who have sex with men but do not identify as gay or bisexual (for a review of these attacks embodied in African American men, see Boykin 2005). Scholars have begun to theorize beyond an inside- or outside-the-closet conversation (see, for instance, Decena 2004). The main criticism of this non–identity-linked behavior has to do with public health concerns over HIV infection within communities of color. Government agencies and the media have framed non–self-identified gay men who engage in same-sex sex as having irresponsible, unsafe sex. These men have become the most recent sacrificial lamb in the government's inability to reduce the prevalence of HIV in the United States. Not surprisingly, these men are most often portrayed as African American or Latinos (Mukherjea and Vidal-Ortiz 2006).

Under President George W. Bush's administration, HIV-specific public health funding has been channeled through faith-based communities of color, thereby diminishing the amount of funds available for other community-based organizations serving more diverse populations. As a consequence, queer-of-color organizations conducting HIV prevention work, to which Cantú refers, have disappeared in the last decade, making the challenge to address HIV prevention among gay Latino men (and other gay men of color) much more difficult. For example, the National Latino/a Lesbian, Gay, Bisexual, and Transgender Organization (or *LLEGÓ*) was established in the late 1980s and became an important source of support for community-based organizations conducting identity-based Latino LGBT organizing, sociocultural community building, and HIV prevention. Originally funded by the Centers for Disease Control and Prevention, the organization closed its doors after financial struggles in the fall of 2004. In various parts of the book (see especially chapter 7), Cantú addresses the important impact of organizations such as *LLEGÓ* and local organizations on the lives of the gay Latino men he interviewed.

Theoretical Context and Its Discontents

Cantú's work speaks to and across three different theoretical perspectives. First, he was strongly influenced by feminist standpoint epistemology, especially as articulated by Dorothy Smith (1987, 1990a, 1990b). He drew on standpoint theory in order to explore the social location and positionality[3] of the Mexican migrant men he interviewed. Second, Cantú was also in dialogue with Queer Theory but was critical of the lack of attention queer theorists paid to the political economy of queer lives.[4] He used capital letters to refer to Queer Theory in order to mark it as an identifiable body of academic literature. And third, Cantú was also critical of political economic analyses of migration that failed to acknowledge the way sexuality shaped the lives of immigrants both before and after they leave their countries of origin to come to the United States.

By integrating key insights from feminist and queer theoretical perspectives with political economic analyses, Cantú deepens our understanding of how sexuality shapes immigration and, in turn, how immigration shapes sexuality. His queer materialist approach stimulates, informs, and emerges alongside groundbreaking research on the history and politics of U.S. border control and sexuality, such as Eithne Luibhéid's *Entry Denied: Controlling Sexuality at the Border* (2002), and on the political economy of heterosexuality within the context of Mexican immigration, such as Gloria González-López's *Erotic Journeys: Mexican Immigrants and Their Sex Lives* (2005). *Queer Migrations*, one of the most significant collections in this new field, coedited by Cantú and Luibhéid (2005), brings together important new analyses of sexuality, immigration, and U.S. policy and includes many insightful essays such as "Sexual Aliens and the Racialized State: A Queer Reading of the 1852 U.S. Immigration and Nationality Act," by Siobhan B. Somerville, and "Mariel and Cuban American Gay Male Experience and Representation," by Susana Peña.

In the next sections, we provide an overview of the three different theoretical approaches that influenced Cantú's work (feminist standpoint epistemology, Queer Theory, and political economy of immigration and sexuality) and discuss how he incorporated insights from these approaches to develop a queer political economy of immigration. He envisioned this project as part of a broader effort to produce a political economic analysis of sexuality and, as evident from the research discussed above, his work contributed much to this new and expanding approach. We then illustrate the contributions of Cantú's work to these and other fields of study. We offer further discussion of his contributions as well as assess contemporary developments in the field of sexuality and immigration studies.

Queer Epistemologies of Border Crossing

Cantú argued for sociological analyses of sexuality that did not limit themselves to essentialist assumptions, or individualized aspects of the self. His interdisciplinary approach included an assessment and critique of sexuality studies that fail to incorporate or attend to issues of race, ethnicity, and national origin in relationship to sexuality. An avid reader and teacher of feminist studies, Cantú had already studied the impact of universalizing practices in the lives of racial/ethnic minorities within the second wave feminist movement and could see this taking place in the development of gay and lesbian studies and in scholarship influenced by Queer Theory.

Cantú drew on feminist, and specifically Chicana feminist, readings to formulate his basic critique. Utilizing Gloria Anzaldúa's *Borderlands* (1987), among the work of other Latina and Black feminist writers like Cherríe Moraga (1981) and Patricia Hill Collins (1991), Cantú emphasized the multiplicity of sexualities as they intersected with class, race, national origin, and other dimensions of social and political life. Cantú was aiming high. He wanted to complicate analyses of sexuality and gender, not merely with a gesture toward intersectionality—the simultaneous study of gender, sexuality, race, and class—but by intentionally illustrating how migration is constitutive of sexuality, and how sexuality is constitutive of migration, and in this way, formulating a distinctive kind of analysis. He refers to his approach as a queer materialist paradigm and his goal, that of producing a queer political economy of immigration.

Cantú utilized feminist standpoint epistemology to argue for the power of a "queer" perspective on sexuality and immigration. "By examining immigration from a queer perspective," Cantú argues in chapter 1, "we can better understand how sexuality impacts migratory processes as a whole and not only those of 'queer' immigrants." Feminist standpoint theorists are critical of positivist scientific methods that reduce lived experiences to a series of disconnected variables such as gender, race, or class. They argue for the importance of starting analysis from the lived experiences and activities of those who have been left out of the knowledge production process rather than starting inquiry with the abstract categories and a priori assumptions of traditional academic disciplines or dominant social institutions.[5] The notion of standpoint is conceptualized differently by different standpoint theorists. Naples (2003) has identified three different approaches to the construction of standpoint: (1) as embodied in women's or other actors' social location and social experience, (2) as constructed in community, and (3) as a site through which to begin inquiry, as in Dorothy Smith's approach. Cantú drew on all three notions of standpoint in his work, and he remained sensitive to the importance of viewing standpoint as a place to begin inquiry into the experiences and organization of the immigrant men's everyday lives.

Theorists who contribute to the embodied strand of standpoint theorizing argue that because of relations of domination and subordination, women, especially low-income women of color or others located in marginalized social positions, develop a perspective on social life that differs markedly from that of men and middle- and upper-income people. Black feminist and Chicana standpoint theorists demonstrate that the political consciousness of women of color develops from their lived experiences.[6] For example, in the preface to *This Bridge Called My Back,* Moraga passionately ties the political consciousness of women of color to the material experiences of their lives. This "politics of the flesh" (Moraga 1981, xviii) does not privilege one dimension and artificially set it apart from the context in which it is lived, experienced, felt, and resisted. Literary scholar Paula Moya (1997) argues that Moraga's "theory in the flesh" provides a powerful "non-essentialist way to ground identities" for the purposes of resistance to domination (150).

Rather than view standpoints as individual possessions of disconnected actors, most standpoint theorists attempt to locate standpoint in specific community and political contexts with particular attention to the dynamics of race, class, and gender. This second strand of feminist standpoint epistemology understands standpoint as relational accomplishment. Using this approach, the identity of "woman" or other embodied identities are viewed as constructed in community and therefore cannot be interpreted outside the shifting community context. For her analysis of Black feminist thought, Collins (1991) draws on the construction of community as a collective process through which individuals come to represent themselves in relation to others whom they perceive as sharing similar experiences and viewpoints. She argues that a standpoint is constructed through "historically shared, *group*-based experiences" (Collins 1991, 375, emphasis in original). Cantú recognizes the significance of group-based experiences as he situates his exploration of the lives of Mexican immigrant men who have sex with men in the political, economic, and social context that shapes their lives. The immigration experiences profoundly shape these men's understanding and expression of their sexuality and they, in turn, contribute to an analysis of these experiences as they interact with each other in various community contexts (see, especially, chapters 6 and 7).

The third strand of feminist standpoint epistemology provides a framework for capturing the interactive and fluid conceptualization of community and resists attaching standpoint to particular bodies, individual knowers, or specific communities or groups. Standpoint is understood as a site from which to begin inquiry. Smith (1990a) explains that her everyday-world approach does not privilege a subject of research whose expressions are disconnected from her social location and daily activities. Rather, Smith starts inquiry with an active knower who is connected with other people in particular and identifiable ways. This mode of inquiry calls for explicit attention to the social relations embedded in specific actors' everyday activities. Cantú begins his analysis in the lived experiences of Mexican immigrant men who have sex with men to demonstrate the complex ways in which sexuality shapes all processes of migration and all immigrants' lives. By viewing standpoint as a mode of inquiry, Cantú was able to explore how power dynamics are organized and experienced in a community context as well as to uncover the complex ways in which sexuality influences the migration experience for the men in his study.

Cantú resisted the reductive reading of standpoint that is often criticized by postmodern critics of standpoint epistemology. Some postmodern theorists argue that the notion of standpoint presumes that it is possible to identify and locate what are in fact socially constructed and mobile social positions (King 1994). While standpoint theorists emphasize that the vantage point of the oppressed remains partial and incomplete, a central problematic of feminist standpoint analyses is to determine how partial particular perspectives are (for example, see Haraway 1988). Cantú addressed this problematic by foregrounding standpoint as a site of inquiry rather than exclusively as an embodied identity and by demonstrating how identity "is constructed and draws meaning from marginality" (chapter 1). Taking inspiration from Anzaldúa's (1987) analysis of *mestiza consciousness* and Moraga's "theory of the flesh," Cantú's queer materialist framework maintains sensitivity to the fluidity of identity and the community context for the development of standpoints, as well as the structural relations of power that contour everyday life.

Queer Materialism and Postmodern Theory

Cantú developed his queer materialist approach in dialogue with queer theoretical analyses of normalization processes as they are accomplished in everyday life through social practices, discourse, and the production of knowledge (see Foucault 1990 [1978]). The significance of Queer Theory for Cantú's work is especially evident in the way in which he resists imposing a fixed sense of identity onto the Mexican immigrant men he interviewed. He shifts between referring to these men as "men who have sex with men," as "gay men," and as "queer men." This slippage should not be seen as an inconsistency in the text. Rather, it should be viewed as an expression of the limitation of existing identity categories in capturing the self-identity of the men in the study—not because they were Mexican, or could not identify as gay, but because Cantú's study included a truly heterogeneous group of men. He was critical of the limited identity categories available in the sociological literature on sexualities, and he tried to capture the shifting sexual identifications of the men in his study by changing the terms he used throughout the text and by calling attention to the limitations of the terms he used. When he did use the identity construction "gay," he typically bracketed the word to reflect his discomfort with the limitations of this label as it applied to the men in his study. We have styled his use of the terms "gay" and "queer" in italics at first, in order to emphasize their contested use.

Many other scholars in the interdisciplinary fields of gay and lesbian studies and Queer Theory have also questioned the intelligibility of a gay or lesbian subject.[7] Given the interest in political representation that served as the cornerstone of gay and lesbian studies within the academy, the limits and possibilities of identity categories are much debated among gay and lesbian scholars. In contrast, Queer Theory does not operate from politics that depend on representational practices. A primary source of Queer Theory's emergence, in contrast to gay and lesbian studies, was the need to destabilize identities that serve as the basis of identity politics (see Butler 1990). As a postmodern epistemology, Queer Theory contends that identities are fluid, and not reduced to biological causality (Sedgwick 1990). Moreover, queer theorists point out that binaries such as homosexual/heterosexual are part of regulatory regimes and that identities flowing from these systems are oppressive (see, for example, Butler 1991). Queer Theory posits that these identities need not be eliminated altogether but should be suspended and challenged (Turner 2000). As a case in point, Butler's (1991) work, as framed in "Imitation and Gender Insubordination," opens up and troubles the use of identity categories that may themselves function as part of homophobic "regulatory regimes" (13–14). Most recently, scholars such as David Valentine (2003) and Vidal-Ortiz (2005) have argued for the bracketing of these identity markers to avoid an automatic imposition of normative definitions of sexuality identities.

As mentioned above, Cantú had already seen the troubled relationship between these categories of identity, and his movement among "gay," "queer," "men who have sex with men," and even the "gay and lesbian" and "LGBT" nomenclatures should be read as an attempt to destabilize the fixed notion of a "gay" identity or a clear-cut relationship between identities and communities. In doing so, Cantú was bridging sociological analyses with those of queer theoretical paradigms of identity, and was challenging the limits of sociological analysis in this regard (for a recent project furthering sociology through Queer Theory, see Valocchi 2005).

In drawing on Queer Theory's skepticism regarding fixed identity categories, Cantú was well aware of the many critiques of queer postmodernism, including the concern that the destabilization of identities signals the impossibility of mobilizing on the basis of gender or sexual orientation (see, for example, Hartsock 1996). Additional skepticism towards Queer Theory includes concerns that queer postmodernism presents some universalizing arguments, focuses almost exclusively on discourse to the neglect of structural and material conditions (Smith 1998), and emphasizes public sex over a multiplicity of other constructions of sexuality. This last critique is interpreted by some scholars as a masculinized and Anglocentric mode of analysis that limits a much broader theoretical and intersectional project (Harris 1996). As Turner (2000, 168) points out in his discussion of Butler's article "Against Proper Objects," if "queer" is left as an unmarked or undefined term, "'queer' could become the gender- and race-blind utopia of white males."

Queer Theory, Race, and Immigration

Early conceptualizations of Queer Theory were marked by an erasure of Black and other minority sexualities.[8] While Cantú acknowledged these tendencies within Queer Theory, he appreciated the sensitivity of Queer Theory to the multiplicity of identities that shape people's experiences, as discussed above, and to discursive and nondiscursive constructions of heteronormativity (see Warner 1993). Cantú found useful for his project the concept of heteronormativity and analyses of discursive systems that maintain a general sense of heterosexuality as a normative regime. He linked heteronormativity to racialization and discussed the intersection of related hegemonic systems of oppression. Cantú was especially concerned with the ways in which family and home served as sites "where normalizing rules of gender and sexual conduct and performance are taught on a daily basis" (chapter 1).[9]

Recent developments such as the critique of universalizing tendencies in feminist and queer studies, as well as queer diaspora analyses, owe much to efforts to theorize the intersection and "interarticulation" (Butler 1993) of heteronormativity and racialization.[10] In the introduction to their edited collection, *Queer Diasporas*, Patton and Sánchez-Eppler (2000) point out,

The debate over identity's essence or lack of essence has been well-re-hearsed both in gender and in lesbian and gay studies. Similarly, the signifi-cance of translocation is taken as a presupposition among scholars of eth-nic diaspora and within postcolonial studies. . . . Now, identity is viewed as strategic, rather than essential, contingent on, reproduced, decaying, co-opted, in relation to material and discursive factors that, especially in the context of sexualities, are always a complex lamination of local onto global onto local. (2)

These intersectional projects are informed by the theoretical work of women-of-color feminism, especially Black and Latina feminist critiques (see Guzmán 2006). A queer-of-color analytic approach in particular engages a similar set of questions as to the placement of queers of color in historical (Ferguson 2004) and popular discourse (Reddy 1998) by looking at their position in society *as people of color*. Cantú was simi-larly committed to discussions about the position of Mexican immigrant men in relation to mainstream gay male communities, HIV/AIDS com-munity mobilization, the exploitative economy of employing immigrants in the United States, and claims of danger in their country of origin. In doing so, his work problematized the relationship between the state and its assumptions about the heteronormativity of its immigrant workers/subjects.

Cantú also drew on Queer Theory to critique the ways in which much of the literature on immigrants and on processes of immigration ren-dered sexuality invisible. Heterosexuality is the unmarked but taken-for-granted premise of this work (see, for example, Portes and Rum-baut 1990; Suárez-Orozco 1999). Heteronormativity also shapes much of the scholarship on sex, sexuality, gender, and gender roles in Latin America up to and including much of the 1980s. Even when researchers turn to same-sex sexual desire, complex sexual desires and behaviors are often understood within the limited gendered lens of *pasivo/activo* (see Almaguer 1993).

In the late 1980s, anthropologists and social scientists began to take a closer look at same-sex practices in Latin America (Lancaster 1992; Murray 1995). The research that resulted emphasized that same-sex rela-tions in Latin American cultures were dominated by the absence of a gay identity (for a recent version of this model, see the discussion on secrecy/disclosure by Strongman 2002). Moreover, this scholarship positioned Latin American culture as imposing oppressive "machista" attitudes on the lives of some men who had sex with men and violated hegemonic gender norms by playing a so-called passive sexual role. The main point of departure regarding this negotiation of sexuality and gender is the presumption that Latin American society and culture are more oppressive and therefore create greater stress for queer individuals. Sex disruptions understood through gender, or gender presentation (public presentation as a "feminine" person) and sexual desire (particularly receptive anal penetration) were lined up to emphasize that it was the "sissy" or the "third-sexed" individual who suffered the most. While Cantú critiqued this research, he also remained in dialogue with it. As a consequence, he reveals some of the contradictions of this work in light of his own research findings. For example, Cantú points out that some of his interviewees discussed the tensions they felt between the way they were able to express their sexuality in Mexico and the way it was experienced and expressed after they came to the United States. Cantú referred to the process of recreation and representation of sexual identity as a "journey to the self" (see chapter 6). He explains that "I do not mean to imply that there is some essential or 'true' sexual nature that awaits 'discovery'; rather, I utilize the term as a means to convey informants' expressed understandings of their sexual journeys." He emphasized that while this process has specific implications for the Mexican immigrants he interviewed, the notion of the "journey to the self" could be used to capture others' narratives and experiences of sexuality, regardless of migration status.

Building on Cantú's work, Katie Acosta (2005), in a study of gay and lesbian Latin American immigrants living in the United States, discusses the way in which U.S. immigration policy participates in reinscribing heteronormativity by failing to recognize same-sex families (also see Luibhéid 1998, Somerville 2005, Acosta 2008). In order to gain some form of legal residency in the United States, some of her respondents chose to enter heterosexual marriages. Acosta's analysis further complicates the construction of Latin America as more oppressive for sexual minorities than the United States.

Another important contribution of Cantú's work is found in his critique of a pattern of research on Latin American sexualities that blurs the distinction between gender and sexuality (see also Gutman 1996). In contrast, he demonstrated that sexual identity and sexual behavior do not have to be congruent. Cantú argues that the blurring of sex and gender in explaining Latin America sexualities left North American sexual configurations outside of any analysis, and, in fact, framed them as normative in relationship to "third-world" sexualities. In other words, Cantú explains, this so-called sexual-object-choice/sexual-aim model prevailed in large part due to the erasure of racial/ethnic identities. Cantú concludes that the relationship between Western constructs of sex/gender/power and those from Mexico, are "more similar than different" than is typically understood in comparative studies of sexuality (see chapter 4).

Recent scholarship confirms Cantú's discussion of the limits of analyses that present totalizing constructions of Latin American masculinity, femininity, and sexuality.[11] For example, Manolo Guzmán (2006, 95) contests the "homophobic" construction of Latino families in popular culture and gay activism. In her pathbreaking study, *Erotic Journeys: Mexican Immigrants and Their Sex Lives*, Gloria González-López (2005, 4) demonstrates that, in contrast to "a generalized belief that Mexican Catholic women value virginity," the majority of married women she interviewed "were not virgins when they married." As Cantú also found in the lives of the men he interviewed, the women in González-López's study experience a "fluidity" in their gendered experiences "that allow[s] [them] to have sexual agency and pleasure but also to be exposed to forms of control and danger" (4–5). The men in her study also "embraced regional expressions of multiple masculinities which were not necessarily hegemonic" (7).

The development of multiple masculine identities is shaped by diverse cultural and material contexts that undergird the experience and expression of sexuality. Cantú's critique of a reductive notion of culture and analyses based on it captures the dangers in homonormative notions of "the closet" and the need for fixed gay identities. His work also anticipates a growing impatience with postmodern critiques of identity that fail to offer a materialist understanding of sexuality (Hennessy 2000). In a chapter entitled "Latino Cultures, Imperial Sexualities," Jose Quiroga (2000) observes,

> These links between sexuality and culture—as well as links between sexuality and empire—have been questioned, problematized, and nuanced in queer studies, and they have been important in the political and activist discourses around Latino sexual identity in the United States. But many of these discourses have to overcome not only generalized cultural homophobia, but most importantly, the homophobia ingrained in the hierarchical structures of minority politics. (201)

In Cantú's analysis, these hierarchical structures are contoured by the political economy of sexuality. By creating a theoretical and empirical project that investigated the mutual constitution of sexuality and immigration, he broadened the scope of investigations in both of these fields of inquiry.

Political Economy of Immigration

Cantú's queer materialist perspective draws on, and is in dialogue with, political economic analyses, including the now classic article by John D'Emilio (1993 [1983]). In "Capitalism and Gay Identity," D'Emilio argues that the development of a gay identity arose alongside the urbanization that accompanied the rise of capitalism (also see Rubin 1992 [1984]). Cantú identifies a similar pattern of collective recognition of same-sex desire among the men in his study as they migrate from rural areas in Mexico to large urban areas in Mexico and asks, "If the literature on the social construction of a Western gay identity is correct in linking sexual identities to capitalist development, then why should our understanding of sexual identities in the developing world give primacy to culture and divorce it from political economy?" His answer is that among U.S. scholars, "culture becomes the mechanism by which difference is reified," reproducing the imagined distance of "the others" in academic discourse itself (chapter 4). In this way, Cantú's queer materialist analysis highlights the ways in which different traditions of academic research perpetuate ethnocentric and cultural-determinist views of sexual difference.

Immigration scholars such as Alejandro Portes and Rubén G. Rumbaut (1996) emphasize the importance of viewing "immigration as a process, not an event, and . . . the diversity of today's immigrants" (xxi; also see Yans-McLaughlin 1990). Despite their attention to the diversity of immigrants, until recently little attention has been paid to the role of sexuality in shaping immigrants' experiences. Portes and Rumbaut attend to the economic motivation for immigration and the role of family and ethnic enclaves in creating the support and economic incorporation of immigrants into different regions of the United States. Among the many aspects of Cantú's queer political economic analysis of immigration is his examination of the relationship between the sexual identity of the Mexican men he interviewed and their economic dependence on, or economic support of, their families. In fact, Cantú's findings illustrate that Mexican men who migrate to the United States have been able to sustain their relationships with their families, as is the case for many immigrants from Mexico as well as many other parts of the world. In other words, a homosexual sexual identity does not necessarily create a rupture in this pattern of economic interdependence, as is suggested in some studies of homosexuality; however, many of the men interviewed for the study had not come "out"—in the confessional way that gay politics often expects—to their families about their sexuality.

Cantú also queers what counts as a family as he examines the living arrangements of the men in his study. In fact, most of the men he interviewed lived with other "gay" Latino immigrants. As he explains in chapter 6, these households served to expand the social networks of the immigrant men who lived there and functioned much in the same way more traditional heterosexual households did; namely, the men shared household tasks and economic responsibilities and gained emotional support from one another. He concludes, "Perhaps more important than the longevity of these household arrangements are their very existence and the spaces they provide Mexican immigrant men to develop as gay men."

Ethnic enclaves provide new immigrants with spaces for economic opportunities and entrepreneurship. Cantú acknowledges the importance of the notion of ethnic enclaves for understanding the experiences of immigrant men who have sex with men. He finds that "gay Latino immigrants' daily lives are in most ways tied more closely to the larger Latino community than to the larger gay one" (chapter 6). Drawing on a postmodern understanding of space, Cantú explores how "spaciality is more than physical location but also the site where social relations are formed and power is exercised; in essence, where social constraints and resistance is lived" (chapter 6). By linking a postmodern view of space with a political economic analysis, Cantú challenges "queer spatial literature" that "focuses on desire, often at the expense of other dimensions, especially race" (chapter 6).

By bringing a political economic analytic framework to the study of sexualities, Cantú shows how migration itself plays a role in the construction of Latin American sexualities. González-López (2005) highlights this process in her study. She explains that "[h]eteronormative models of sexuality are fluid and vulnerable to forces such as migration and modes of social and economic incorporation" (251). She demonstrates that "regional patriarchies . . . explain how women and men are exposed to diverse, fluid, and malleable but regionally uniform and locally defined expressions of hegemony and their corresponding sexual moralities" (6). With this more complex understanding of the construction and experience of diverse gendered sexualities, it is possible to examine how changes in sexual identities and practices shift throughout the migration process.

Cantú reveals this complexity by exploring the sexual and gendered identifications of his informants in Southern California as well as in Guadalajara. However, he did not stop there. He furthered this exploration in his analysis of sexual tourism (chapter 5) and political asylum (chapter 3). As a consequence of his multisited approach, his analysis demystifies and dislocates the idea of a border. Building on Anzaldúa's (1987) "border theory" and the work of social geographers who emphasize the importance of space and place (see, for example, Rose 1993; Massey 1994; and Soja 1996), Cantú highlights the significance of shared space, or spaciality, as a central aspect of his queer materialist approach. He explores what he calls "landing pads" developed by the *gay* immigrants, which include the more traditional sites such as households and community groups as well as bars and advocacy organizations.

Cantú's political economic approach demonstrates the importance of contextualizing analyses of migration patterns, the law, and policy making with attention to national origin, sexuality, gender identity, race, and ethnicity. Dennis Altman (2001) explains that "a political-economy perspective means we have to recognize class, gender, race *but also* the role of the state; that is, we need to think in terms of structures rather than specific issues or identities" (34). In Cantú's intersectional approach, structures and identities are mutually constitutive. The state constructs identities as well as structures how identities can be performed, shaping what can be understood as a deserving immigrant, an "authentic" asylum case, or a recognizable "gay" identity. Cantú anticipates Altman's call for "a political economy of sexuality, one which recognizes the interrelationship of political, economic, and cultural structures, and avoids the tendency to see sexuality as private and the political and economic as public" (157). Furthermore, Cantú's analysis demonstrates that "changes in our understandings of and attitudes to sexuality are both affected by and reflect the larger changes of globalization" (Altman 2001, 1).

Conclusion

The Sexuality of Migration explicates the power of a queer materialist analysis of immigration to illuminate the intersection of immigration and sexuality in the lives of Mexican men who have sex with men. As emphasized throughout this introduction and as further discussed in the text that follows, literature on the political economy of immigration typically ignores issues of sexual identity, and scholars writing in gay and lesbian studies too often privilege the cultural and local features of identity formation and resistance over the social structural context that informs individual constructions of identity. However, as Cantú persuasively demonstrates, sexual identity is shaped by the immigration experience as well as constitutive of it. Once the standpoint on these two areas of study is shifted to the experiences of gay and lesbian immigrants, scholars are forced to reconceptualize the relationship between economic and political process and national and sexual identities.

Of course, Cantú did not produce his analysis in isolation. He drew on feminist and queer theoretical writing alongside political economic analyses of immigration and theories of racialization. Among his many contributions is the demonstration that Queer Theory is advanced through a strong empirical research project. Furthermore, Cantú's analysis provides a rich, theoretically driven empirical resource that speaks to more recent work on "queer globalizations" and "Latino homosexualities" (Manalansan and Cruz-Malavé 2002; Guzmán 2006), which we will elaborate more fully in our concluding chapter. By developing a materialist analysis of identity, his work also highlights the ways in which the men he interviewed engage in "border crossings" of many different varieties with diverse consequences for themselves. The many important insights revealed in this analysis provide a rich resource for activists and academics concerned with immigrant rights and sexual citizenship.

1

Sexuality, Migration, and Identity

This book concerns the experiences of sexual migrants who cross the imagined physical, social, and cultural boundaries of normative sexuality, gender, and institutions of the state. It offers a *queer* analysis of immigration, gender, and sexuality that is informed by a *queer* theoretical paradigm that attempts to destabilize models based on heterosexuality and to make "regimes of normalization" visible, particularly as they relate to relations among sex, gender, and sexual desire.[1] In many respects my project is a *queer* transgression of academic boundaries. I cross what have traditionally been defined as distinct and separate subjects of inquiry—sexuality and international migration. My goal here is to *queer* migration studies, that is, to expose how migration research and literature is framed by heteronormative assumptions that not only deny the existence of nonheterosexual subjects but also cloak the ways in which sexuality itself influences migratory processes. This is especially challenging, for I seek to examine sexuality not as an additive component or characteristic of analysis (such as with demographic variables of sex or age) but rather as an axis of power relations.

This book also offers a new way to frame the construction of sexuality in a migratory context. I argue that sexuality, as a dimension of power, shapes and organizes processes of migration and modes of incorporation. In turn, the contextual and structural transitions that mark the migration experience impact the ways in which identities are formed. Identity is understood, therefore, as a social construct wherein the sexual identities of *gay* immigrants assume multiple and shifting meanings informed by structural variables, institutional policies, cultural influences, and the dynamics of migration. In my work to understand these processes I develop a "queer political economy of migration."

It must be noted that as in most (if not all) discussions of sexuality, the issue of terminology and labels is extremely problematic. My use of the term "queer" in this text is for the most part academic; that is, "queer" is not a term commonly used by Mexicans as an identity label. "Queer," as used in this text, is a theoretical and analytical tool. In addition, my use of the term "gay" is a matter of convenience. "Gay" does not necessarily mean the same thing in Mexico as it does in the United States but there are similarities. In this text, when I use the term "queer" in the Mexican context I am referring to sexual minorities. Terminology for sexual identities in the Mexican context (and in my research) is complex in part because of translation but also due to the diverse identity labels used by Mexicans. In addition, the social, cultural, and political changes that the *gay* and *lesbian* community is experiencing adds to the fluidity of these labels. The politics of translation is a problem of which the reader should be aware.

This chapter provides an overview and a theoretical outline of the research project. In the following pages I first address the question of relevance—i.e., why is it important to study *gay* immigrants? While my focus is on Mexican immigrant Men who have Sex with Men (MSM), I have also conducted research on a more general population of lesbian, gay, bisexual, and transgender (LGBT) immigrants to the United States through my work with LGBT immigrant rights organizations and the individuals who work with this population (see chapter 2). In this way, I am able to provide a more informed general context of LGBT migration by which I can more closely examine the role that sexuality plays in processes of immigration and identity formation from the social locations of Mexican male immigrants to the United States who have homosexual relations. Because sexual identities are fluid and are shaped by structural and cultural influences, there is no monolithic "natural" label that can be used to categorize a group of men who engage in homosexual relations and have a variety of identities. Therefore, terms such as "gay," "homosexual," and even "MSM" as used within this text denote unstable categories and are adopted for ease of presentation. They do not indicate unquestioned acceptance of these terms by the men in this study who have same-sex sexual relationships.

My primary focus on men is not meant to imply that women's sexuality is irrelevant to the study of migration. On the contrary, I believe that, like men's, women's sexuality constitutes a very important dimension of migration but that it does so in gendered ways. My focus on men is therefore intended as an effort to control to a certain extent these intersecting dimensions of gender and sexuality so as to enable clearer analysis of the way gender, race/ethnicity, culture, and socioeconomics intersect with "sexual migration" among one of the largest ethnic immigrant groups to the United States.

Viewing the immigrant experience from the standpoint of the gay immigrant raises critical questions regarding sexual identity formation in a transcultural setting and the linkages among human sexuality, state institutions, and global economic processes. I examine the following research questions: (1) How is Mexican migration to the United States influenced by sexuality? (2) Do gay Mexican male migrants have alternative reasons for migration and modes of incorporation (e.g., social networks and ethnic enclaves), as a result of their sexual orientation, than those posed by the current research on migration? (3) How do gay Mexican immigrants adapt to, negotiate, and resist the constraints of their marginalization (in terms of their sexual orientation, gender, race/ethnicity, class, and legal status)? (4) How is sexual identity among Mexican men shaped by sociostructural and migratory factors? (5) What is the relationship of sexual identity to gender identity and definitions of masculinity?

I employ a multimethod approach for gathering and analyzing data that was collected from January 1995 to December 1998. There are in essence four separate but related components to the research project: ethnographic research, interviews with key informants in the United States, interviews with Mexican MSMs in Guadalajara, and oral histories of gay men who migrated to the United States. In the United States, there were two main ethnographic sites where this study was conducted. The primary site was the greater Los Angeles area. Most of the research was conducted in Los Angeles and Orange Counties, but some data was also collected in San Bernardino and Riverside Counties. The greater Los Angeles area is an ideal site for this research due to its large Mexican immigrant communities and the existence of various "gay neighborhoods" and commercial locations that serve gay Latino[2] populations. In addition, the area is home to several community organizations that serve either gay immigrants or Latino MSMs. There are also several gay community centers throughout the area, including the L.A. Lesbian and Gay Community Center, which make the area an ideal location for this research.

Although my primary research site was within the United States, I also collected ethnographic data in Guadalajara, Mexico, in the state of Jalisco, for a little over two weeks in June 1998. While this is, of course, a very short period in which to conduct an in-depth ethnographic study, I had several relative advantages that aided immensely in my data collection. First, I was able to stay with a gay male couple who lived on the outskirts of the city. I had befriended one of the pair during his visit to the United States a year earlier and as "luck" (my luck) would have it, his partner had recently quit his job and was more than happy to escort me throughout the city. The second advantage I had was that research participants and friends in the United States linked me with their contacts in the city. Guadalajara was chosen as an ethnographic site for three main reasons: (1) Guadalajara has a significant gay and lesbian population (it is sometimes referred to as the San Francisco of Mexico because it has significant social spaces for gays and lesbians, however, unlike in San Francisco, there is an overall intolerance towards gays and lesbians in Guadalajara), (2) previous research on homosexuality in Mexico has, for the most part, been conducted either in Mexico City or Guadalajara, and (3) approximately two-thirds of my U.S.–based participants were from the state of Jalisco, of which Guadalajara is the capital.

The ethnographic research techniques used throughout the research project included participant observation, field notes, and archival research. Participant observation techniques were employed during the monthly meetings of Immigration Equality, the Los Angeles chapter of the Lesbian and Gay Immigration Rights Task Force, and fieldnotes were taken during special events sponsored by the L.A. Lesbian and Gay Community Resource Center and other events attended by LGBT immigrants. These same methods were employed with other organizations with which I did research, including the Delhi Center and Bienestar. Archival resources of the L.A. Lesbian and Gay Community Resource Center, the Lesbian and Gay Immigration Rights Task Force, Inc. (New York), and other LGBT resources also informed this project.

Interviews with key informants who work with LGBT immigrants, in particular LGBT Latinos and/or LGBT HIV-positive clients, were conducted to gain a greater understanding of the characteristics and issues that are important to this segment of the LGBT immigrant population. I conducted interviews with twelve key informants who work with either the more general gay immigrant or the Latino immigrant communities. For several years I fostered relationships with Latino organizations that work with MSMs, such as the Delhi Center of Santa Ana, California, and Bienestar, which has offices throughout the greater Los Angeles area. In addition, I've worked with a gay immigrant rights group named Immigration Equality that meets out of the L.A. Lesbian and Gay Center in Hollywood.

In-depth interviews with ten Mexican MSMs and ethnographic research in Guadalajara allowed me to explore the experiences of men who have *not* emigrated to the United States. The interviews were collected through both a snowball sampling technique and direct requests for interviews of men whom I met in Guadalajara. This formal interview data is supplemented by field notes of my observations and informal conversations from the various sites in the everyday lives of Guadalajaran MSMs. In this way, I am able to provide a more informed context by which I can examine the role that sexuality plays in processes of immigration and identity formation from the social locations of Mexican male immigrants.

Oral histories of twenty Mexican immigrant MSMs were collected utilizing a snowball sampling technique through contacts made with gay Latino organizations. The interview schedule was informed by both the literature on sexuality and migration and the information gathered from the other research components of the research project, such as key informant interviews. Oral histories provide a more in-depth study of the everyday lives of a segment of the LGBT immigrant population by uncovering dimensions of sexuality, gender, and migratory processes as part of the transcultural experience and included the following themes: childhood experiences, family relations and activities, religion, education, employment history, social networks, intimate relationship histories, reasons for migration, intended purpose of migration, adaptation to the new environment, changes in self-perception, and self-perceived important life events.

Why Study Queer Immigrants?

A common reaction I first received when I expressed my interest in studying LGBT immigrants was, "Why?" To some, the subject seemed too specific and not generalizable. In essence, the LGBT immigrant population could not possibly represent a "significant" proportion of all immigrants and thus the research project itself could not bear any "significance." I believe that the study of LGBT immigrants is indeed significant, in terms of both policy and theory, and it is in part the aim of this project to reveal *why*.

Although my interest in gay immigrants arose in 1992, my research with gay and lesbian immigrants actually began to take shape in January 1995 at a meeting held at the Los Angeles Gay and Lesbian Community Center. A legal seminar was conducted at that time to educate queer immigrants about immigration law and the effects of Proposition 187 passed less than two months prior to that meeting. Proposition 187, the ballot initiative passed by California voters on November 8, 1994,[3] denied public social services, publicly funded health care, and public education to people who are suspected of being illegal immigrants. Soon after, a support and education group named Immigration Equality was formed by lesbian and gay immigrants. This group continues to meet at the center on a monthly basis. These immigrants are not a homogenous group by any definition. Differences in class, nationality, legal status, and motivations for seeking U.S. citizenship rights exist among them—and they also differ in the ways in which they identify themselves and their relationship to gay and ethnic communities.

By examining immigration from a queer perspective we can better understand how sexuality impacts migratory processes as a whole and not only those of queer immigrants. The knowledge gained from this perspective is perhaps best articulated by Dorothy Smith (1987). Smith's formulation of everyday-world standpoint epistemology offers keen insights into understanding, from a feminist perspective, the institutional workings of power that she calls "the relations of ruling." She explains,

> "Relations of Ruling" is a concept that grasps power, organization, direction, and regulation as more pervasively structured than can be expressed in traditional concepts provided by the discourses of power. . . . When I write of "ruling" in this context I am identifying a complex of organized practices, including government, law, business and financial management, professional organization, and educational institutions as well as the discourses in texts that interpenetrate the multiple sites of power. (1987, 3)

Thus, the "queer standpoint" perspective makes visible the heteronormative power infused not only into U.S. immigration policy but also into the academic discourses of migration itself. This means that sexuality, as a dimension of power, has in fact shaped *all* migration in its practice, regulation, and study in profound yet "invisible" ways. The queer standpoint reveals not only how "homosexuality" as a marginal sexuality influences migration but also how "heterosexuality" as a normative regime shapes the social relations and processes of migration.

In the following section, I provide a theoretical outline for an understanding of the sexuality of migration. In order to examine the multiply constituted dimensions of identity and their relationship to the structural influences of a global political economy, it is necessary to integrate and dialogue with what are conventionally the disparate literatures of sexuality, gender, migration, geography, and feminist critiques of the state. My aim in this chapter is not to review these bodies of literature (greater emphasis on select works are discussed in other chapters) but rather to provide a skeletal framework from commonalities between them. Despite the seeming disparity of the literatures mentioned, there are some continuities that have become more apparent over the course of this project. The process of being able to "see" these continuities was aided by Edward Soja's (1996) conceptualization of Thirdspace. As he describes it, Thirdspace is a transdisciplinary project that examines the "simultaneity and interwoven complexity of the social, the historical, and the spatial, their inseparability and interdependence" (1996, 3).

Queering the Political Economy of Migration

A queer theoretical framework by its very logic resists definition and stability (Jagose 1996). As a result, it has become both an area of growing influence and an entrenched resistance in the social sciences. These tensions and contradictions are due in part to an increased focus on issues of identity (including that of nation, race/ethnicity, gender, and sexuality) among scholars from a variety of disciplines with different theoretical perspectives and empirical concerns. Yet these tensions are rooted in Queer Theory itself, descended from the more modernist concerns of early gay and lesbian studies scholars and the postmodern influence of semiotics and the work of Michel Foucault.

Queer theorists more closely aligned with the semiotic tradition have built upon Foucault's assertion that sexualities and identities can only be understood through discursive strategies and an "analytics of power" that examines the multiple sites where normalization occurs through discourse and knowledge production.[4] However, an "analytics of power" restricted purely to an examination of textual discourse, void of a material context, is obviously limited. There are, of course, numerous normalizing sites, including the body (which has received particular attention as an inscribed "text"), but my concern here lies with that of the family. As I demonstrate below, the family and the home (or household) is a site where normalizing rules of gender and sexual conduct and performance are taught on a daily basis.

More recently there has been a move toward a queer materialist paradigm that asserts that "all meanings have a material base" from which cultural symbols and identities are constructed (Morton 1996).[5] Furthermore, it is "the examination of the complex social conditions (division of labor, production, distribution, consumption, class) through which sexual preference/orientation, hierarchy, domination, and protest develop dialectically at a particular time and place" (Bennett 1996, 382). Thus, in this section I briefly outline a queer materialist paradigm for analyzing the social relations among family, migration, and sexual identity.

The link between "gay" identity and socioeconomic forces[6] has been asserted by gay and lesbian studies scholars since at least the late 1960s with the work of Mary McIntosh (1968) and Jeffrey Weeks (1977). In his seminal article, "Capitalism and Gay Identity," John D'Emilio (1993 [1983]) asserts that the modern construction of a gay identity is the result of capitalist development and the migration of homosexuals to urban gay communities in San Francisco, Los Angeles, Chicago, and New York after World War II. In a similar vein, Gayle Rubin argues that gay identity is a result of the rural-to-urban migration of "homosexually inclined" men and women where communities and economic niches (which Rubin calls a "gay economy") were formed on the basis of a shared identity as an "erotic minority" (1992 [1984]).

Key to these arguments is an understanding of how capitalist development has shaped and transformed family relations and structure. D'Emilio argues, "Only when individuals began to make their living through wage labor, instead of parts of an interdependent family unit, was it possible for homosexual desire to coalesce into a personal identity—an identity based on the ability to remain outside the heterosexual family and to construct a personal life based on one's attraction to one's own sex" (1993 [1983], 470). D'Emilio's argument thus expanded the historical materialist understanding of the patriarchal heterosexual family structure long argued by feminists (see, for example, Donovan 1992; Hennessy and Ingraham 1997) and even Engels (1993 [1942]) and made more evident the relationship between the political economy of the modern family and sexual identity, asserting that the economic interdependence of family members constrained "gay" identity formation and that these bonds were loosened by capitalist development.

Yet, the "capitalism/gay identity" argument is limited in several important ways. First, it fails to capture the complexity of stratified power relations beyond a simple class argument even if held to the Western industrial experience. Racial/ethnic dimensions are notably absent and must also be considered, especially when family economic interdependence plays so central a role in the paradigm. In the case of international migration, family economic interdependence may continue to play an important role in social relations and identity even while reconfigured through migratory processes and while new systems of support are created. Second, while most social constructionists agree that gay identity is linked with capitalist development, this body of literature fails to capture the multiplicity and fluidity of sexual identity and fails to conceptualize capitalist development as an international phenomenon with implications for sexuality and migratory patterns on a global scale. Unfortunately, migration studies scholars have in turn ignored this literature marked as "gay studies" and have not examined how sexuality may shape migratory processes.

A queer materialist paradigm is central to my analysis, for such a paradigm allows identity to be understood not only as a social construction but also as fluid—that is, constructed and reconstructed depending upon social location and political economic context. Furthermore, my analysis is informed by what Anzaldúa (1987) refers to as "*mestiza* consciousness" (also sometimes referred to as "border theory"), in which the incongruities of binary systems are made visible, as are the intersections of multiple marginal positions and relations of power. My analysis is thus centered on "the borders" in its conscious effort to incorporate structural dimensions of "the borderlands" into an identity that is constructed and draws meaning from marginality.

Sexuality, Migration, and Citizenship

While there are a number of theoretical paradigms that are relevant to this project, in this section I highlight three broad areas of study that are particularly relevant to my theoretical formulation. These bodies of work are (1) the social construction of sexuality,[7] (2) the literature on international migration, and (3) critical studies of the state and citizenship. Taken together, these three areas of study provide the basis for analyzing the relationship among citizenship, (homo)sexuality, and reasons for migrating.

Following the political economic approach developed by D'Emilio (1993 [1983]) and Rubin (1992 [1984]), Murray (1996) showed, in a study of gay men who moved to San Francisco, that the migratory experience is a diverse one. Reasons for migration and experiences of incorporation varied according to such factors as year of migration, sexual orientation prior to moving, and ethnicity.[8] Social networks were also found to play an important role in the migratory experience. Murray (1996) explains,

> Contrary to claims that gay chain migration does not occur . . . a third of gay men queried moved to San Francisco with or to love with someone they knew before moving. This someone was a gay man in 78.4 percent of these cases. Nearly half stayed with someone they previously knew when they first moved to San Francisco; 81.5 percent of the persons with whom they stayed were gay, and 83.0 percent were strong ties . . . nearly half the gay male émigrés to San Francisco mobilized a preexisting network upon initial arrival. (230)

However, Murray does not distinguish between international and intranational migrants,[9] and his work has received little attention (if any) from migration scholars. Yet other "gay studies" scholars have also suggested linkages between sexuality and international migration.

In Mexico, the international component of gay migration seems to have had an effect on sexual identities themselves. In his research on homosexuality in Mexico, Joseph Carrier (1995) reports that the traditional dichotomous sexual categories of *activo/pasivo* or "active/ passive" among men who have sex with men in Mexico is being transformed by a third category of *internacional,* suggesting a cross-cultural or international influence on identity. In addition, scholars argue that the combination of increased migration between Mexico and the United States, in conjunction with a resistance to discussing homosexuality in an informed manner, has contributed to the prevalence of AIDS among gay Mexican men (Alonso and Koreck 1993; Wilson 1995). These international exchanges contribute to the way sexual categories migrate and to the migration of sexual minorities.

In an attempt to highlight and illustrate part of the theoretical framework of my research and my ideas for "queering" it, I consider it important to point out that there are a number of theoretical migration models that postulate the reasons why migration begins or what the conditions are that perpetuate migration in general. Traditionally, micro level theories focus on the rational choice of either the individual or the household,[10] while macro level theories examine the structural forces of capitalist societies such as the labor market, trade relations, or economic intervention by nations.[11] The neoclassical economic model of migration argues that migrants choose to migrate (or not) on the basis of an individual cost-benefit analysis of such a decision.[12] That is, individuals weigh the costs and the benefits of migrating and base their decision on whichever "side" weighs heaviest. On the other end of the spectrum, world systems theory[13] views international migration as an effect of the disruptive forces of global capitalist expansion. Immigration scholars, working within a world system framework, argue that labor migration is linked to the recomposition of the economic, political, and social structures of a global economy. They argue that the migration of labor is representative of the internationalization of the reserve army of labor and the effects of global economic restructuring (Cohen 1987; Sassen 1988).

Neoclassical economic and world-systems approaches foreground the complex economic aspects of migration. However, influenced greatly by Latin American dependency scholars,[14] students of international migration began in the 1970s to realize that colonial legacies, including economic ties and the political economy of race, were influencing migration patterns (Blomström and Hettne 1984). In the 1980s other "social" factors began to receive analytical attention. For example, Sylvia Pedraza's (1991) "Women and Migration: The Social Consequences of Gender" foregrounded feminist concerns about the gendered process of migration. Part of the reason for the delay in recognizing gender as an important dimension of analysis within migration studies (and the continued resistance to this recognition) has been the limited scope by which migration scholars have viewed the "economic" realm. For many, gender was perceived as a social factor subsumed by the economic or as a variable of analysis, like age or education. Yet, feminists have shown that gender is a significant factor that influences the migration process and experience in complex ways.

While migration scholars argue that social networks link migrants to social, cultural, familial, and economic resources, most studies have conceptualized social networks in terms of either familial relationships or men's labor networks without theorizing how gender itself might shape these relations. Pierrette Hondagneu-Sotelo (1994) demonstrates in her book *Gendered Transitions* that gender is more than a variable of migration. It is a dimension of power relations that shapes and organizes migration. Similarly, sexuality is a dimension of power that I contend also shapes and organizes processes of migration and modes of "incorporation." I want to stress here that gender and sexual orientation are not merely unidimensional variables that should be added to migration studies. They are dimensions of power in a system of stratified relations that need to be theorized and incorporated analytically into analyses of migration.

Space plays an important part in this formulation as well, for in rural-to-urban migration, sexual minorities migrate from a space perceived as constraining to one imagined as more liberal. Furthermore, in his article "Gay Ghetto," Martin Levine (1979) utilizes Robert Park's and Louis Wirth's operationalization of the characteristics of an immigrant "ghetto"[15] to demonstrate empirically that the "gay ghetto" is a spatial reality in the cities of Boston, New York, Chicago, San Francisco, and Los Angeles. Stephen O. Murray (1995, 1996) has also argued that the gay community assumes what he calls a "quasi-ethnic" community formation and that within this community are "homosexual occupations"— that is, a specific gay labor market. However, Murray points to the fact that this "labor opportunity" may in fact lead to downward mobility as positions are characteristically unstable, competitive, and low-wage, largely as a result of the marginal status of gays and lesbians.

Although the literatures on citizenship and on migration are not commonly integrated, they are integral to understanding the social location of gay immigrants both as a marginal group (i.e., homosexual) within the United States's tiered system of citizenship rights and as a "peripheral" migrant group within a tiered global capitalist system. The marginality of gays and lesbians can be better understood if we examine how they are further stratified by gender, race, and class, and how these intersectional dimensions are constructed in the state and in ideas of citizenship. The relationship between citizenship and marginality has become the focus of an increasing number of feminist theorists. For example, with her emphasis on access linked to marginality, Nira Yuval-Davis (1991) argues that a formulation of a feminist theory of citizenship must examine "the differential access of different categories of citizens to the state and the implications this has on relations of domination" (58). She further argues that Marshallian theories of citizenship miss the inclusionary/exclusionary criteria based on ethnic, racial, class, and gender divisions and is also critical of feminist and antiracist critiques of citizenship for their treatment of "both women and ethnic/racial minorities as homogenous categories." She concludes by making the following suggestions for a theory of citizenship: (1) it "should not take the state as a unitary given, but should retain the notion of the state as the focus of the intentionality of control," (2) it "should not assume 'society' or 'the community' as a given, but should see struggles over the construction of their boundaries as one of the major foci of struggles on the nature of citizenship within a specific society," (3) it "should not accept the boundaries between the public and private domains as a given but again as a focus for struggles which determine gender divisions of labour as well as ethnic patterns of cultural hegemony within the society," and (4) it "should develop a notion of difference" in terms of identities and power (66–67).

The analysis of citizenship as a "boundary project" (Jones 1994, 260), offers another useful framework for exploring immigration processes and incorporating immigrants into the national imaginary. Kathleen Jones (1994) critiques the idea of citizenship as "an action practiced by people of a certain identity in a specifiable locale" (260). She argues that "identity should be understood as the contingent effect of citizenship instead of its necessary precursor" (261). That is, citizenship depends upon the idea of the "foreign" or "alien" for its rationale. This notion of the "alien" is, of course, also central to Foucault's notion of the "regimes of normalization"; that is, the gay immigrant is an "alien" on more than one count.

In his study of undocumented Mexican immigrants in San Diego, Leo Chavez (1992) argues that the experience of migration is similar in some respects to a rite of passage (especially as an experience of transition). "Territorial passage," according to Chavez, "can be divided into three important phases: *separation* from the known social group or society, *transition* (which is a liminal phase), and *incorporation* into the new social group or society" (1992, 4–5). As undocumented persons, Mexican migrants assume an "illegal" status that marks them as "liminal" and "outside" an imagined legitimate community (Chavez 1992, 1994). Chavez further argues that the liminality phase of the undocumented immigrant, as an "illegal" and "foreign" subject outside of the imagined community of "Americans," may never end and that incorporation is prevented by social and structural constraints.[16] However, if a Mexican man is marked as marginal (i.e., outside the imagined "Mexican" community) *before* migrating, then a very real *social separation* may precede the actual physical separation of migration. In addition, if the Mexican immigrant is "outed" after migrating to the United States, then a new social separation may occur. Moreover, a gay immigrant's liminal phase may persist regardless of his or her legal status. The gay immigrant is an outsider in more than one respect, for as an "erotic minority" he or she has transgressed society's moral, sexual, and even gender borders.

"Homosexuals" have historically been marginalized by the dominant religious, medical, legal, and cultural discourses. Judeo-Christian religious beliefs demonized homosexuals as "sinners." Medical discourse pathologized gays and lesbians for their "sickness." Legal discourse criminalized homosexuals for their "deviance." Social-cultural belief systems mythologized and dehumanized gays and lesbians as abnormal perverts who posed a threat to "the family" and "society" as a whole. While these examples demonstrate the mechanisms by which institutions of the state regulate the lives of lesbians and gays, a contradiction arises as well. For example, how can sexual repression coexist with the development of "erotic minority" communities?

In *The History of Sexuality* (1990 [1978]), Foucault argues that contrary to what he calls "the repressive hypothesis," modern industrial societies have not increased sexual repression over the past two centuries but, rather, there has been a "deployment" and multiplication of sexualities through the "transformation of sex into discourse," particularly medical discourse (1990 [1978], 36). Foucault finds fault with theories of social inequality that focus on the policing functions of the state through laws and censorship (what he calls the "juridico-discursive" theory of power). He asserts that sexualities and identities can only be understood through discursive strategies and through an "analytics" of power that examines the multiple sites where normalization occurs through discourse and knowledge production.[17] While I examine multiple "sites" where normalization occurs, or where relations of ruling are practiced, I argue that the policing functions of the state are indeed important. This is not a contradiction to Foucault's polemic because I am concerned not with "repression" but rather with regulation and its relationship to identity production. One such "site" where processes of normalization occur for the gay immigrant is that of immigration and citizenship laws and other state policies that I examine more closely in chapter 2. For my purposes here, however, I want to briefly focus on the issues of identity, liminality, and citizenship.

Scholars who adopt a queer performative understanding of identity contest the view offered by historical materialist scholars who argue that sexual identity is constructed from the material conditions of unequal relations of power in a capitalist system. In the performativity model, identity is a discursive formation. In *Gender Trouble,* feminist philosopher Judith Butler critiques psychoanalytic discourse and employs a Foucauldian analysis to argue that gender is a social construction that is inscribed in the body. Butler (1990) argues that

> [a]ccording to the understanding of identification as an enacted fantasy or incorporation, . . . it is clear that coherence is desired, wished for, idealized, and that this idealization is an effect of a corporeal signification. In other words, acts, gestures, and desire produce the effect of an internal core or substance, but produce this *on the surface* of the body, through the play of signifying absences that suggest, but never reveal, the organizing principle of identity as a cause. Such acts, gestures, enactments, generally construed, are *performative* in the sense that the essence or identity that they otherwise purport to express are *fabrications* manufactured and sustained through corporeal signs and other discursive means. (136)

This focus on "the body" as a text is central to the queer ludic paradigm's analysis of identity performances. Here "resignified" gender displays such as butch/femme or drag[18] are subversive "performances" of gender. Like other scholars,[19] Butler envisions the marginal or deviant location as a site for political potential: "resignification marks the workings of an agency that is (a) not the same as volunteerism, and that (b) though implicated in the very relations of power it seeks to rival, is not, as a consequence, reducible to those dominant forms" (ibid.). Performativity describes this relation of being implicated in that which one opposes, of turning power against itself to produce alternative modalities of power, to establish a kind of political contestation that is not a "pure" opposition, a "transcendence" of contemporary relations of power, but a difficult labor of forging a future from resources inevitably impure (Butler 1993, 241).

Latina feminists have contributed a more intersectional queer analysis than is evident in Butler's work. For example, in her book *Borderlands/ La Frontera: The New Mestiza,* Gloria Anzaldúa (1987) theorizes (albeit in a nontraditional way) the political implications of the subject position that she refers to as "*mestiza* consciousness." She writes,

> Because the future depends on the breaking down of paradigms, it depends on the straddling of two or more cultures. By creating a new mythos—that is, a change in the way we perceive ourselves, and the ways we behave—*la mestiza* creates a new consciousness.

> The work of *mestiza* consciousness is to break down the subject-object
> duality that keeps her a prisoner and to show in the flesh and through the
> images in her work how duality is transcended. (80)

Anzaldúa asserts that the liminal "borderland" position, like the performativity model, serves as a site for both political resistance and theoretical analysis. She argues that from the "*mestiza*" position the incongruities of binary systems are made visible, as are the congruities, the intersections, of multiple marginal positions and relations of power. Anzaldúa's argument differs from the performativity model, however, in its conscious effort to incorporate structural dimensions of "the borderlands" (such as the colonial history of the Southwest, racial and class dynamics, and cultural dimensions) into an identity that is constructed and draws meaning from marginality.

Returning to the issue of citizenship, we can better understand how these queer borderlands models inform one another. For example, American citizenship itself impels a performance, a fabricated act by which an actor must convince others that she/he is what she/he purports to be. To function, the performance depends upon both difference and similarity. Immigrants to the United States are impelled to perform certain acts or gestures in order to make claims as if they were "citizens"—whether a citizenship "test," the manner of their dress, or the language they speak. This queer borderlands approach questions binary systems of identity; it allows for fluid and shifting identities that may be context-specific; it allows for a greater agency than the phenomenologically influenced approaches of symbolic interactionism,[20] which tend to be more deterministic (Blumer 1986); and it "fixes" an analytical eye at the precise point where binary systems are challenged and where gay immigrants are socially located—at the margins. Yet, as previously mentioned, queer performativity does not incorporate a historical materialist framework in its analysis—identity is constructed by discourse.

Although not an extensively articulated part of the theory of queer performativity, the queer materialist paradigm provides an integrated concern with place, history, and the social. This latter approach evokes Soja's (1996) formulation of Thirdspace (discussed earlier in this chapter), where those three elements are linked—as in the historical relationship between the citizen and the immigrant, the socioeconomic and political reasons for migrating, and the concepts of the border between

Mexico and the United States. In summary, these are some of the basic tenets of this book's project:

1. Sexuality is understood as a dimension of power that permeates all social relations and institutions.
2. Sexual identities, explicitly "gay" identities, are linked to capitalist development and urban migration. Yet the effects of globalization are missing from this equation.
3. Due to the heteronormativity of mainstream literature, migration studies scholars have ignored scholarship on sexuality and gender and, therefore, failed to recognize sexuality as an important dimension of analysis.
4. Feminist and queer critical studies of the state have linked identities to the power of the state and its mechanisms of regulation and normalization—including citizenship and immigration policies.
5. Spatiality must be included, along with historical and social dimensions, in order to better capture the complex and specific relations that shape the sexuality of migration.

Throughout the chapters of this book, I develop these ideas further and examine more closely how sexuality shapes the lives and migratory processes of Mexican men who have sex with men.

Organization of the Book

The next chapter serves as a historical background by which to understand how sexual norms are an ingrained part of immigration policy that marginalize immigrants who do not "fit" the profile of a "desirable" immigrant. In the case of Mexican immigrants, race, class, and historical legacies obviously shape these relations as well. This chapter analyzes the development of U.S. immigration policy and highlights the shifting heteronormative and racialized assumptions of border control and immigration policy and practices.

In chapter 3, I utilize both discourse analysis and ethnographic data to demonstrate how the U.S. state has in effect created the "gay immigrant" through its efforts to control its borders and regulate its citizenry through what Foucault calls "regimes of normalization."

In chapter 4, I examine the premigration issues that affect the lives of "gay" Mexican immigrant men, including the sociopolitical context for gays and lesbians in Mexico and how Mexican male sexual identity is influenced by normative constructions of masculinity. Previous studies of Mexican male "homosexuality," archival materials, and ethnographic data gathered in Guadalajara, Mexico, serve as the source by which to understand not only the conditions that give rise to migration but also those that privilege (or constrain) the men who remain.

Chapter 5 examines queer tourism "south of the border" and the effects of gay tourism on Mexican sexualities.

In chapter 6, I highlight six of the oral histories that I have conducted that are representative of the different experiences of Mexican immigrant MSMs. Ethnographic data, especially life histories, are analyzed to examine the processes and experiences of migration that relate to the sexuality of migration. I examine such issues as background, sexual identity, reasons for migration, social networks, and adaptation in the lives of these men.

In chapter 7, I take a closer look at life in the United States by focusing on the issue of community among gay Latinos in the greater Los Angeles area. My main concern here is with the issue of space and its importance not only for the formation of gay Latino community but also for the adaptation of gay immigrant Latinos. I argue that gay Latino communities are being shaped by four distinct but intersecting factors: (1) demographic changes, (2) the commodification of Latino sexuality, 3) the institutionalization of both the gay and the Chicano movements, and (4) HIV-prevention programs.

In chapter 8, I conclude with a summary of my research findings and discuss both policy and theoretical implications of queering immigration and analyzing the political economy of sexuality.

2

Border Patrol

Sexuality, Citizenship, and
U.S. Immigration Policy

It has long been held that the Congress has plenary power to
make rules for the admission of aliens and to exclude those who
possess those characteristics which Congress has forbidden. Here
Congress commanded that homosexuals not be allowed to enter.
The petitioner was found to have that characteristic and ordered
deported. . . . It may be, as some claim, that "psychopathic personality" is a medically ambiguous term, including several separate and
distinct afflictions. But the test here is what the Congress intended,
not what differing psychiatrists may think. It was not laying down
a clinical test, but an exclusionary standard which it declared to be
inclusive of those having homosexual and perverted characteristics.
It can hardly be disputed that the legislative history of 212 (a)(4)
clearly shows that Congress so intended.

—Justice Clark, *Boutilier v. Immigration
and Naturalization Service*[1]

Although the literatures on citizenship, gay and lesbian studies, and migration are not commonly integrated, they are integral to
understanding the multiply constituted social locations and identities of
"gay" immigrants. Gay and lesbian immigrants' varied social locations
are sites where processes of marginalization and resistance, nationalism,
and globalization intersect and shape the lives not only of these immigrants but also of others who are in positions categorically relational to
them and whose positions rely upon the logic of difference.

American history is replete with examples of how various definitions
of difference (including race, gender, class, and sexuality) have been uti-

lized to legitimize exclusion, inequalities, and violence. The passage of California's anti-immigrant Proposition 187 in 1994 is but a contemporary manifestation of the xenophobia that periodically infects the nation's psyche. (As mentioned in the previous chapter, Proposition 187 intended to deny public social services, publicly funded health care, and public education to people who are suspected of being illegal immigrants.) The immigrant, as "outsider," is a common scapegoat for the problems of society in times of economic slump, and exclusionary movements provide a means by which unscrupulous politicians can direct attention away from the structural conditions and policies that are causing the decline. While implementation of the bill was overturned by the courts, the passage of Proposition 187 had its effects. The racist sentiment behind the legislation transformed into practice as Latinos and Asian Americans immediately became "suspect" to the extent that some individuals, citizen and immigrant alike, were asked to provide identity papers to prove that they were in fact "legal." Such xenophobia illustrates the contradictory ideas that Americans have over who may actually claim the rights and privileges of being "American." While such ideas have cultural and ideological influences, they become legitimized through definitions of citizenship and the mechanisms by which the state maintains them.

Citizenship is a socially constructed identity that delimits an individual's relationship to a political community (in this context the nation-state).[2] It is a legal identity constructed by the state to distinguish the "native" from the "foreigner," the inside from the out. Yet citizenship should not be conceptualized in simple binary terms but rather as a continuum of stratified relations and legal statuses shaped by dimensions of class, gender, race, ethnicity, and sexuality. Citizenship is a concept that is key to understanding how difference is constructed and maintained by the state and has been the focus of an increasing number of studies that examine the racial and gendered dimensions of citizenship (Orloff 1993; Skocpol 1992). Yet only recently have scholars begun to examine citizenship's sexual dimensions (Evans 1993; Berlant 1997).

Conventionally, democratic citizenship is conceptualized as a relationship of rights and obligations between an individual and the state. In his seminal essay "Citizenship and Social Class" T. H. Marshall (1964 [1950]) examines the relationship between capitalism and democratic citizenship in the British welfare state.[3] He defines citizenship as a status imbued with certain powers, rights, and duties, and as a mechanism by which citizens of a nation progress towards a supposed equality, a process associated with modernization. Marshall argues that citizenship (as a mechanism of equality) works diametrically against the capitalist social class system (which is dependent upon inequality) but that the two can coexist in equilibrium. He asserts that certain inequalities are "legitimate" (for example, income inequality) as they maintain this "balance" (1964, 103). Marshall's work has had a profound influence as a theoretical starting point for much of the current theories of citizenship. However, Marshall's model of citizenship is limited in several important ways, including the fact that gendered dimensions of citizenship are largely neglected, as are racial differences. Sexuality is, of course, not part of his analysis. I assert, however, that there is much to gain from bringing a queer theoretical perspective to citizenship studies, including an understanding of the mechanisms by which identities are constructed within "regimes of normalization."

Feminists have long argued that citizenship, as a site from which to make claims on the state, is an exclusive category that treats women differentially from men (Nelson 1984; Jones 1990; Sarvasy 1994). From this realization has arisen a feminist debate over whether women should argue for the rights of citizens as women who are equal to men (sameness) or as women who are different yet worthy of rights (difference) (see, for example, Rhode 1990). As I will discuss below, this debate also plays an important role in the gay and lesbian movement and in particular the political strategies that gay immigrant organizations "choose" in their struggle for equality. More recently, feminist scholars, especially those situated within Critical Race Theory, have broadened the sameness/difference debate by seeking to deconstruct the notion of citizenship and the ideologies upon which it is vested, such as patriarchy, racism, colonialism, and compulsory heterosexuality (see, for example, Luibhéid 1998). These scholars seek to understand the ways in which the constructions of gender, as well as race, ethnicity, class, and sexuality, intersect across multiple systems of oppression. Examining the heteronormative practices of U.S. immigration policy helps to illuminate the stratified nature of citizenship.

In the following section, I examine how the state, through immigration policy, has produced identities in order to regulate groups of people located within and across national borders. I examine the historical conditions that gave rise to the gay immigrant "problem" and how it relates to other systemic patterns of exclusion, for as Luibhéid (1998) argues, once one exclusion is legitimized, others are easier to create. Thus, while

I focus on sexuality, these mechanisms of exclusion are related to other forms of exclusion such as race and class.

Citizenship: The Borders of Identity

The main mechanism for controlling movement across the national borders of the United States today is, of course, the Immigration and Naturalization Service (INS). The mission of the INS is divided into four major areas of responsibility (INS 1997):

- facilitating the entry of persons legally admissible as visitors or as immigrants to the United States;
- granting benefits under the Immigration and Nationality Act, as amended, including providing assistance to those seeking permanent resident status or naturalization;
- preventing unlawful entry, employment, or receipt of benefits by those who are not entitled to them; and
- apprehending or removing those aliens who enter or remain illegally in the United States and/or whose stay is not in the public interest.

Behind the succinctly stated mission of the federal agency of the Department of Justice lies an inherent tension: the responsibility of "facilitating the entry of *persons*" and that of "apprehending or removing *aliens*." To many, this may not seem a tension at all, but when one examines the history of the INS and questions the processes by which the agency determines what *type* of immigrant is in the "public interest," then these tensions or contradictions become more evident.[4]

The power to define "the public interest" lies, of course, in the hands of the state and immigration restrictions and exclusions are historically rooted in the concern for maintaining that power. The processes by which the state, through the INS (and now Immigration and Customs Enforcement [ICE]), legitimizes migration across its borders depends on its ability to differentiate the citizen from the foreigner, the welcome immigrant from the threatening alien, and thus its ability to identify and categorize people. These processes, however, are shaped by power relations and normative discourses of race/ethnicity, gender, class, and sexuality within the laws and policies of immigration and citizenship.

In her analysis of citizenship and immigration laws, feminist scholar Chandra Mohanty (1991a) asserts that "[h]istorically, citizenship and immigration laws and social policies have always been connected to economic agendas, and to the search for cheap labor. These state practices are anchored in the institutions of slavery, capitalist neo-colonialism, and, more recently, monopoly, multinational capitalism" (23–24). In the United States, the linkages between economic agendas (i.e., the transformation from an agricultural to a post-Fordist global economy)[5] have influenced U.S. citizenship and immigration policies and laws in three important ways: (1) as the labor demands of industrialization grew, the state's role in controlling the quality of this labor also grew; (2) in order to regulate movement across its border, the mechanisms of identification, categorization, and distinction developed by the state became more important; (3) related to these first two dimensions, the state needed to identify "undesirable" migrants who might pose a "threat" to social order and the modernization project; exclusionary policies and the regulation of sexuality through immigration policies were utilized to meet this need (see, for example, Calavita 1992).

By 1790, the U.S. federal government had already set a uniform rule for naturalization, which had formerly been under individual state control. Yet the act of 1790 addressed only naturalization concerns, not immigration. In 1791, Alexander Hamilton warned the nation's leaders that immigration should be encouraged in order to meet the labor needs of the time and ensure the future development of the growing American economy (Calavita 1992). It wasn't until the Aliens Act of 1798, however, that Congress passed the first federal law concerning immigration by authorizing presidential power to arrest and/or deport any alien deemed "dangerous," a power facilitated by the Naturalization Act of 1798, which required the registry of all aliens residing in or entering the country. This early legislation and subsequent immigration laws that would be passed by Congress were justified via section 8, article 3 of the Constitution, which gives Congress the power "to regulate commerce with foreign nations" (INS 1975). In addition, while the INS is currently under the authority of the Justice Department, immigration concerns were formerly under the Treasury Department and then the Department of Commerce and Labor. The very rationale for immigration laws and policies, therefore, has historically been rooted not so much in a concern for national sovereignty but rather in the interests of a capitalist agenda.

While systems of servitude and slavery assisted in meeting labor shortages in the early part of the nation's history, changes in the country's socioeconomic system, including industrialization and expansion, brought new demands, and labor immigration became more important. Immigrant labor helped to satisfy the needs of a growing capitalist economy in two ways: the immediate needs of industry were met by the productive power of immigrants, and future needs were met by the reproductive potential of immigrant families. However, it soon became evident that while America wanted immigrant labor, not all immigrant labor was equal. The productive and reproductive power of labor became a double-edged sword for a state that was also attempting to protect the status quo.

The short history of the first immigration bureau serves as an example of these tensions. Created in 1864 by an act of Congress, the bureau was headed by a commissioner of immigration who was appointed by the president and served under the authority of the secretary of state. The bureau was meant to facilitate immigration and regulate new "contract labor," elements that had also been part of the legislation passed in 1864. The type of labor that this early contract labor law attracted, however, proved problematic, especially under the racialized economic conditions of the Civil War; subsequently, the act of 1864 was repealed in 1868. Biases against certain "types" of immigration had actually started before the 1864 legislation; in 1862 Congress had already passed legislation that prohibited the transportation of Chinese "coolies" on American vessels.

The repeal of the act of 1864 served as little more than a symbolic gesture as tensions increased. The second half of the nineteenth century, marked by economic problems and xenophobia, led to the institutionalization of immigration control. While cheap labor was desired by industry, "Americans" did not welcome the settlement of non-European immigrants in their communities. The 1870s and 1980s were marked by legislation that specifically targeted "Orientals" (i.e., Chinese immigrants), criminals, and prostitutes for exclusion. Thus, as the nation's immigrant labor pool became more diverse, the need to regulate and restrict immigration demanded more formal state interventions. The continuing debates over immigration, contract labor, and race led to the first comprehensive law for the federal control of immigration in 1891. Created by an act of Congress in 1891, the Bureau of Immigration, which was then under the authority of the Treasury Department, was renamed the Immigration and Naturalization Service (INS) in 1906.[6]

Since its creation, the agency's concern with identification, categorization, and distinction among different types or classes of immigrants and their surveillance seems to have grown exponentially. John Torpey (1998) argues that, as a consequence of capitalist development, modern states have expropriated from individuals the legitimate means of movement not only through the policing of borders but also by requiring individuals to depend on the state for an identity. Passports, visas, and other types of "identity papers" are necessary for legitimate movement through the boundaries of state-controlled space, and as Torpey stresses, all other forms of movement become illegitimate (i.e., "illegal"). Identity papers are one component of citizenship and serve the preservation of the status quo—in a stratified system of "citizenship," some are "more equal" than others.

The citizen, therefore, should not be conceptualized as one category but rather as a stratified system that follows an order along these lines: (1) "native born," (2) "naturalized," (3) legal resident alien, and (4) "illegal" or undocumented alien. Each of these categories is in turn stratified along dimensions of race, class, gender, and sexuality. Thus, historically, the white heterosexual native-born American male citizen represented the most "legitimate" of state-constructed identities and subordinated or delegitimized those of other groups, including immigrants. The immigrant categories are in turn subcategorized into desirable and undesirable classifications.[7] It is important to note the extraordinary number of visa classifications. These classifications fall into three general types: visitor, worker, and family member. It should come as no surprise that "family" as used here follows strict biological and legal definitions and does not include any "alternative" relationships, including those of gays and lesbians. Before elaborating on this point, however, it is necessary to return to the matter of how the INS has historically identified and distinguished between desirable and undesirable immigrants.

Restrictions and exclusions have historically been organized along five distinct but intersecting dimensions of race, class, gender, sexuality, and political ideology. Thus restrictions and exclusions have been biased not only against non-European groups but also against those who posed a political or ideological threat (such as Communists and anarchists), those of lower socioeconomic status who might become a "public charge," women (who potentially posed a double threat of economic liability and sexual menace by reproducing inferior races), and "sexual deviants."

The Chinese exclusion acts that were passed in the 1860s and were not repealed until 1943 serve as an example of how these dimensions intersect. Legislation that either limited or excluded Chinese migration was defined along not only racial lines but also those of gender and sexuality. Because Chinese male immigrants were prevented from bringing their families or fiancées to join them, the Chinese population in the United States became disproportionately male. The racist rhetoric at the time warned of the "yellow peril" and often portrayed Chinese males as a sexual menace who prowled after white women—the "peril" was not only racial but sexual as well. The threat eventually led to antimiscegenation laws (in order to protect white women), and further restrictions were placed on Chinese women, who were portrayed as potential prostitutes (see Almaguer 1994). Thus sexuality became a dimension within immigration policy through a concern with race and reproduction and slowly became explicitly codified through processes of identifying undesirable groups and categorizing them. The logic that allowed for one type of exclusion would also allow for others; they need only be identified. This process started with the use of simplistic categories of moral and mental fitness but in time became an elaborate and detailed system of identification.

The Moral Peril

In 1917, the INS banned the entry of "constitutional psychopathic inferiors," a category that included those with "abnormal sexual instincts" (Luibhéid 1998). But sexual deviants, such as prostitutes and homosexuals, might also be prevented entry by moral reasoning or criminal histories. The growing power of science and the medical establishment, which used the rhetoric of science to justify social inequalities (including those of race, gender, and sexuality), was utilized to justify restrictions and exclusions of "deviants" in immigration policy.

In order to prevent such deviancy or ambiguities, Congress categorized immigrants for exclusion. In doing so, it identified the desirable immigrant by naming the undesirables. The McCarran-Walter Act, also known as the Immigration and Nationality Act (INA), was passed by Congress in 1952 in the midst of the Second Red Scare (the first occurring between 1917 and 1920) and was promoted in the Congress by Senator Joseph McCarthy. The restrictions and exclusions of the legislation reflect the politics of the time and elucidate the process by which categories of exclusion and identity are deployed and multiplied by the state. Section 212(a) of the INA lists four general categories of exclusion:

1. Aliens who are of the undesirable class
2. Aliens who arrive in an improper manner
3. Aliens who present improperly issued, fraudulent, or invalid visas or documents in lieu thereof, presented at time of entry or who have no entry documents
4. Aliens who are ineligible to [sic] citizenship

These general categories are in turn broken down into thirty-six classes of excludable aliens, twenty-two of which fall under the "undesirable class" category. These twenty-two classes are organized by six subcategories: (1) physical or mental deficiency (six classes), (2) economic factors (four classes), (3) criminal or moral grounds (six classes), (4) illiteracy (one class), (5) being contrary to the best interests of the United States (four classes), and (6) aiding others to enter in violation of law (one class).

According to section 212(a), subsections 1182 (a) (4) and (9) of the INA, "aliens" (i.e., persons who are not citizens or nationals of the United States) could be denied entry if they were found to be "afflicted with psychopathic personality, or sexual deviation" or "convicted of a crime involving moral turpitude." Lesson 3.2 of the INS's Extension Training Program, entitled "Grounds for Exclusion" (1987, 8), explains, "Crime involving moral turpitude refers to a criminal act which is basically wrong (malum per se), evil, depraved, and offensive to society. . . . It is not criminality that creates moral turpitude, but the inherent evil or offensiveness of the action. Moral turpitude for the purpose of our law must be judged by American standards." However, not all morally offensive acts were to be considered "crimes involving moral turpitude." Rape, incest, prostitution, and polygamy were defined as such, but "fornication" and "extramarital relations" were not. Homosexuality was also included, but to emphasize this, the U.S. Supreme Court determined in *Boutilier v. INS* (1967) that the subsection was meant to prohibit all homosexuals from immigration to the United States (*Boutilier v. INS*, 387 U.S. 118, 123 [1967]).

Tables 2.1 and 2.2 summarize data on the number of aliens excluded by cause from 1892 to 1984 and aliens deported by cause from 1908 to 1980. I only include those causal categories that may have involved sexual deviation. Because the INS does not have statistics that differentiate homosexuals from other sexual deviants and because a homosexual may have been excluded or deported as either a "criminal, an immoral, or a mental defect," I provide statistics for those categories and collapse all others under the "Others" category. Several characteristics of the tables should be highlighted.

In table 2.1, "Aliens Excluded by Cause, 1892–1984," three periodic trends are of note: first, there is a significant increase in exclusion cases after 1900, in the 1901–1910 decade, across categories; second, the increase is even more marked in the 1911–1920 decade but subsequently decreases except for the increase in the 1950s in the "immoral" category; and third, there is a general decrease of "immoral" and "mental or physical defect" cases after 1960. The general increase across categories in the first four decades (except for the significant increase in the "mental or

TABLE 2.1

Aliens Excluded by Cause 1892–1984

Year	Total	Criminal or Narcotics Violation	Immoral	Mental or Physical Defect	Others
1892–1900	22,515	65	89	1,309	21,052
1901–1910	108,211	1,681	1,277	24,425	80,828
1911–1920	178,109	4,353	4,824	42,129	126,803
1921–1930	189,307	2,082	1,281	11,044	174,900
1931–1940	68,217	1,261	253	1,530	65,173
1941–1950	30,263	1,134	80	1,021	28,028
1951–1960	20,585	1,791	361	956	17,477
1961–1970	4,831	383	24	145	4,279
1971–1980	8,455	837	20	31	7,567
1981–1984	3,425	700	24	3	2,698
Total	633,918	14,287	8,233	82,593	528,805

Source: U.S. Immigration and Naturalization Service, *Statistical Yearbook of the Immigration and Naturalization Service, 1995*, U.S. GPO: Washington, D.C., 1997.

TABLE 2.2

Aliens Deported by Cause 1908–1980

Year	Total	Criminal violation	Immoral	Mental or physical defect	Others
1908–1910	6,888	236	784	3,228	2,640
1911–1920	27,912	1,209	0	178	26,525
1921–1930	95,127	8,383	4,238	8,936	73,570
1931–1940	117,086	16,597	4,838	6,301	89,350
1941–1950	110,894	8,945	759	1,560	99,630
1951–1960	129,887	6,742	1,175	642	121,328
1961–1970	96,374	3,694	397	236	92,047
1971–1980	231,762	2,524	67	38	229,133
Total	812,915	48,330	16,582	27,305	720,698

Source: U.S. Immigration and Naturalization Service, *Statistical Yearbook of the Immigration and Naturalization Service, 1995*, U.S. GPO: Washington, D.C., 1997.

physical defect" category from 1911 to 1920, which may be attributable to physical disabilities incurred during World War I) may be a result of the bureaucratization of the INS, which included more attentive surveillance of port-of-entry immigrants. It also seems probable that the significant increase in alien exclusions in the "immoral" category (the number more than quadrupled) from 1951 to 1960 is in no small part due to the effects of the INA in 1952. The linkage seems all the more probable when we look at the deportation statistics in table 2.2.

The number of deportations under the "immoral" category for the 1951–1960 decade in table 2.2 forms a marked contrast against other categories for the same decade, which decreased in number. It is not clear why the 1920s and '30s have such significant deportations based on immorality, but this may be linked to significant increases in deportations for criminal violations and, although not shown here, an increase in deportations due to anarchist or communist affiliations. As in the 1950s, the immoral argument may have been a "catch-all" by which to deport "undesirables" who could not easily be targeted under other categories. As I mentioned, statistics for those either excluded or deported explicitly for homosexuality are not kept by the INS, but the fact remains that the preoccupation with "sexual deviance" across the three categories included here resulted in a significant number of immigration exclusions and deportations.

It is important to note, however, that while the number of immigrant exclusions and deportations is significant, they should be understood as disciplinary or regulatory mechanisms and not as a repressive forces in an absolute sense. That is, only a small number of "undesirables" was actually excluded or expelled. But the threat of exclusion and especially deportation has also served as a disciplinary measure in its own right. Selective enforcement is a means by which immigrants may be used for cheap labor, intimidated by the threat of exposure, and, if in the "public interest," eventually deported (Sassen 1988). Thus, through the manipulation of citizenship regulations by the state, certain migrants can be kept permanently "marginal" and dispensable (Eades 1987; Cohen 1987). This particular form of power, the threat of "discovery" and expulsion, served to discipline even those who were fortunate enough to have avoided detection.

The problem of "detection" points to the flaws of the logic of this modernist project, which relied upon essential characteristics. The essentialist logic of the INS nomenclature is revealed in the Supreme Courts argument in *Boutilier v. INS* that "[t]he petitioner is not being deported for conduct engaged in after his entry into the United States, but rather for characteristics he possessed *at the time of* his entry" (1967, 71). The emphasis on characteristics, rather than conduct, was particularly important for the logic of homosexual exclusion at this historical period. In 1948 Kinsey et al. published *Sexual Behavior in the Human Male*, in which they estimated that at least 37 percent of the American male population had had at least one homosexual experience. The Supreme Court cited Kinsey in their argument (*Boutilier v. INS*, 387 U.S. 118, 123 [1967]) and thus helped to affirm the exclusion based on an essential characteristic. However, while the logic supported the exclusion, it did not solve the problem of determining resolutely who exactly had this characteristic—*who exactly was the "homosexual"?*

The process of identifying "homosexuals" depended on various filters, including criminal records, psychiatric records and examinations (which also included physical exams), and self-disclosure. Criminal records were not "full proof" simply because not all "sexual perverts" had criminal records, despite the criminality of their behavior, and could more easily avoid detection. Thus, a second filter aided in detection. In the first half of the century, as immigrants were required to take physical and psychiatric evaluations, the psycho-medical model of homosexuality was thought to be an effective mechanism of detection. However, over time, a decreasing number of mental health professionals subscribed to the "homosexuality as mental illness" paradigm and finally, in 1973, the American Psychiatric Association removed homosexuality from the Diagnostic and Statistical Manual III. The third filter depended upon self-disclosure. Following the passage of the INA in 1952, immigrants were directly asked about their moral character on immigration forms and explicitly asked if they were "homosexuals." Due to the gendered ways in which homosexuality was constructed and understood, these filters tended to detect men more than women. In addition, these filters were cultural constructions, that is, "homosexuality" was understood through a Western perspective.

Despite these filters, in the opinion of some, detecting homosexual immigrants was still problematic, and with the advent of AIDS in the 1980s, detection seemed all the more important. Thus, in 1987 immigration became even more exclusive when Congress enacted a law preventing the immigration of those infected with HIV. In 1990, in a surprising turnaround, Congress dropped the exclusion of gays based on the old moral reasoning of the INA (Harvard Law Review 1990).[8] A prominent lawyer and activist of gay immigration rights shed some light on the 1990 legislation in an interview I had with him in the mid-1990s. The passage of this legislation appeared especially unlikely under the first Bush administration. My informant explained that right-wing political elements were never completely satisfied with the policy since most gays and lesbians could simply lie about their sexual orientation to avoid exclusion. The 1987 HIV policy was assumed to be a much more effective exclusionary policy by the right wing since HIV/AIDS was believed to be a predominantly gay disease anyway. Thus the action, according to this informant, was less an act of goodwill than an effort to delete a redundancy. In addition, I would argue that with the growing number of U.S.–based multinational corporations that employed gays and lesbians, economic concerns and the influence of business may well have contributed to the policy change. The hypothesis is supported, in part, by David Evans's (1993) assertion that the commodification of the gay and lesbian movement serves capitalist interests in a variety of ways, including forming an identifiable market.

Contemporary Policy

With the repeal of homosexual exclusion from U.S. immigration law in 1990, a year in which profound changes were made to INS structure and policies, one might be led to believe that discrimination against gay and lesbian immigrants became a thing of the past. It might very well have been were it not for a fourth "filter" (alluded to earlier) that remains firmly intact—the heteronormativity of U.S. immigration laws and policies.

Gay and lesbian immigrants are overtly discriminated against through the heteronormativity of U.S. immigration law by the following means: (1) family definition, (2) HIV status (which also applies more broadly than to homosexuals), and (3) political asylum. Immigrants who apply for U.S. residency on the basis of a family petition must be the parent, child, sibling, or spouse of a U.S. citizen. While a number of countries currently permit same-sex partners to immigrate, including Australia, Canada, Denmark, New Zealand, Norway, Sweden, and the Netherlands, in the United States gay relationships are not recognized as legitimate means by which an American "spouse" can claim citizenship rights for his or her non-American partner. Proponents of gay immigrant rights argue that gay and lesbian immigrants have the right to maintain loving and supportive relationships that should be recognized as legitimate by the state. They argue that same-sex marriage should be recognized and/or that the definition of family should be extended to include gay and lesbian families. The power of this immigrant class is more evident when one considers that in the 1994 fiscal year 520,000 of 700,000 legal immigrants were granted their status via a family-based argument (Lambda Legal Defense and Education Fund 1995).

Individuals who are HIV positive are still excluded from immigrating to the United States. However, this exclusionary policy may be waived for heterosexual spouses. No such waiver exists for same-sex partners as those relationships are not recognized by the state. Several national and international organizations have publicly denounced this ban, including the National Commission on AIDS, the Centers for Disease Control, the American Medical Association, and the World Health Organization.

The move towards recognizing sexual orientation as placing people in a persecuted class began in 1986 when a Houston immigration judge barred the INS from deporting a Cuban gay man on the grounds that he faced a threat of persecution in Cuba due to his sexual orientation. In 1993, another immigration judge in San Francisco granted asylum to a Brazilian man. In 1994, for the first time, the INS granted asylum directly to a gay Mexican man. In response to this case, that year Attorney General Janet Reno formally announced that homosexuals would be recognized as a persecuted class for claims of political asylum, and a growing number of exiles are seeking asylum based on that claim.

However, while the INS has officially recognized sexual orientation and HIV serostatus as factors that place homosexuals in a persecuted class for the purpose of granting political asylum, this status is difficult to prove and is only for immigrants from specific countries who can demonstrate "well-founded fears of persecution"—a term discussed more in the following chapter. Countries included in this definition to date are Cuba, Brazil, Mexico, and several Islamic countries. Between 1994 and 1997 approximately sixty petitioners were granted asylum by U.S. judges, but there were reportedly over one thousand petitions in this same time frame (Dorf 1998). Cases are difficult to prove. Take for instance the example described by Keen (1995), in which a request for asylum for a Russian lesbian who was threatened with forced psychiatric incarceration and electroshock was denied because both the court and a board of appeals ruled that Russian authorities had "good intentions" in trying to cure her lesbianism. Ironically, the INS conduct/characteristic argument holds but in an almost reverse logic: in order to be *granted* asylum one must prove that one's queerness is an essential characteristic. In the Russian case, when the Board of Immigration Appeals representative was asked if he thought that sexual orientation was an immutable characteristic, he responded "that he had no evidence on the point but was willing to concede that a person's sexual orientation is closely identified with their fundamental identity" (as cited in Queer Immigration 1995). The irony, of course, is that the "immutable characteristic" evidence that the BIA representative needed to grant asylum seems to have been sufficient to exclude gays and lesbians in the past.

These examples also point to ways in which gender shapes asylum processes. Luibhéid (1998) argues that sexism blocks many lesbians from being granted asylum; we do not know to what extent gay women's social locations in their home countries or in the United States may also decrease their chances of "successful" migration. In addition, applying for political asylum became much more difficult on April 1, 1997, when a new policy went into effect that requires immigrants to file asylum claims within one year of entry to the United States.

Conclusion

My emphasis, thus far, has been on how identities are produced by the state and the ways in which immigration law serves to regulate and discipline sexuality. However, queer immigrants are not merely pawns in a game of sexual politics. While each migrant is constrained differentially by these mechanisms, migrants also resist these constraints in a variety of ways. In the following chapter, I examine how gay and lesbian immigrants and their advocates negotiate the system of border control and immigration policy.

3

Border Crossers

Seeking Asylum and Maneuvering Identities

Over the approximately 100-year history of the INS, the "homosexual immigrant" has evolved from being a nonexistent entity to being an ambiguous yet clearly undesirable sexual deviant to being a specifically named individual designated for exclusion. In recent history a 180-degree turn was made, and the "gay asylee" identity has been created under a new politics of inclusion. As mentioned, the irony is that queer immigrant petitioners who once had to prove that they were not homosexual must now do the opposite and prove not only that they are gay but also that they have a "well-founded fear of persecution" for being so. The INS serves as gatekeeper and promoter of ideologies through which agents of the state dispense the "land of liberty" myth. Only a select few gay men (and even fewer lesbians) have been granted political asylum on the basis of sexual orientation. A far greater number has not only been historically excluded but is in fact discriminated against today by U.S. immigration policy.

On August 24, 2000, the Ninth Circuit Court of Appeals in Los Angeles granted political asylum to Geovanni Hernández-Montiel, a Mexican national, overturning a prior rejection of the applicant's case by the Board of Immigration Appeals (BIA). In its verdict the court announced that as a transgendered gay man,[1] Hernández-Montiel had a "well-founded fear of persecution based on past experience or risk of persecution in the future if returned to the country of origin because of his membership in a particular group" (*Hernández-Montiel v. INS*, 225 F.3d 1084 [9th Cir. 2000]). Furthermore, the court stated that "sexual orientation and sexual identity are immutable" and that "sexual identity is inherent to one's very identity as a person." The court ruling was a precedent, as Shannon Minter, senior staff attorney for the National Center for Lesbian Rights, expressed: "It is the first time a federal court has affirmed that persecution on the basis of sexual orientation is a basis for receiving asylum under U.S. law. It is also a powerful recognition of the links between sexual orientation and gender identity" (ACLU 2000). In its decision the court not only made a 180-degree turn from the BIA decision but, in effect, made a 360-degree turn in immigration law—that is, the very logic that had once been used for exclusion was now being used for "inclusion."

While dimensions of sexuality and gender were obviously important factors in this case, there is an*other* important dimension that played a central role; quite literally, it is that of the "Other." Cultural studies scholars such as Edward Said (1978), James Clifford (1988), Homi Bhabha (1990), and Paul Gilroy (1992), to name but a few, have argued that "culture" is a means by which the specificities of non-Western Others are homogenized and the power of the center is masked. In addition, third world feminists argue that through discursive practices in the production of knowledge such scholarship reproduces the colonial project (Mohanty, Russo, and Torres 1991).

In this chapter, I utilize scholarly literature, archival, participant observation data, and interviews with leaders of organizations invested in the topic of immigration and asylum based on sexual identity to examine the historical and contemporary dimensions of sexual orientation in U.S. immigration policy, with a focus on political asylum. I am particularly interested in the discursive practices that have transformed the concept of the "homosexual Mexican" from one outside the nationalist imaginaries of Mexico and the United States to one of immutable essence in contemporary political discourse. I argue that in the process, the boundaries of sexual identities have become entrenched in nationalist discourse even while the borders of sexual politics between the two nations converge. Theoretically central to my argument are the Foucauldian notions of "deployment" and discursive analysis. More specifically, I am interested in examining how dimensions of gender, sexuality, and race/ethnicity are discursively constructed through four distinct yet overlapping narratives: (1) Mexican sexuality and gender, (2) U.S. sexuality and gender, (3) the "immigrant" in U.S. immigration policy, and (4) discourses of sexual rights. In the following sections I examine the social construction of the gay asylee in U.S. immigration policy.[2] In the first section of this chapter, I briefly summarize the discursive practices by which the "homosexual immigrant" was created and then transformed into the "gay asylee." I then follow with a discussion of gay Mexican asylees and the politics of identity in immigration courts.

With the repeal of homosexual exclusion from U.S. immigration law in 1990, a year in which profound changes were made to INS structure and policies, one might be led to believe that discrimination against gay and lesbian immigrants became a thing of the past. While some of the most overt forms of discrimination against gays and lesbians in U.S. immigration policy have eased, the heteronormativity of U.S. immigration laws and policies remains firmly intact. However, the processes by which this heteronormativity manifests itself are also shaped by normative constructions of race/ethnicity, gender, and class.

The period after World War II served as a time of codifying what had long been part of America's popular image, its "protection" of refugees. This first took the form of ad hoc refugee legislation designed to handle the resettlement of World War II refugees. In 1965 the INA was amended to enact permanent refugee legislation in which the category of "conditional entrants" was created and "refugees" were defined as "persons fleeing communist or communist dominated countries or the Middle East" (INS 1999, 2). In 1968, the United States consented to the 1967 United Nations Protocol Relating to the Status of Refugees and adopted the United Nations's "well-founded fear" definition of a refugee (INS 1999). The United States took another step towards bringing its national laws in synch with international ones through the passage of the Refugee Act of 1980. However, through the Refugee Act, the United States actually expanded its definition of "refugee." The new definition had a time dimension that allowed for the inclusion of individuals who have a history of persecution or a "well-founded fear" of future "persecution"—a term never defined.

As Philip Schrag (2000) has recounted in his book *A Well-Founded Fear: The Congressional Battle to Save Political Asylum in America*, the congressional victories of the Republican party in 1994 placed U.S. immigration policy in dire straits. The anti-immigrant fervor reached a zenith in 1996 as the battle, led by Newt Gingrich, over restrictive legislation was fought out in the 104th Congress. Of particular concern for human rights activists was the move by the Congress to restrict the entry of refugees of political or religious persecution, as well as the rights they had gained through the Refugee Act of 1980. In the end Congress passed the Illegal Immigration Reform and Immigrant Responsibility Act (IIRIRA), which placed drastic restrictions on refugee cases, although not as severe as its author Alan Simpson had originally proposed. The legislation required that after April 1, 1997, immigrants must file asylum claims within one year of entry to the United States (Simpson had originally wanted one month after entry) (Schrag 2000).

The question of how the "gay asylee" was born during this historical period is somewhat complex, with periods of progress followed by regress. Although in 1994 homosexuality was recognized by Attorney General Janet Reno as a persecuted class for claims of political asylum, the move towards recognizing sexual orientation as a persecuted class actually began in 1986 when a Houston immigration judge barred the INS from deporting a Cuban gay man, Fidel Armando Toboso-Alfonso, on the basis of the threat of persecution due to his sexual orientation. In this particular case the petitioner had not sought asylum because of a criminal record, which made him ineligible; however, when the INS appealed the case in 1990, the BIA affirmed the prior decision, which had established gays as a "particular social group" (Keen 1995). In 1993 another immigration judge in San Francisco granted asylum to a Brazilian man, Marcelo Tenorio. And in 1994, for the first time, the INS granted asylum directly to a gay Mexican man.

The fact that these precedent-setting cases involved migrants from Latin America is more than coincidence. Part of the reason clearly lies in the numbers alone—not only is the number of immigrants from Latin America proportionately large when compared to that of other migrant groups in the last two decades, but also the majority of petitions for asylum are from Latin American immigrants. However, as with all political stories, the issues are more complex. For example, the Toboso-Alfonso case was complicated by U.S.-Cuban politics. Deporting a Cuban refugee, whatever his sexual orientation, was not expedient during the Cold War. After 1994, it behooved the Clinton administration to take a stance on "gay rights" in an arena that was less controversial than the military and at the same time seem to be supporting "human rights" issues in Latin American countries with governments once supported by Republican administrations.

While the INS has officially recognized sexual orientation and HIV serostatus as conferring membership in a persecuted class for the purpose of granting political asylum, this status is difficult to prove and only for immigrants from specific countries who can demonstrate "well-founded fears of persecution," as I discuss in brief. However, it is important to locate Mexico-U.S. border relations historically before discussing the current effort to establish a "well-founded fear."

Alien Desires and Tolerance Zones

The U.S./Mexican border is, without doubt, one of the most contradictory geopolitical lines in the world—a militarized border with a "good neighbor." (The "Good Neighbor Policy" was the term given to the efforts by the Franklin D. Roosevelt administration to improve relations with Latin American in the 1930s.) The U.S./Mexico relationship is perhaps best summarized in the famous quotation from Mexican president Porfirio Diaz—"Poor Mexico! So far from God, and so close to the United States"—that was a common phrase used by Diaz during his time as president of Mexico, which lasted over thirty years in a two-time presidency, between 1876 and 1911. The roots of this contradictory relationship are deep and vexed by the violence of the U.S.-Mexican War that created what Anzaldúa (1987) has referred to as the "open-wound" of the border. Indeed, the war itself was justified through the complementary ideologies of "manifest destiny" and racism, which portrayed Mexicans as a "mongrel race," lazy and unworthy of a land so obviously meant to be dominated/conquered by the United States (O'Rourke 1998; King 2000).

Perhaps this view of the "lazy Mexicans" is what permitted the border between the countries to be largely ignored by U.S. immigration authorities for half a century following the war. In 1893, there was but one immigrant inspector along the entire border (at El Paso, Texas). Soon thereafter, more immigration ports were opened, but border surveillance focused not on Mexicans but rather on the Chinese, who were an excluded class. Years later, the Immigration Act of 1907 created what was to be officially known as the Mexican Border District (which included Arizona, New Mexico, and most of Texas) (INS 2000). The newly appointed director of the district, Frank Berkshire, released a report in 1908 wherein immigrants crossing the border at Mexico were divided into two classes: legitimate and illegitimate. Contrary to contemporary wisdom, however, Mexicans were considered to be "legitimate" immigrants. It was other immigrants, such as the Chinese, who attempted entry into the United States via Mexico, who were "illegitimate." The paradox, of course, is that it was precisely the exclusion of the Chinese that created the demand for Mexican labor. The difference in their "legitimacy," however, was in reality based on both the perception and, for many, the fact that Mexicans were likely to return to their country of origin; that is, despite the racism that existed against both groups, Mexicans were seen as truly "migrant labor." As the 1910 Report of the Immigration Commission related, "in the case of the Mexican, he is less desirable as citizen than as a laborer. The permanent additions to this population, however, are much smaller than the number who immigrate for work" (as cited in Acuña 1972, 132).

As a nearby source of reserve labor—labor that returned home—Mexico truly was a "good neighbor" from the U.S. perspective; but the U.S.-Mexican border wasn't a white picket fence either. Over time, the border served as a gate by which to both control Mexican migrant entry and deport migrants when they were no longer needed, as in the 1920s and '30s, and again during the early 1950s through "Operation Wetback" (Acuña 1972). More recently the contradictions of U.S.-Mexico relations are exemplified through economic policies such as the North American Free Trade Agreement (NAFTA) and anti-immigrant sentiment and legislation such as California's Proposition 187 (Lipsitz 1998). Even more dramatic and tragic examples of these "border tensions" are the hundreds of undocumented immigrants who die attempting to get to the low-paying jobs that await them and the hundreds of murdered female Mexican *maquiladora* workers around the Juarez/El Paso border.

However, the desire to cross the border runs in both directions. During the early twentieth century the border also came to be known as an unruly and unsavory place—where many Americans could themselves "migrate" temporarily to whet their repressed appetites. Arising in Mexico's postrevolutionary period, *zonas de tolerancia* (tolerance zones or red light districts) were conceived as a way to spatially regulate various forms of social deviance, including prostitution and homosexuality. In their study of *zonas de tolerancia* in the Northern Mexico border area, Curtis and Arreola argue that *zonas* provided a space wherein deviance (including the potential spread of sexually transmitted diseases, or STDs) could be controlled and through which profits could be derived from both Mexican and U.S. patrons. The *zonas* of the border region proved particularly attractive to Americans during the Prohibition era. Border towns such as Tijuana, Nuevo Laredo, and Juarez continue to serve similar roles, especially for American youth; in the 1980s and '90s Mexican resort towns such as Cancún, Acapulco, and Puerto Vallarta became the favorite destinations of many Americans, including gay and lesbian tourists. This situation creates its own set of border tensions; that is, thousands of gay and lesbian tourists vacation in a country that has been vilified for its treatment of homosexuals. I return to this topic in more detail in chapter 5, where I discuss Mexican tourism and the shifting meanings of sexuality.

Thus, the relationship between these different forms of border crossings is impacted by social scientific knowledge production and the interaction between local and international organizing around sexual rights. More specifically, our (North American) understanding of homosexuality in Mexico is based primarily on the work of anthropologists and, more recently, NGOs such as the International Gay and Lesbian Human Rights Commission (IGLHRC). As I argue in the next chapter, according to both the NGOs and the anthropological work in Latin America on Mexico, the act of having homosexual relations is not, in and of itself, sufficient to cause a person to be considered homosexual (Almaguer 1993; Carrier 1995; Lancaster 1992; Murray 1995). At least in the context of political asylum, suffice it to say that such anthropological reports of homosexuality asserted that a "gay" identity, as understood in an American context, did not exist in Mexico. "Gay" identity and culture were understood, therefore, as American constructions—alien to the Mexican social landscape.

Fear and Loathing and Other Border Tensions

Since 1999, I have served as expert witness on five political asylum cases for Mexican immigrant petitioners; all five cases were in California and all five men were granted asylum. My experience on these cases has given me some insight into the asylum process and has informed my analysis of other cases. In each case the court scenarios are remarkably similar, as are the arguments of both INS and petitioner lawyers. In this section I provide an overview of these scenarios and the discursive practices by which the "gay Mexican asylee" is created.

As mentioned, the years 1990 and 1994 were turning points for "gay" immigrants to the United States. In March 1994, INS officials granted asylum to "José García" (pseudonym), a Mexican national seeking asylum on the basis of his persecution in Mexico as a gay man. His attorneys argued that his history of being ostracized, harassed, and beaten by fellow Mexicans and raped by Mexican police was grounds for asylum. The courts agreed, but as INS spokesman Duke Austin made clear, "This does not mean that homosexuals in Mexico are persecuted. This means that this individual, due to the facts and circumstances, convinced an asylum officer that he had a well-founded fear of persecution that would justify asylum. It only relates to him. It doesn't relate to a class of people" (Warren 1994). However, only two months later, Attorney General Janet Reno announced that sexual orientation could indeed relate to a class of people.

In 1995, in a report written for the INS and the Department of Justice entitled "Mexico: Democracy and Human Rights," Andrew Redding asserted that although certain homosexuals in Mexico had a history of persecution, the situation was improving, and he pointed to the rise of a Mexican gay and lesbian movement as evidence. However, in that same year the INS granted asylum to fifty-four Mexican petitioners who claimed asylum for a variety of reasons—a major political shift from years past when such appeals were rejected. This shift signaled a broader ideological change in which Mexico was juxtaposed to the United States along lines of democracy and human rights issues. Thus in 1998, Redding wrote a second report entitled "Mexico: Treatment of Homosexuals" in which he reversed his previous statements and argued that homosexuals were indeed persecuted in Mexico.

The first asylum case I served on was in 1999 in Los Angeles, and the 1995 Redding report was used as part of the INS case against the petitioner. Yet his 1998 report was also present in terms of the contradictions of the arguments and the narratives of the courts. These narratives have been repeated in each of the cases I have served on since 1999. The first narrative defines for the court the context for gay men in Mexico. The irony of the narrative is that it depends upon anthropological research from the '70s and '80s that argues that a gay identity does not exist in Mexico. Instead, the literature argues, there is an active/passive dichotomy by which only those men who assume a sexually passive position (gendered as nonmasculine) are labeled as homosexual. In fact, in the *Hernández-Montiel* case (described at the beginning of this chapter), the court stated, "The primary issue we must decide is whether gay men in Mexico constitute a protected 'particular social group' under the asylum statute" (*Hernández-Montiel v. INS*, 225 F.3d 1084 [9th Cir. 2000]).

As in the cases I've served on, the lawyers of Geovanni Hernández-Montiel utilized a combination of petitioner and expert witness testimonies, human rights reports, and court precedents to argue that gay men are indeed a "particular social group" that is persecuted. Thus, Mexico is represented as an oppressive country where homosexual relations exist but where only the passive partner is stigmatized. In the Hernández-Montiel case, an expert testified that

> "in most of Latin America a male before he marries may engage in homosexual acts as long as he performs the role of the male." A male, however, who is perceived to assume the stereotypical "female" i.e. passive, role in these sexual relationships is "ostracized from the very beginning and is subject to persecution, gay bashing as we would call it, and certainly police abuse." (*Hernández-Montiel v. INS*, 225 F.3d 1084 [9th Cir. 2000], 5)

The second narrative, juxtaposed to the first, represents the United States as a bastion of freedom and liberty and a haven for the oppressed, including gays and lesbians. It is only in this context, in the United States, that a Mexican man can be his true self, his gay self. An essentialist notion of sexuality is therefore needed for the argument. This is not an easy task given the fact that the anthropological literature utilized for the first part of the argument is in fact a social constructionist paradigm. A more fluid concept of sexuality must then be fixed and made in the likeness of a U.S. understanding of "gayness." The current legal stance for political asylum is in fact taken from the Supreme Court case of the *Boy Scouts of America v. Dale*; the argument is that "sexual orientation and sexual identity are immutable; they are so fundamental to one's identity that a person should not be required to abandon them" (*Hernández-Montiel v. INS*, 225 F.3d 1084 [9th Cir. 2000], 12).

In the Hernández-Montiel case the original immigration judge found the petitioner's female gender identity not to be immutable, stating, "If he wears typical female clothing sometimes, and typical male clothing other times, he cannot characterize his assumed female persona as immutable or fundamental to his identity" (*Hernández-Montiel v. INS*, 225 F.3d 1084 [9th Cir. 2000], 6). In their appeal to the Ninth Circuit, Hernández-Montiel's lawyers conflate gender, sexual orientation, and identity to argue that "[h]omosexuality is as deeply ingrained as heterosexuality" (14) and that, "too often homosexuals have been viewed simply with reference to their sexual interests and activity. . . . Sexual identity goes beyond sexual conduct and manifests itself outwardly, often through dress and appearance" (13). In its opinion, the court agreed, stating, "This case is about sexual identity, not fashion" (17).

Finally, the petitioners' argument relies on establishing a history of persecution and a threat of harm should the petitioner return, namely, a "well-founded fear" of future persecution or harm. The most common way that this is accomplished is by presenting the court with evidence that the petitioner was teased and harassed for being homosexual, was discriminated against, was the victim of violence such as rape because of his sexual orientation, and was threatened with mortal danger *and* would continue to suffer such victimization and threats should he return to Mexico.

This part of the discursive construction of the "gay Mexican asylee" is not only fundamental to the overall argument but also the most difficult to prove, largely because of the contradictions of the earlier narratives. It is here that the discursive and political process of "othering" becomes complete. The spotlight of the court theatrics shines upon the homophobia of Mexico, a homophobia constructed as foreign to the "American way of life"—as foreign as the Mexican himself. Thus, the "gay Mexican asylee" is reborn as an "American," that is, should the petitioner be granted asylum.

Resistance Strategies

Gay and lesbian immigrants do resist the constraints placed on them by U.S. immigration laws and policies through either individual or organized efforts and by utilizing a variety of strategies. There are two main organizations that deal with gay and lesbian immigration issues in the United States: the International Gay and Lesbian Human Rights Commission (IGLHRC) and the Lesbian and Gay Immigration Rights Task Force (LGIRTF).[3] IGLHRC is a nongovernmental human rights organization that was founded in 1991. The main objective of the San Francisco–based organization is to "monitor, document and mobilize responses to human rights abuses against lesbians, gay men, bisexuals, transgendered people, and people with HIV and AIDS, and those oppressed due to their sexual identities or conduct with consenting adults" (Rosenbloom 1995). The international monitoring that the group conducts has been an essential resource for queer immigrants seeking political asylum on the basis of their sexual orientation. In a 1998 interview, Julie Dorf, founder and then director of IGLHRC, reported that the organization had to date worked on over two thousand sexual orientation cases.[4] She explained that political asylum is one of the main priorities of the organization and that [it] comes out of our core work which is working with activists world-wide and helping them, wherever it's appropriate and possible, to make change there. And then because we have this information, everyone wants it [for a variety of reasons]. So it's our effort to sort through all the various requests and try to prioritize those that in many cases truly help save people's lives. So our asylum project is really one key [aspect] of what we do.

While assisting with asylum cases has become a priority for IGLHRC, Dorf explained that asylum cases received more attention from the organization partly because of the INS sending "new kinds of messages that it was okay to consider sexual orientation a reasonable [asylum] claim, membership of a particular social group." Furthermore, there is a rush to get cases in with the new asylum legislation, as discussed above. The problem, of course, is that despite the opening of this "window of opportunity" for gay immigrants, it is an "opportunity" that is open for only a select segment of the queer immigrant population—those in relationships with American citizens.

The Lesbian and Gay Immigration Rights Task Force (LGIRTF) has focused on another aspect of gay immigration—binational same-sex relationships. The LGIRTF was created in 1992 through the joint efforts of the International Lesbian and Gay Association (ILGA) and the Lambda Legal Defense and Education Fund (Lambda, also abbreviated as LLDEF), which believed that the repeal of homosexual exclusion from U.S. immigration policy in 1990 was an "opportunity" for action. The group was initially organized by gay and lesbian immigrants in New York who felt that their concerns were not being addressed by other gay and lesbian organizations. The founding mission of LGIRTF was to challenge the discrimination against gay and lesbian immigrants, recognizing that these issues were rarely discussed within the gay and lesbian or immigrant communities. The national organization is now called Immigration Equality and has a dozen chapters throughout the United States.

It soon became clear to LGIRTF leaders that immigration was a concern for one segment of the "mainstream" gay and lesbian community, in particular, gay and lesbian Americans involved in intimate relationships with non-Americans. As director Lavi Soloway (a gay immigrant himself) explains,[5]

the focus changed in 1995. When the first development in the Hawaii marriage case arose, the membership saw marriage, legalizing marriage, as the solution to the immigration problem. And that was distinctly different from where it began when it was just talking about immigration categories being too restricted because they didn't recognize different kinds of families. So, what we were trying to push for was opening it up to the idea that the same kinds of relationships were called different kinds of things between different kinds of people, who should warrant benefits as well. It was of course different politically in part because there was no reason to believe that talking about marriage meant anything. So, it was the encouraging news in the Hawaii marriage case [that caused] a great deal more interest in organizing around marriage as a solution, which I have to say not everyone was excited about in the beginning but with time more became excited about the idea, and it wasn't just binational couples either. Immigration became another vehicle to argue for marriage.

Soloway's comments point to two important dimensions. First, "marriage" as a state-sanctioned relationship could in effect be coopted to "mean something" for gays and lesbians (a strategy that, as I will demonstrate below, is not limited to "gay marriage"). Second, the focus on marriage, while serving some immigrant interests, was more directly of interest to members of the mainstream gay movement. The restricted definition of "spouse" and "family member" in immigration law illustrated how queer American citizens were being discriminated against.

Soloway further discussed how the group worked to improve documentation for gay and lesbian asylum seekers and why it contributed to a split between group members:

> Until 1994, there weren't really any asylum cases and then in the summer of 1994, the Janet Reno thing happened; there was a lot of publicity about gay people winning asylum. A lot of other things changed. The IGLHRC established an asylum project and it quickly became very well known and very active in documenting asylum. So, we also had a lot of people who were looking right in the eye at a veritable solution to their problem, so asylum became much more interesting. It also divided north and south, . . . or those people who came from all the great Western European privileged places and the people who came from places where gay people were persecuted—because for them that was important but for others it was less important.

While it is unclear whether the LGIRTF was more diverse prior to 1994, it is clear that the subordination of asylum to marriage was influenced not just by the politics of the group but also by the political economy of sexuality on a global scale. That is, factors that shape the experiences and identities of Western queers are different from those of non-Western ones, and these differences have shaped not just the strategies that the LGIRTF employs but also the type of immigrants who are affiliated with the group. Thus, the differences in focus that the IGLHRC and the LGIRTF have given to queer immigration are but two of numerous concerns that this population faces. These different foci are due in part to the specialized concerns of their respective members, but even more so, they are due to the diversity of queer immigrants themselves.

Accurately describing the U.S. queer immigrant population is a nearly impossible task. Queer immigrants in the United States are not a homogenous group by any definition. Differences in class, nationality, legal status, and motivations for seeking U.S. citizenship rights exist among gay immigrants. However, intake statistics for 1996 documented by the immigration program of the Legal Services Department of the Los Angeles Gay and Lesbian Community Center reveal that of approximately five hundred clients, 81 percent were men, 19 percent were women, and the clients ranged in age between twenty and forty-four. Immigrants from Latin American countries comprised the majority of the clientele at 70 percent, followed by Europe (20 percent), Asia and the Pacific Islands (7 percent), and Africa (3 percent). Most of the clients searching for immigration assistance are either the partners of U.S. citizens who are seeking a way to legitimize the migration status of the immigrant partner and preserve their relationship or are HIV positive and face the very real possibility of death should they be deported to their countries of origin due to a lack of access to adequate health care in those countries. For example, Manuel explained that one "very strong reason for migrating" to the United States was the opportunity to get "more advanced treatment" for HIV than a person could get in Mexico. In addition, a small but steady number of clients are seeking information on political asylum. Clearly, queer immigrants are a diverse group. As Jeff Kim, immigration law coordinator for Legal Services of the Los Angeles Center elucidates,

> One thing I've learned from working on this project, on and off for the past four years [1996–1999], is that there is no one kind of client profile that we have. And I think it would be surprising to a lot of people who make assumptions about who the immigrants are in the community, what

they're about, and why or why not it should be a concern to us. They come from all kinds of backgrounds, all demographics, not just the racial/ethnic but all classes, from poor, indigent to people who can afford to hire an attorney and pay the thousands of dollars to help them out of their bind.

This reported diversity is parallel to that reported by both Dorf for IGLHRC and Soloway for the LGIRTF. Yet it is important to remember that these organizations are located in cities with extremely diverse populations: Los Angeles, San Francisco, and New York. Gay and lesbian populations in other areas of the country may be smaller and less diverse. It is also important to remember that not all of the immigrants who seek help from the Los Angeles Center's Legal Service are members of Immigration Equality. At a national level, the LGIRTF claims a membership of approximately four thousand, but my research with the organization leads me to believe that the members of LGIRTF are a distinct, class-differentiated subgroup of queer immigrants. Soloway himself stated,

> We know for example that many, many people are HIV positive and indigent and that many people are involved in illegal situations like marriage fraud, or just working illegally, or being in an unlawful status. Many more than who report their status to us, so if you took a sample that looks at that information you would think that most people are in status or were privileged enough to be able to fly around all the time or go to school, but that's actually a small number.

There is another major difference between IGLHRC and LGIRTF immigrants and the larger gay and lesbian immigrant population: their sexual orientation is a salient characteristic of their identities by which they are making "rights" claims upon the state. I emphasize this aspect because this population of "queer immigrants" differs from other immigrants who may also be gay, lesbian, or bisexual but do not make rights claims from a "queer" location; that is, they assume a specific political identity, constructed in part vis-á-vis their relationship to the state, from which they contest notions of citizenship and make "rights" claims.

The position that Immigration Equality and LGIRTF assume in making rights claims is couched within a discourse of both national (U.S.) citizenship rights and human rights (global citizenship). Critiquing the heterosexist language of immigration policy and the INS's definition of "spouse," the organization claims that queer binational couples (where

one partner is a U.S. citizen) are denied the rights that heterosexual binational couples have. In discussing his experience with such couples, Jeff
Kim explains,

> I was just speaking to a couple. One is American and one is from England
> and they're out of status. And you know they're a couple and they cite the
> discriminatory treatment that queer people get in terms of the marriage laws
> and INS nonextension of benefits to queer couples. That is clearly a big prob-
> lem. I've seen male and female couples from all across the board. They have
> fallen in love with an American, the non-U.S. citizen. You know, what can
> they do? They have to play games, go through many other hoops that straight
> couples don't have to do. And just to barely stay legal, I mean, a lot of those
> couples, they do not even have legal status. And they're freaking out.

The group thus employs the notion of human rights to defend gay and
lesbian immigrants' rights not only to love (as a universal human right)
but also to exist in a community free from persecution, which allows
gays and lesbians to develop their human potential and the recognized
civil rights of American citizens. The citizenship strategy projects an
image of "sameness," that is, it is a project that in many ways attempts
to mask, if not deny, its "queerness." This is demonstrated, in part, by
the LGIRTF's mission of "supporting marriage as a vehicle for lesbian
and gay immigration," which is exemplified in a video produced by the
LGIRTF entitled "Love Knows No Borders." In the video the group constructs and projects an image of "sameness" in which all-American men
and women (four binational couples) have fallen in love with "foreign-
ers," but unlike other U.S. citizens they cannot bring their spouses home
because they are of the same sex. Film director Elizabeth Bird explains,

> The purpose of this documentary is to demonstrate how our lives and re-
> lationships are being destroyed because we cannot marry. We have to edu-
> cate ourselves and the public to understand why we are fighting for the
> freedom to marry. The couples depicted in the documentary just happened
> to be from different countries, and they are trying, against all odds, to stay
> together. (Immigration Equality 1995)

Along with "just happening" to be from different countries, the couples
also "just happen" to be the same sex. The issue of "equal rights," of
freedom of movement, is silenced to a large extent by the demand for

marriage "rights." The fact that marriage is an institution of privilege and inequality is overlooked, and only a certain kind of relationship and immigrant (one who is involved in a monogamous relationship with a U.S. citizen) is legitimized or "sanctioned" by such an approach; the strategy is thus an exclusive one.

This exclusivity is elucidated by the fact that many of the immigrants who come to Immigration Equality meetings seek information that the organization cannot legally give (i.e, how to succeed at "fraudulent" marriage). Many gay and lesbian immigrants come to meetings in the hopes of meeting people, or finding out how to meet people, of the opposite sex, who are U.S. citizens and are willing to marry them, and thus help them to become legal residents. It is illegal in the United States to either commit such a "fraudulent" marriage or assist in one, so organizations like Immigration Equality are greatly restricted in giving their members the kind of help they want most. Yet among themselves, the members do meet and talk and assist one another in finding persons whom they can marry in a state-sanctioned ceremony. This is more reflective of individual strategies to maneuver the system.

Just as immigrants attempt to navigate within the confines of an organization's policies, their advocates attempt to navigate within the confines of the state policies, which in turn further complicate organizational practices. Gay immigrant advocates have assumed what has become a "legitimate" position and identity—a voice of "authority" to which state officials are increasingly listening. Serving in a sort of "watchdog" capacity, members of the LGIRTF work with other queer, immigrant, and/or human rights groups to report institutional improprieties. In one case, agents of the INS raided an HIV clinic in Los Angeles in search of "illegal" immigrants. Working together, Immigration Equality, the L.A. Center's Legal Services department, and AIDS organizations brought the case to the attention of the public and INS officials themselves. The INS activity reportedly was not repeated.

The relationship that gay immigrant groups now have to the INS's identification procedures has taken a queer turn. There are instances in which the INS sought educational or training information from gay immigrant groups and vice versa, cases in which gay immigrant groups got assistance from the INS. In one example Kim reports,

> There are some unique issues which come up and I've dealt with them, several times, and the one that I can cite, that comes to mind readily is

transgender . . . somebody who may have became a permanent resident under one gender and then in the time that transpired between then and when they apply for naturalization they change their genders and they're wondering what they should do when they apply for naturalization, if it's going to be a problem, what they should do in the interview. . . . I'm planning on writing a position paper for cases like that to inform the INS. Another example is someone who is naturalized and wants to get a passport and they want to know what they should do. The level of sophistication of the passport process is amazing; to handle these kinds of situations, I was told that if someone is leaving the country to perform the surgery they can give a one-year passport for a pre-op and change it later for a post-op.

Kim's illustration of the sort of "give and take" collaboration that can occur between state institutions like the INS and gay immigrant rights organizations also illustrates how the state's attempts to regulate identity, in this case gender, are actually informed by queer immigrant organizations. Thus, the organizations are legitimized and become part of the process by which identities are reformulated and produced. In this particular case, "transgender" is named and becomes another category that the state may regulate.

Immigrant categories or identities, like any identity, are more than a means of description; they are socially constructed locations that can serve as sites of resistance. In *The Power of Identity*, Manuel Castells (1997) argues that dominant institutions create legitimizing identities and that resistance identities are created by marginal communities (along the lines of Calhoun's [1994] conceptualization of identity politics). But I assert that resistance may also reproduce the legitimizing identities of dominant institutions. Butler's work on performativity is particularly useful for understanding the subversive potential of "legitimizing identities." She argues that

> resignification marks the workings of an agency that is (a) not the same as volunteerism, and that (b) though implicated in the very relations of power it seeks to rival, is not, as a consequence, reducible to those dominant forms.
>
> Performativity describes this relation of being implicated in that which one opposes, this turning of power against itself to produce alternative modalities of power, to establish a kind of political contestation that is not a "pure" opposition, a "transcendence" of contemporary relations of

power, but a difficult labor of forging a future from resources inevitably impure. (Butler 1993, 241)

The "fraudulent marriages" practiced by some individual queer immigrants are perhaps most illustrative of what I mean by resistance from within "legitimizing identities." In these cases, queer immigrants enter into state-sanctioned relationships (i.e., marriages) with persons of the opposite sex who are American citizens and perform the straight role for an audience that is the legitimizing authority of the state. Thus, gay immigrants' strategies to achieve "equal rights" must be understood in light of the "impurity" of the cultural articulations in which they are embedded. Although far from an institution of equality, marriage—or rather its performative resignification—may serve to actually subvert it. In this instance, this "strategic mode of articulation" can be linked to Fredric Jameson's (1992) concept of pastiche as "a parody that has lost its humor." As a political strategy, a mode of articulation, the method is questionable, but as a performative act, it leaves room for a subversive reading that destabilizes the concept of citizen and the binary structures that support it.

Since the 1990 change in immigration law that repealed homosexual exclusion, it has also become easier for gay and lesbian immigrants to strategically use other immigration categories as well, especially if they obtain legal assistance. If a gay immigrant has a profession or skill, he or she can arguably make a case for professional entry, and in these cases, immigration lawyers advise that such efforts be made. The difference with these strategies, again, is that they do not make claims from a "queer" location but rather from "legitimate" sites. In addition, these types of strategies are more accessible to immigrants who are better informed and have the means to successfully utilize them, so class shapes not only identity in these cases but also the strategies by which identity may be utilized to ensure successful passage through the immigration boundaries.

Conclusion

By examining the social locations of gay and lesbian immigrants to the United States we can begin to unmask the mechanisms of social regulation more broadly. In the preceding pages, I have examined the historical and contemporary mechanisms by which the state produces identities through normative discourses and administrative practices, as well as its attempts to regulate its borders and discipline those who cross them. The state, through its immigration laws and policies, works to meet the demands of capitalism and discipline both the productive and reproductive power of its migrant labor force. It is these very processes of immigration regulation, of "border patrol," by which the state attempts to differentiate and name the strata of "desirability" that have created the "gay immigrant" identity. While stratified practices of citizenship in many ways demand a "performance," the failure of their logic provides some room for agency and resistance, space by which queer immigrants can maneuver the system with varying degrees of success. This resistance is carried out both at individual and organizational levels, and at times it is from the very location that is supposedly illegitimate that the "gay immigrant" makes claims against the state.

It is still too early to say to what extent the strategies of gay immigrant rights groups such as Immigration Equality have been "successful." Towards the end of increasing visibility, the LGIRTF has met with some success with major lesbian and gay media as well as the mainstream press, which has come to recognize and cover gay immigrant issues. Yet even this "success" may also be attributed to an increase in binational gay relationships that arises from dimensions of globalization such as tourism, multinational corporations with migratory executives, and communications advancements. There is hope, however, that through international pressure from other governments who have recognized same-sex relationships, from transnational corporations who have queer employees whom they relocate, and from organizations like the LGIRTF, the U.S. government may eventually recognize same-sex partnerships for immigration purposes. In light of the nation's current anti-immigrant sentiment, it may take some time to succeed in this regard. In conclusion, by focusing on state practices of immigration regulation and stratified citizenship, I have examined but one dimension of the way sexuality influences migratory processes. In the following chapters, I will examine other dimensions of the sexuality of migration with a focus on Mexican men who have sex with men.

4

De Los Otros

Mexican Sexual Borderlands

On June 14, 1997, I crossed the U.S.-Mexican border at San Diego to observe (and celebrate) Tijuana's third annual gay and lesbian pride parade. Standing on the sidelines of Avenida Revolución, in the heart of the city, I cheered as the march began with mariachis leading the procession. The parade was small[1] compared to Los Angeles and San Francisco gay pride events, but for many reasons, it seemed so much more important than those now heavily commercialized events. So, when members from the East Los Angeles group Las Memorias[2] motioned for me to join, I too marched in the parade. Soon after I joined the group, a heckler on the sidelines began shouting homophobic slurs at us, when suddenly a lead member retorted, "Pancho Villa was bisexual!" The nearby crowd and parade participants alike burst out in laughter and the contingent continued unfazed.

Whether the legendary revolutionary had sex with men or not, the comment and its context help to illuminate the paradox and complexity of Mexican constructions of sexuality and gender. For if Villa had sexual relations with men (an act that is conceivable), he would not have been, according to Mexican definition, "*de los otros*." The term, which translates "of the others," is used by members of the dominant group[3] to refer to "homosexuals" and thus to mark difference. The act of having homosexual relations is not, in and of itself, sufficient to cause one to be defined as homosexual or *de ambiente*.[4] For although homosexuality, per se, is stigmatized, bisexuality is a common practice among Mexican men.[5] This is, in part, why the label "men who have sex with men," or "MSM," is often applied to Mexican men by researchers. The question this raises in discussions of homosexual identities is, who exactly are "the others" and what are the boundaries that define them as such?

As noted in the previous chapter, traditional explanations emphasize cultural differences in order to explain how homosexuality is defined in non-Western cultures. Through such a framework "culture" becomes the mechanism by which difference is reified and the distance of *los otros* is reproduced. If the literature on the social construction of a Western gay identity is correct in linking sexual identities to capitalist development (as discussed in chapter 1), then why should our understanding of sexual identities in the "developing world" give primacy to "culture" and divorce it from political economy? Should not Mexican sexual identities also be understood as multiply constituted and intimately linked to the structural and ideological dimensions of modernization and development? In my view, sexuality must be understood as a dimension of power relations. This chapter examines the complexities of Mexican sexualities from a political economic perspective in order to clarify how these dimensions shape migratory processes.

The Gender/Sex/Power Axis

Much of the scholarship on Latino gender[6] roles has perpetuated gender stereotypes and constructs male and female roles in terms of a "machismo/marianismo" sex role model.[7] In this view, Latino cultures are marked by "traditional" views of gender in which women are supposedly submissive, maternal, and virginal; and men are characterized by "extreme verbal and bodily expression of aggression toward other men, frequent drunkenness, and sexual aggression and dominance" of Latinas (Hondagneu-Sotelo and Messner 1994). These gender paradigms became reinforced in the 1970s in research on gender inequality in Latin America conducted mostly by anthropologists who were concerned with cultural constructions and differences (see, for example, Nash and Safa 1986). Subsequent research built upon these frameworks with the supposition that "Latino" gender role norms are rooted in Mexico's pre-Colombian Aztec and colonial Spanish patriarchal heritage and thus are steeped in tradition. Ironically, social scientists, in an effort to be more "culturally sensitive," adopted these cultural frameworks, which gave rise to interpretations of the problems of Latino cultural gender constructions such as the following:

> An interpretation of American values such as assertiveness (a socially desirable traditional male attribute) that have no cultural counterpart in behaviors of Hispanic women may be needed . . . the concept of assertive behavior for Hispanic women is an alien one. (Napholz 1994, 508)

It is noteworthy that while such arguments may sound dated, these cultural stereotypes were still influential in gender scholarship on Latinos in the 1990s.[8] Culture, through these conceptual frameworks, becomes not only reified and monolithic (Latino culture is defined as static regardless of location) but is also called on as an explanation of the "symptoms" of social inequalities. The solution then is to make "them" more like "us" not by socioeconomic remedies but by "cultural adaptation." Only recently have scholars begun to question these ahistorical, monolithic, and one-dimensional constructions.

Problematizing "Gay" Latino Men

In his treatise on sexuality, Foucault (1990 [1978]) argues that theories of sexuality that focus on the policing functions of the state through laws and censorship (which he calls the "juridico-discursive" theory of power) are misleading. He asserts that sexualities and identities can only be understood through discursive strategies. In addition, Foucault asserts that it is necessary to have an "analytics" of power that examines the multiple sites where normalization occurs through knowledge production. I utilize Foucault's analytics of power conceptualization in this chapter, but drawing on feminist theory, especially Dorothy Smith's "relations of ruling" (1987), I extend his approach to account for the ways in which processes of identity deployment and multiplication are not simple top-down relations but rather are contested and negotiated by individual actors.

To examine the lives of gay Latino men as an "abstracted and generalized" group is to reproduce some of the very social relations that I wish to challenge. Similarly, contemporary scholarship in Queer Theory examines how these normative discursive practices operate in terms of binary oppositions (i.e. natural/unnatural, normal/abnormal, heterosexual/homosexual) at sites of production such as medical texts, literature, film, and television. Thus informed by these conceptualizations of normative discourse, knowledge production, and the "relations of ruling," I review the literature on gender and sexuality as it relates to gay Latino men and examine its discursive role in a normative project of sexuality, race/ethnicity, and gender.

This literature exemplifies how a focus on "culture" limits our understanding of Latino masculinities and sexualities through a discourse of two cultures—the normative and the "exotic." I am not arguing that this literature is without merit; on the contrary, such scholarship has shed light on a topic that few were willing to investigate. However, by giving primacy to culture in order to explain difference, this literature in effect creates difference. Through such discourse the dominant culture is made nearly invisible while Latino cultural differences are placed in a critical spotlight. I am not arguing against non-Latino scholarship. Such an argument would be too simplistic. What I am arguing is that as researchers and scholars (producers of knowledge), we are all directly implicated in "relations of ruling" even as we challenge them through our research on sexuality and gender.

One of the aims of recent scholarship in men's studies is to examine how some men have power over others in what Carrigan, Connell, and Lee (1987) refer to as "nonhegemonic masculinities." Nonhegemonic masculinities are types of masculinities (i.e., those of gay men and men of color)[9] that are subordinated by the ruling or hegemonic masculinity of Western, white, heterosexual, middle-class men. By examining nonhegemonic masculinities, we are better able to understand not only the gendered relations between men and women but also the multiple and intersecting axes among men themselves, such as the axes of race/ethnicity, class, and sexuality (Brod and Kaufman 1994; Hondagneu-Sotelo and Messner 1994).

While attention has been paid to the existence of multiple masculinities, rarely has this framework been applied to an intersectional understanding of gender, sexuality, and race/ethnicity in such a way that the different masculinities among Latino men would come into focus. "Latino masculinity" continues to be represented as a cultural singularity that as a "nonhegemonic" masculinity pluralizes the hegemonic—providing an exotic Other relational to the normative one. "Culture" thus serves to reify difference in a sort of "one-size-fits-all" representation of the Other. We must then ask to what extent such cultural arguments serve a cultural hegemony rather than counter it. By this, I mean to say that "culture" has been used uncritically in at least three ways in much of the literature on Latino men, particularly with respect to gender and sexuality. Specifically, the discourse regarding "culture" in general often perpetuates homogenization, the assumption that "culture" is static, and exoticization.

The first analytical problem is rooted in the homogenization of Latino culture (Nolan and Nolan 1988; Clancy 1999). Latinos are commonly represented as a homogenous entity without cultural differences. Even with respect to the most simple of cultural characteristics such as language, religion, music, and food, there are innumerable differences within the Latino cultural category, which is not to argue that similarities are nonexistent. Ignoring differences among Latinos, however, shadows the extent to which Latinos are drawn together by the material conditions in which they share a sociopolitical space rather than a shared essentialized "culture." By ignoring differences within, essentialist cultural arguments reproduce, through the knowledge production discussed before, the distance between "hegemonic" and "nonhegemonic" men (as well as women). As Mohanty argues, "the idea of abstracting particular places, people, and events into generalized categories, laws, and policies is fundamental to any form of ruling" (1991a, 16).

The second problem is that Latino culture is commonly represented as if it were fixed or static. Contemporary scholarship on U.S. Latinos often refers to past anthropological scholarship on Latin American cultures, implying that culture does not change either with time, with context, or with global influences. Cultural arguments, (ab)used in this manner, suggest that "what is different about [marginal peoples] remains tied to traditional pasts, inherited structures that either resist or yield to the new but cannot produce it" (Clifford 1988, 5). As previously mentioned, one example lies in scholarship on Latino gender roles that perpetuates stereotypes of male and female roles according to a "machismo/marianismo" sex role model (see Madsen Camacho 2000). Some scholars have argued that "macho" performances of masculinity are a response to feelings of inferiority (Peña 1991; Mirandé 1997), but such arguments are deterministic and maintain a static concept of Latino culture.

Matthew Gutmann (1996), in his ethnographic study of the residents of the *colonia popular* (urban, poor, and working-class neighborhood) of Santo Domingo in Mexico City, critiques this static view to argue that the traditional macho stereotype is inappropriate for describing the multiple and changing meanings of contemporary Mexican masculinities. He asserts that gender identities must be understood as historical constructs (in a Marxist sense) that are shaped by changing political, social, cultural, and economic conditions. Thus, the static and monolithic definition of the Mexican "macho" is problematic both in its failure to capture the diverse social locations of Mexican men and in its assumption that Mexican gender identities transcend time. Furthermore, Hondagneu-Sotelo and Messner (1994) argue that varying displays of masculinity are shaped by both the power relationships of men over women and the power relationships of some men over other men so that "marginalized and subordinated men tend to overtly display exaggerated embodiments and verbalizations of masculinity that can be read as a desire to express power over others within a context of relative powerlessness" (214) and in which men in powerful positions may project more "egalitarian" images of masculinity.

Finally, I refer to the "culture as Other" to describe a third problematic, which is a more general characteristic of the literature that examines subordinated racial/ethnic groups. "Culture" in this (mis)application becomes a defining characteristic of the Other that explains "exotic" behavior and positions dominant social forms as normative (i.e., Western civilization). As Abu-Lughod (1991) states, "Culture is the essential tool for making other" (143). While culture is important analytically, its importance is not necessarily greater for nonhegemonic groups. When "culture" is used as a factor of analysis only of U.S. minorities or non-Western peoples, there is a tendency to either directly or indirectly imply that their "culture," which is a "backwards" culture, is to "blame" for what are represented as pathological traits[10] or what may be called "cultural pathologization."

While scholarship on Latino sexuality is relatively sparse, the sociological and anthropological literature suggests that Latino men's sexual identity is determined not by the biological sex of the sexual partner but rather by the culturally defined roles of *activo/pasivo* (i.e., dominant/submissive) assumed by the actors.[11] For example, Tomás Almaguer (1993, 257) argues that

[u]nlike the European-American system, the Mexican/Latin-American system is based on a configuration of gender/sex/power that is articulated along the active/passive axis and organized through the scripted sexual role one plays. It highlights sexual aim—the act one wants to perform with the person toward whom sexual activity is directed—and only gives secondary importance to the person's gender or biological sex.

Almaguer further argues that this system genders and devalues the "passive" as feminine. Thus, according to this framework, as long as Latino men maintain an *activo* (active) or dominant sexual script, their masculinity, as culturally defined, remains intact. The passive role is defined as feminine and is thus denigrated. The problem, of course, is that the basis of the model relies on a static understanding of culture and gender (Gutmann 1996).

A number of important studies offer more complicated cultural read-ings. For example, as noted in the first chapter, Joseph Carrier (1995) illustrates how the traditional "dominant/submissive" dichotomy of Mexican sexual identity is being transformed by U.S. migration through factors such as a more versatile definition of sex roles that includes a third category: *internacionales* (internationals). Annick Prieur's (1998) work on *travesti* (transvestites) in Mexico City demonstrates as well that social class plays an important dimension in shaping the gender identi-ties of men who have sex with men. Such findings point to the impor-tance of examining structural influences such as class, globalization, and migration upon constructions of masculinity and sexuality.

The problem of "cultural" arguments becomes more evident when juxtaposed to studies of what might be called "mainstream" homosexu-ality in the United States. While the "active/passive" typology seems to fit a culturally defined differentiation between Mexican/Latin American and European American homosexuality, other research suggests this culturally based dichotomy is too simplistic. Scholars such as Kinsey, Pomeroy, and Martin (1948), Albert Reiss (1961), Laud Humphreys (1970), George Chauncey (1994), Seymour Kleinberg (1989), and Brian Pronger (1990) demonstrate that both in the past and in the present European Ameri-can males' meanings of homosexuality are multiple and shifting depend-ing upon the context. Alfred Kinsey's early survey research showed that not all American men who experienced sexual relations with other men defined themselves as "homosexual." Laud Humphreys demonstrated as well (albeit in a highly controversial manner) that married profes-sional men who identified as heterosexual participated in sexual encoun-ters with other men in public bathrooms. Furthermore, in his study of homosexual prostitutes in Tennessee, Reiss argued that a homosexual identity was very much influenced by power relations nearly identical to the gender/sex/power system that Tomás Almaguer discussed. Likewise, Chauncey argues that European immigrants in New York in the early part of the twentieth century had a meaning system similar to that which Almaguer describes as a Latin American one. In a more contemporary light, Kleinberg (1989) and Pronger (1990) both argue that today's gay man displays a hyper-masculine "straight" behavior with an overt gay identification. These examples suggest that the Latin American gender/ sex/power system described by Almaguer and previously discussed may be organized by intersecting dimensions of class, race, gender, and sexu-ality. Almaguer's formulation of the gender/sex/power system remains a powerful analytical concept, but culture (i.e., Latino culture) may be less of an axis of organization than posited.

This research on American masculinity and sexuality suggests that differences in the gender/sex/power system may *not* be culturally determined. In other words, social class and capitalist development shapes gender and sexuality. Such an argument is supported by Prieur's (1998) scholarship on transvestites in Mexico City in which she argues that stricter definitions of gender roles seem to be held by those of the lower socioeconomic strata and, furthermore, that sexual roles are not as strict as previous research has suggested. Thus, while culture may play an important role in shaping constructions of gender and sexuality, cultural primacy masks structural dimensions that are also important. This understood, the gender/sex/power axis proposed by Almaguer remains a useful analytical model in which a political economy of Mexican sexuality may be formulated.

Yet, culture remains central to most analyses of gay Latino masculinity, creating a language of difference that has material consequences in the everyday lives of gay Latino men. The focus given to culture by most literature on gay Latinos has thus served to create an "Other" by suggesting that deficiencies in "Latino culture" are responsible for non-normative forms of sexuality, race/ethnicity, and gender. In "Chicano Men and Masculinity" Maxine Baca Zinn (1991) challenges these cultural-deficit models of Latino masculinity and argues for research on Latino masculine roles and identities that examines sociostructural factors that shape these identities rather than "cultural" differences between Latinos and non-Latinos.

A central aspect for this stagnant position is that scholarship on Latino/a sexuality, particularly Mexican male sexuality, has for the most part maintained these ahistorical representations of gender in Latino culture as the basis for understanding sexuality. This literature suggests that for Latino men sexual identity is not determined by the object choice (i.e. the sex) of the sexual partner but rather by gendered "dominant" or submissive" roles assumed by the actors (Lancaster 1992, Almaguer 1993, Carrier 1995, Murray 1995). Carrier's research with Mexican men who have sex with men, has been the most influential scholarship on Mexican male sexuality and descriptions of the activo/pasivo roles and their relationship to identity. The argument is perhaps best described by Almaguer (1993) who writes, "The structured meaning of homosexuality in the European-American context rests on the sexual object choice one makes—i.e., the biological sex of the person toward whom sexual activity is directed" (257).

Although Carrier's (1995) research is perhaps the most often cited scholarship on Mexican homosexuality, Ian Lumsden has also conducted extremely important research on Mexican homosexuality. In *Homosexuality, Society, and the State in Mexico*, Lumsden (1991) takes a political economic approach towards the understanding of Mexican sexuality; unfortunately, however, the book has not received wide circulation. Lumsden argues that "[t]hree distinct but connected social processes are taking place in Mexico which will affect the construction and regulation of homosexuality in the foreseeable future" (85). To paraphrase, these processes include (1) tensions between Mexican traditional sex-gender identities, roles, and values and new ones that are shaped by the increased commodification of sexuality, (2) the diffusion of mass American culture among youth through technology, the media, and foreign capital, and (3) linkages with the U.S. Latino population, particularly in the Southwest. In the following sections I expand on and elaborate these processes and move more closely towards a political economic understanding of Mexican sexuality.

The Socioeconomic Context

Mexico's position as a developing nation in the world system can be traced back to the growth of liberal political empowerment beginning in the 1850s and fortified in the era known as the Porfiriato that dates from 1877 to 1910 and is named after Porfirio Diaz's dictatorial reign. The Porfiriato was a period of imposed "law and order" in which the seeds of modernization were planted and foreign investment dominated the Mexican economy. The resulting social inequalities eventually led to the Mexican Revolution (1910–1920) and the subsequent years of power struggle (1920–1940). President Lazaro Cardenas's (1934–1940) government promoted extensive land reform, the expropriation and nationalization of foreign oil companies, and the entrenchment of the Partido de la Revolución Mexicana (PRM), renamed the Partido Revolucionario Institucional (PRI) in 1945.

The PRI dominated Mexican politics for over seventy years and remained in power despite recent economic setbacks and moves toward political pluralization. The PRI lost control of the presidency to National Action Party (PAN) candidate Vicente Fox in 2000. The PRI's downfall can be traced in part to the debt crisis of 1982 that followed a period of economic boom and increased foreign debt. "La Crisis" led to a period of economic restructuring under the presidencies of Miguel de la Madrid (1982–1988), Carlos Salinas de Gotari (1988–1994), and Ernesto Zedillo (1994–2000). Under these presidencies, the Mexican government made concerted efforts to economically integrate the nation more closely into a globalized capitalist system. To achieve this goal, Mexico increased efforts to privatize industry and services, strengthen international ties, and increase tourist development. The United States played an important role in each of these efforts.

The uneasy relationship that Mexico has had with the United States dates to the 1800s, when tensions and contestations led to the U.S.-Mexican War in which Mexico "sold" nearly half of its territory to the United States under the Treaty of Guadalupe-Hidalgo in 1848. In addition the United States and Mexico have had tenuous relations due to labor programs (such as the Bracero program)[12] and the treatment of Mexican migrant labor in the United States. It is for this very reason that scholars such as Anzaldúa (1987) see the two thousand miles of the geopolitical border that the two nations share as more of a scar, a visible wound that joins, rather than a border that separates two autonomous nations. It is, therefore, impossible to discuss the socioeconomic context of Mexico outside of this relationship.

The economic relationship between the United States and Mexico can best be described as a "codependent" one. Economic ties between Mexico and the United States have been strengthened through economic treaties such the General Agreement on Tariffs and Trade (GATT 1986) and the North American Free Trade Agreement (NAFTA 1994), as well as its membership in the Organization for Economic Cooperation and Development (OECD). In 1997, Mexico became the United States's second largest trading partner, surpassing even Japan with $70 billion in trade a year (CTCA 1997).[13] In addition, the economies of the southwestern U.S. states are dependent upon Mexico for exports and labor, thus making U.S.-Mexican linkages particularly important for border economies. California is the top-ranked U.S. exporting state. In 1997 the state's exports were valued at $109.54 billion (CTCA 1997). Mexico is California's second largest trading partner (after Canada) and again in 1997 this trade was reported to "directly or indirectly support approximately 169,400 jobs in the Golden State" (CTCA 1997).

Table 4.1 summarizes how Mexico's socioeconomic landscape has changed between 1982 and 1998. Several variables are particularly worth noting for the purposes of this discussion. First is the increased amount of trade that Mexico developed between 1982 and 1998 and an even more substantial increase between 1990 and 1998. By 1998, 85 percent of Mexico's exports and approximately 75 percent of its imports were to and from the United States. Secondly, while unemployment rates seem to have improved between 1990 and 1998, underemployment remains a major concern. Finally, while the top three employment sectors seemed to be stable, the numbers are misleading. For example, in 1998 while agriculture employed 21.8 percent of the labor force, it produced only 8 percent of the gross domestic product (GDP). Comparatively, the service sector employed 28.8 percent of the work force but produced 59 percent of the GDP. This was due in part to the increasing importance of the service sector, which grew along with Mexico's increased urbanization and development of the tourist industry.

As in other developing countries of the world, the latter half of the twentieth century was a period of increased urbanization in Mexico. Rural-to-urban migration increased by about 4.4 percent per year between 1965 and 1980. Between 1980 and 1995 Mexico's urban population increased by 7.2 percent (from 66.3 percent in 1980 to 73.5 percent in 1995)[14] so that nearly three-fourths of the population now lives in an urban area. The four largest cities are Mexico City (15 million), Guadalajara (3.2 million), Monterrey (2 million), and Puebla.[15] With implementation of its 100 Cities Program as part of its 1995–2000 National Program for Urban Development, the Mexican government tried to divert urban migration from impacted metropolitan areas to other locations by refocusing development programs to other parts of the country (Castill 2004).[16] Thus, by developing its tourism industry, Mexico hoped to draw labor away from urban centers and to new tourist development sites.[17]

The social and economic changes that this development brings with it are begging to receive the attention of scholars from a variety of disciplines, yet sexuality has been largely overlooked (see Madsen Camacho 2000). Clearly, the socioeconomic linkages between Mexico and the global economy, and the United States in particular, have grown stronger since Mexico's early attempts in the late nineteenth century, especially in the past two decades. But, what do these political economic factors have to do with Mexican sexuality and gender? And how do they relate to the sexuality of migration?

TABLE 4.1

Mexican Socioeconomic Profile since 1982

CATEGORY	1982	1986	1990	1994	1998
Population (millions)	71.3	81.7	87.9	92.2	98.5
Growth Rate	2.4	2.5	2.2	1.94	1.77
Net Migration Rate			-2	-3.09	-2.89
Gross Domestic Product	170	176	187	740	694.3
Exports (millions)	$15,308	$23,727,000	$23,100,000	$50,500,000	$110,400,000
% with U.S.	62%	53%	66%	74%	85%
Imports	$18,572	$11,870,000	$23,300,000	$65,500,000	$109,800,000
% with U.S.	65%	60%	62%	74%	74.80%
Labor Force					
Total (millions)	18	24	26.1	26.2	36.6
Unemployed	10%	10%	20%	10.70%	3.70%
Top 3 sectors	agriculture	services	services	services	services
(% of labor force)	(33.0%)	(31.4%)	(31.4%)	(31.7%)	(28.8%)
	manufacturing	agriculture	agriculture	agriculture	agriculture
	(16.6%)	(26.0%)	(26.0%)	(28%)	(21.8%)
	services	commerce	commerce	commerce	commerce
	(16.6%)	(13.9%)	(13.9%)	(14.6%)	(17.1%)

Source: CIA World Factbook, 1982, 1984, 1990, 1994, and 1998.

Political Economy of Mexican Sexuality

The move towards modernization in the later part of the nineteenth century and Mexico's subsequent strategies to attract capitalist investment in the twentieth century have profoundly influenced sexuality. Although reports of "sodomy" and homosexual acts date back to the Spanish conquest (with subsequent actions of the Church to eradicate such behavior), my focus here is on the effects of capitalist development on sexuality, particularly sexuality between men. A growing number of scholars are beginning to examine these issues. Hondagneu-Sotelo (1994) and Gutmann (1996) have demonstrated how gender norms are being transformed among Mexicans both in the United States and in Mexico. In addition, Espin (1999) and González-López (2000) have demonstrated that sexual norms, behaviors, and identities among Mexican men and women are also transformed through the experiences of migration. However, it is important to remember that, as a geopolitical boundary and militarized zone, the U.S.-Mexican border is a line that is difficult to cross if you are moving north and relatively easy if your destination is south. For a variety of complex reasons (including immigration laws and policies and the politics of gender and sexuality), the crossing is made more difficult for Mexicans who might be branded "homosexual" (see also Luibhéid 1998). Thus, for many Mexican "queer" men and women, migrating to urban areas within Mexico proved to be a better alternative (see Sanchez-Crispin and Lopez-Lopez 1997).

Beginning with the Porfiriato period, in its efforts to modernize the nation, the Mexican state began to link development to moral and social order. Buffington (1997) argues that

> [i]n the Porfirian period, social scientists had been obsessed with the problem of "order," which seemed the necessary first step toward capitalist economic development. Criminal activities represented a grave threat to public order, threatening economic development by disrupting commerce, encouraging capital flight, and discouraging foreign investment. Crime was therefore a source of considerable concern to Mexican policy makers. This concern translated into a scientific investigation not just of crime and criminals per se but of a generalized state of being, "criminality," that included sexual deviance. . . .
>
> Post-revolutionary criminologists shared Porfirian concerns about public order and capitalist economic development but with one significant dif-

ference. Ideologically linked to the idea of an inclusive (if not democratic) modern state, their agenda stressed the redemptive possibilities of the new regime. And thus doubly condemned congenital (probably unredeemable) states like homosexuality. Criminals might be the by-products of social injustice; homosexuals were (especially in the biological sense) unproductive degenerates whose perversion threatened the moral health of the newly reborn Mexican nation. . . . In the new "revolutionary" Mexico: criminals maybe, homosexuals definitely not. (124–25)

It is important to reiterate here that in this context, the term "homosexuals" refers to a particular type of man who has sex with men. "Homosexuals" may be interpreted to mean openly effeminate men who made their "shameless" desire publicly known through dress, behavior, and/or identity. Over time an elaborate "system" of identity labels has been created by the Mexican homosexual subculture to differentiate the types of sexualities that men have (see also Murray 1995; Murray and Dynes 1995). These range from the *vestidas* who dress as women (who are assumed to play the feminine role but who do not necessarily assume *pasivo* sexual roles) to the *mayates*[18] (who display masculine performances and assume the *activo* sexual role), from the more versatile *internacionales* to the strictly heterosexual *bugas* (see also Prieur 1998). The importance of these terms lies not in their subcultural etymology, per se, but rather in that they demonstrate a system of social stratification and the creation of a subcultural lexicon by which to name power differentials.

This construction of sexuality as a continuum, rather than a binary system of stratified relations, nears institutionalized status when one considers that consensual sex between adult (age eighteen and above) members of the same sex is not a crime in Mexico.[19] While this may seem contradictory, I would argue that given the prevalence of bisexuality, sodomy laws would have been counterproductive (if enforced) because they would have criminalized the sexual activities of a large portion (if not the majority) of the male masses. How, then, to control *los jotos*?[20]

Even though there are no federal antisodomy laws, public "decency" laws are frequently applied against homosexuals. Queer Mexicans have been subjected to legal persecution under Article 201 of the Mexican penal code for "Transgressions against Morality and Public Decency," which is supposedly meant to protect minors. However, as Lumsden (1991) argues, the underlying purpose of Article 201 is not to "protect" minors from "sexual depravity," but to stigmatize anyone whose values and behavior question Mexico's machista and heterosexist order. Thus, Article 201 associates homosexuality with drug addiction, alcoholism, prostitution, and crime in terms of the possible outcome resulting from the "sexual corruption" of minors. (52)

Thus, while explicit laws that criminalize homosexuality per se are not found in Mexican penal codes, queer Mexicans become the target of the implicit and subjective reading of other codified "crimes." Locally, more direct policies against homosexuals have been implemented. In 1997, the mayor of Guadalajara, a member of the conservative PAN issued new police codes punishing "practices implying a deviant life" and "offending public morality or practicing obscene exhibitionism in public places" with a fine of 21–30 days' minimum wage or 25–36 hours in jail (Wockner 1997a). In addition, Mexican informants in Guadalajara explained that although the political environment has improved for gays and lesbians, the police still employ intimidation techniques such as "raiding" gay bars on occasion, asking patrons for identification, and then departing.

Thus, for middle- and upper-class homosexuals who might have been more concerned with appearances and rumor, private parties were often held in the homes of well-known persons.[21] Santiago, a man in his forties and a former professor of drama, describes queer life in Mexico before the commodification of "gayness":

> Twenty years ago I started in *el ambiente*. The *ambiente* in Guadalajara was something magical, it was sensational. There weren't any of the places that we have today. Before, the parties were at regular houses. The richest men of *el ambiente* would give you an invitation. They made invitations for everyone. Most of us in *el ambiente* knew each other, we were like a family. Some treated us well, depending on whether you were good looking you would end up going to bed with the most rich and famous. . . . As one of my friends of *el ambiente* says, "Before, being a *joto* was a privilege, now it is a vulgarity, anyone can be *gay*."

Santiago's comments illustrate not only the fact that class and physical appearance (in all likelihood race is part of this) were factors in constructing the strata of Mexican homosexuality but perhaps more importantly that a dramatic change has occurred by which the boundaries that constrained *los jotos* have been reshaped to give rise to a "gay" identity that "anyone" can share. The creation of gay and lesbian bar space, which has largely replaced private parties, is the result of at least two factors: (1) the growth of the Mexican gay and lesbian movement, which has made gays and lesbians more visible in Mexico, and (2) greater market demands for gay bars, which are strengthened through foreign gay tourism. The bars range from upscale discos to more humble cantinas, and although the majority of patrons were men, women were also present in the establishments I visited in Guadalajara, as I discuss in the next chapter. The most salient feature of these different bars is their class stratification. Cantinas are open to practically anyone who walks through the door while upscale discos cater to a wealthier clientele. Santiago's sense that "anyone can be gay" does not mean that social stratification no longer exists in Mexico's *ambiente*. On the contrary, "otherness" remains a marked facet of life among *los otros*, but its meaning is reformulated within a context of sexual commodification and queer tourism. In such a context, class remains an important marker, but I would argue that there is a greater mixing across not only class but also male and female social worlds than that which existed in private party events.

Lumsden (1991) asserts that Mexico's gay and lesbian movements have their roots in the student movement of 1968 that rocked Mexico and the rest of the world. The firing of a Sears department store employee in 1971 served, according to Lumsden, as "the catalyst that brought together the first group of gays and lesbians in Mexican history that would question their stigmatization and social oppression" (1991, 60). Since that momentous occasion various gay and lesbian organizations have been created (and disbanded) throughout Mexico, including the Nancy Cardenas Lesbian Documentation Center and Historical Archive for Mexico, Latin America, and the Caribbean, in Mexico City. Gay pride festivities are held in various Mexican cities, including Ensenada, Mexico City, and, of course, Tijuana. And in 1997, lesbian activist Patria Jimenez won a seat in the Chamber of Deputies (a federal position). These examples illustrate that a "gay" (and lesbian) identity exists in Mexico. While not a clone of the contemporary American construction of "gay," it does exhibit more similarities than differences. The rise of a "gay" identity and social movement is rooted in part in response to attempts by society and the state to regulate and repress homosexuality, which has become more visible due to the effects of capitalist development (D'Emilio 1993 [1983]). The rise of a gay identity is also linked to the transnational ties of globalization that link Mexico to the United States, in particular the gay United States, as shown in the next chapter.

My interviews with several of my informants in Guadalajara were useful in shedding light on this matter (as were my interviews with Mexican migrant men detailed in the next chapter). Some informants explained that they had information about gay life in the United States from a number of different sources, including magazines, newspapers, videos, the internet, and travel. Middle- to upper-class Mexicans were able to travel to the United States (as well as other countries) and experience the "gay lifestyle" first-hand. These individuals would then return and share stories of their experiences. As Santiago put it, "the majority were interested in going to the United States to experience it and change their social status because traveling gave them a certain characteristic, the ability to say they were a very traveled, worldly person." Information on gay life in the United States is also disseminated through contacts with gay travelers to Mexico. With its proximity to the United States and the relatively low cost, Mexico has become a common destination for many gay and lesbian tourists. *The Ferrari Guides Gay Mexico: The Definitive Guide to Gay and Lesbian Mexico* (Black 1997), which provides tourist information for gay and lesbian tourists, lists over forty businesses that offer travel arrangements to Mexico aimed at gay and lesbian clientele. How this tourism is influencing the lives and sexual identities of Mexican men and women remains to be researched; however, Murray (1995) and Black (1997) report that the hospitality industry is a common employer of Mexican gays and lesbians (Córdova 1999).

Homosexuals in Mexico have responded to social regulation and oppression in a number of ways that depend on their social locations. These responses range from the creation of a subculture and communities to social protest and even an "escape" of sorts through travel to other countries such as the United States. As I will discuss later, tourism is of course one type of migration and is also a response to the marginalized status of homosexuals in Mexico. But first, I want to focus on why it is that not all queer Mexicans pack their bags and migrate to a "safer space" such as the United States.

Holding Their Ground

Very soon after I arrived in the Guadalajara area for my fieldwork, it became clear to me that, despite the fact that Mexico may not be as "liberal" as the United States in terms of sexual politics, gay life was indeed part of the city's landscape. Gay bars, cruising areas, bath houses and *travesti* clubs are part of the visible *ambiente,* albeit at a relatively less visible level than the *buga* one. Given these circumstances, one might be tempted to surmise that Mexican men can just as easily be "gay" in Mexico as in the United States and that sexuality has little to do with migration at all. Being "gay," however, is in many ways the crux of the matter. As I've argued, the meanings and identities associated with homosexual sex are varied, complex, and influenced by intersecting social dimensions. In part, it was through my questioning of these sexual categories and meanings that I began to notice some of the differences between Mexican MSMs who migrate to the United States and those who don't.

Marcos

Among the men I met in Guadalajara were those who can best be described as financially stable gay men, who are professionals, are self-employed, or come from well-to-do backgrounds and identify as either homosexual or gay. For instance, Marcos is an insurance coordinator in his late twenties who works for a hospital in Guadalajara. A key informant introduced me to him and I interviewed him in his office. Like most of the men I met in Guadalajara, Marcos felt that there was no reason to be "out of the closet" as we would define it here in the United States. He self-defines his sexuality as homosexual and lives with his family but has never directly told his family members of his sexual orientation. As he explained,

> I imagine that my whole family knows, but not from my mouth or because they've asked me. I think that they intuitively know. They prefer not to ask me and prefer that I don't tell them. It's not necessary, it's only my sexual preference.

Despite the fact that Marcos has never "outed" himself to his family, he considers himself to be an "out" gay man. Most of his friends are gay and he does not, according to his definition, lead a double life. Marcos explained that he does go out to gay bars rather frequently and feels very much to be part of Guadalajara's *ambiente*. His social class position has allowed him to live a comfortable life as a gay man despite social constraints that American gay men might find oppressive.

In addition, Marcos mentioned that travel was one means by which he could explore gay life more freely. Marcos explained that he travels often and is able to enjoy the gay scene in other parts of Mexico, including Puerto Vallarta, as well as in other countries. Marcos's class position allows him to keep his private and public lives separate by negotiating his identity through and across space and "zones of tolerance." When I asked if he had ever considered migrating to the United States, he exclaimed,

> No, no that country doesn't agree with me! Not its people, nor its customs, nothing. Better said, it just doesn't call my attention. The first chance I got I went to Canada, I've always been interested in Europe and I've gone there too. I've been to the U.S. but I've always seen it as something complicated. I know that immigrants are not looked upon favorably, so I don't have any reason to go to a country that mistreats people, especially my people.

For Marcos, the United States does not represent a space for tolerance in large part because it is a space that racially marks him as Other and allows no room for negotiation. Thus, Marcos's references to American racism were not unrepresentative. Many of the people whom I spoke to in Mexico, both formally and informally, mentioned racism and how Americans mistreat Mexicans as a matter of concern and at least one of the reasons why they preferred to stay in Mexico.

Jorge

While class plays an important role in mitigating the marginalization and stigmatization of homosexual sex, "heterosexuality," or rather the ability to "pass" as heterosexual, is another factor. Bisexual men who are married and maintain a public heterosexual persona and performance are able to maintain sexual relationships with men with minimal social repercussions. Jorge is one such man. In his fifties, Jorge is a married man with four children who works as a bartender in one of Guadalajara's all-male bath houses, where he has worked for the past seventeen years. The bath house is located in the heart of the city, tucked away in the subterranean floors of an office building. I interviewed Jorge one weekday afternoon in the bath house while he was working. The establishment was fairly busy and men of various physical descriptions would occasionally wander in, wrapped in a towel, and either survey the room or order a drink. When I asked Jorge what kind of men patronized the baths he smiled and replied, "Married gay men like me, we're all married and gay too." Jorge seemed to have no qualms with his "married and gay" identity (in fact, few of the people whom I met did) and explained to me that his wife knew where he worked and never asked him questions about it. As Jorge explained, "What do I do here? A blow job, a hand job, a quick screw. I always go home. Why should she care?" Jorge also explained to me that he had been to the United States several times to work but that he had never wanted to migrate permanently. Jorge viewed Guadalajara in a manner similar to the way he viewed his wife: Guadalajara was his home and always would be; there was no reason to leave.

The ease with which Jorge discussed sexuality was perhaps accommodated by the setting of the bath house itself, which provides a relatively safe space where men can have sexual encounters with other men, but my sense was that his comfort level is in no small way supported by his public status as a "straight" man. The ability to pass as heterosexual is not, of course, limited to married bisexual men; many "gay" men also pass, but marriage does provide, perhaps, the greatest level of legitimacy to that performance.

Santiago

Santiago was one of my key informants and played an important role in my understanding of gay life in Guadalajara. A friendly and articulate man who has been "in the life" since his teens, Santiago was able to provide me not only with insights into his life as a gay man but also with his perspective on Guadalajara's contemporary gay history (as discussed above). Although he spoke of the United States with an air of longing, Santiago explained that he had remained in Mexico due to familial responsibilities.

Santiago explained that since his first visit to the United States in 1986, he has always wanted to move there, in part because of its relatively more liberal sexual environment, which he jokingly referred to as the "phallic dream," but also because age is not a barrier to employment as it is in Mexico. However, he points to two reasons why he has not emigrated to the United States: first, a concern for racism and discrimination; and second, familial obligations. Since 1996 when his mother had a stroke, Santiago has been responsible for her care. He took an early retirement from his job in order to provide her with the care that he feels that she deserves, but for which he could not afford to pay. His siblings help with modest financial support and he provides the daily assistance that is needed. He expressed concern, however, that he would not be able to find a job when his mother dies due to age discrimination in the Mexican job market. Santiago's concern is a real one in many senses, as job applicants are required to give their date of birth and a photo with their résumés, and it is common for employers to place employment ads with an age range (commonly under forty). In fact, Santiago specifically asked me if I thought a man his age could find work in the United States. I replied that it was not necessarily a question of if, but rather at what cost. The likelihood that he would enter the United States as an undocumented immigrant would mean not only constant stress and anxiety but also that his job options would be limited, unless he could either find a way to migrate legally or use his social networks to help ensure better possibilities.

Francisco

The question of cost is a relative one. Among my contacts in Mexico were several men who entertained the thought of migrating to the United States but did not. A common reason is what I term "lack of support systems"; that is, these men lacked the sort of support systems and social networks that migration scholars have asserted facilitate the migration process.

Francisco is a 30-year-old gay man of modest means who sells fruits and vegetables from a stand in an industrial area of Guadalajara during the day and at night sells hamburgers from the front of his home in one of the poorer districts of the city. Somewhat shy, Francisco is what most Mexicans might consider stereotypically gay. He is a relatively effeminate man with long bleached hair that he keeps in a ponytail, and I noticed that although he seemed to be at least tolerated in his environment, he was also stared at frequently. Francisco explained to me that he *had* immigrated to the United States earlier and spent two months with family members in Santa Monica, California. However, Francisco related that his family members gave him a hard time due to his sexuality and appearance, and when he couldn't find work they sent him back to Mexico. He hopes to try again in the year 2000, but the next time he knows he can't depend on the support of his family.

Conclusion

In the preceding sections of this chapter, I have argued that cultural conceptual frameworks for understanding homosexuality in Mexico mask the structural dimensions that shape Mexican sexualities through a discourse of difference and cultural primacy. Almaguer's thesis of the sex/gender/power axis has been particularly helpful in my thinking about Mexican men's sexualities as shaped by intersecting dimensions of power. The variety of labels that the homosexual subculture has created to name types of men and male sexualities points to these stratified relations. They also exemplify Foucault's (1990 [1978]) notion of the multiplication of sexualities that result as the state attempts to regulate them.

My research in Mexico supports Lumsden's (1991) arguments for a political economic understanding of sexuality in Mexico. The state's early strategies to create an environment conducive to capitalist development led to a push to create social and moral order through legal regulation. Urbanization, the development of queer communities, and the rise of a Mexican gay movement have supported the development of gay identities.[22] The creation of gay organizations, gay pride events, and the ensuing commercialization of "gayness" in Mexico are examples that illustrate that a "gay" identity exists in Mexico. Though not clones of the American model, Mexican gay identities are more similar to than different from the gay identities in the United States. The point here is not to argue that "gays" in Mexico are just like "us" but rather to demonstrate that among the variety of sexual identities that exist in Mexico is a gay identity. This identity is linked to capitalist development, and depending upon the social locations and sexual identities of men who have sex with men, there are a number of responses to social attempts to regulate and repress homosexuality.

Men who either are able to maintain a relatively secure status or have strong emotional or financial ties are less likely to emigrate from Mexico. For many of these men migration would in all probability lead to downward social mobility. In addition, there are men who because of their social locations do not have the support mechanisms necessary for migration even though it is an aspiration. Social class location is obviously an important factor in determining these outcomes and to what extent an alternative space exists for a queer existence.

5

De Ambiente
Queer Tourism and Shifting Sexualities

> The coastal regions all around the country are noted for their sensual ambience. Perhaps it's the heat but just about anywhere there's a beach and a city there's action. Acapulco, Cancún, Vallarta, Mazatlán, and Veracruz are all hot, and so are the men.
> —Eduardo David, *Gay Mexico: The Men of Mexico*

"Do you know Mexico?" coyly poses the opening page of Mexico's official tourist web site.[1] Do you? Perhaps not. This is not a Mexico of social inequality, economic turmoil, indigenous uprisings and mass emigration. No, this is a different Mexico—a sexy Mexico. Additional headers entice the reader to "Come Feel the Warmth of Mexico" where "...beaches are such as moods: bays that with happy smiles, beaches that spread in straight line, as to remind its steadiness, female beaches, smooth and with cadence, frisky beaches, that open and close, decline and go up [sic]." The sexual imagery of the web site leaves the reader (presumably heterosexual) with a sort of coquettish frustration and a desire for more than a "virtual tour" can provide. While it may seem otherwise, Mexico's flirtation with tourists is not limited to straight travelers. As previously mentioned, the nation has become a major destination of gay and lesbian tourists, particularly Americans, in a growing global tourism industry. In turn, Mexico's *ambiente* (homosexual subculture—see chapter 4, note 4) is undergoing its own transformation, intimately linked to queer tourism.

The purpose of this chapter is to examine two sides of queer tourism "south of the border": (1) the development of gay and lesbian tourism in Mexico and (2) the effects of this industry on Mexican sexualities. As a point of clarification, I should also state up front that I refer to gay and lesbian tourism as an identity-based industry, and queer tourism as a larger market that encompasses a multitude of identities, including both native and foreign heterosexuals, bisexuals, and transgendered people. I argue that the relationship between gay and lesbian tourism and Mexican sexualities is a complex one in which dimensions of both sexual colonization and sexual liberation are at work. Furthermore, I assert that in order to understand Mexican sexualities we must move away from one-dimensional cultural models and instead examine them from a more complex and materialist perspective that recognizes that culture, social relations, and identities are embedded in global processes.

Although my original research interests focused on migration in a stricter sense, I soon realized that tourism was not only an important factor in the lives of the men I interviewed but also a form of migration itself (in a broader sense of the word). While my ancestry is Mexican and I am fluent in Spanish, I am a Chicano—I am not Mexican. Thus, although my purpose in Mexico was entirely academic, I was a tourist. Despite the voyeuristic tendencies of both, there is a difference between my roles as ethnographer and as tourist that I think is relevant to this chapter and my analysis. My gaze as an ethnographer was aimed at understanding the political economy of sexuality in Mexico as it differentially shapes the lives of men. I was not in Mexico on vacation; nonetheless, Mexicans often read me in the public spaces of the plazas, the bars, and the streets, not as a researcher but as a tourist. Thus, it is the intersection of my ethnographic and tourist roles that informs my analysis of queer tourism in Mexico. Following a brief discussion that links my analysis of tourism with the previous chapters, I discuss various dimensions of Mexico's political economy that contributed to the development of queer tourism in the country. I then utilize archival and ethnographic data to examine more closely the relationship between gay and lesbian tourism and Mexican sexualities in these sexual borderlands.

As discussed in the previous chapter, according to anthropological accounts, including the important work of Carrier (1995) and Murray (1995), homosexuality in Mexico is defined not by the biological sex of the participants but rather by the gendered role that they perform in the sexual act. According to this model, it is only the *pasivo* (passive) participant who is marked as homosexual. However, it is not clear if this gendered construction only applies to men. It should come as no surprise, given the relative historical invisibility of lesbian sexuality in academic discourse, that there is a dearth of literature on Mexican female homosexuality (see Yarbro-Bejarano 1997; Mogorevejo 2000). The literature that does exist focuses not on sexual behavior but rather on public gender performance, and here too it seems that it is the non-normative role that is marked—that of the "masculine" *marimacha* (both *marimacha* and *marimacho* are used to refer to masculine lesbians). In addition, and as discussed in chapters 3 and 4, anthropological reports of male homosexuality asserted that a "gay" identity, as understood in an American context, did not exist in Mexico.[2] I emphasized that "gay" identity and culture were understood as American constructions—alien to the Mexican social landscape.

Among U.S. gay and lesbian scholars in the late twentieth century, "gay" identities were understood to be the socially constructed results of a combination of factors related to modernization. These included industrialization, greater economic independence from family as a result of wage labor, urbanization, and a greater concentration of people with similar erotic inclinations in larger cities (see D'Emilio 1993 [1983]; Rubin 1992 [1984]). This view of homosexuality in the industrialized world stood in stark contrast to that of less developed countries. In the previous chapter, I asked whether the matching of gay identities and capitalist development by social constructionist arguments could stand in sharp contrast to social scientists' understandings of sexual identities in the "developing world." Arguing that Mexican sexual identities should also be understood as multiply constituted and intimately linked to the structural and ideological dimensions of modernization and development, I address the following questions in this chapter: First, to what extent are Mexican sexualities and the dimensions that shape them "Mexican," and to what extent are they global? Furthermore, if tourism is to be understood as a modernist project built upon mediated representation and space, as Dean Mac-Cannell (1999 [1976]) asserts, then how might these dimensions shape "native" identities and experiences? This chapter attempts to examine the complexities of Mexican sexualities from a political economic perspective, with a particular focus on queer tourism, in order to understand, in turn, how these dimensions are shaping the sexual identities of Mexican men.

Enclaces/Rupturas Fronterizas *(Border Linkages/Ruptures)*

The border that delineates the nations of Mexico and the United States has been since its creation with the Treaty of Guadalupe in 1848 "an open wound." But as Anzaldúa (1987) makes clear, *la frontera* is both real and imagined. It is a geopolitical boundary that links even as it separates the two nations, but it is also a metaphor for the spaces in which hybridity is created (in an often violent manner). In this section, my purpose is to highlight the political-economic linkages between the United States and Mexico that have given rise to the development of gay and lesbian tourism in Mexico. In addition, I highlight the border ruptures that are created through "tolerance zones"—a sexual "borderlands" in which Mexican male sexualities are fixed even as they are transformed.

Tourism has become an increasingly important sector of the Mexican economy. Beginning in the late 1960s Mexico created its own Ministry of Tourism (SECTUR), which is responsible for tourism as a whole, and FONATUR (in the early 1970s), which is responsible for infrastructure development projects in particular and has sponsored annual tourism trade fairs since 1996. In 1999, the World Trade Organization ranked Mexico seventh among the top ten destinations and tenth in foreign currency generated from tourism, and a majority of Mexican tourists continue to be from the United States (Guenette 2000). More precisely, more than 90 percent of Mexican tourists are from the United States (Arellano 1996). While it is impossible to know in any definitive way what proportions of Mexican tourists are gay, lesbian, or bisexual, there are factors that point to the development of queer tourism in the country.[3] These include the development and commodification of Mexican "gay" culture and space, and the rise of a Mexican gay and lesbian movement.

Gay bars in Mexico are a relatively new phenomenon, although they seem to be historically linked to urbanization and the development of *zonas de tolerancia* in the early part of the century. As discussed in chapter 3, *zonas de tolerancia* (tolerance zones, or red light districts) developed after the revolution to control what were defined as forms of social deviance that included prostitution and homosexuality. The *zonas* were thus both gendered and sexualized spaces for those who transgressed gender norms and where men could satisfy their "licentious" desires. The spaces included areas where both male homosexual and transvestite bars were located and provided an escape from moral restraint for men who otherwise led more public heterosexual lives. Once established, the *zonas* became a legitimized space for "immoral activity" that attracted sexual tourism from north of the border where morality was more closely policed. For example, "Boys Town" brothels on the Mexican side of the border remain to this day rites of passage for young American men who cross the border looking for mostly heterosexual adventure. Thus, by the mid-twentieth century, the Mexican border towns were already firmly established as sites of sexual tourism for men on both sides of the border.[4]

Various scholars have mentioned the growing popularity of the term "gay" as an identity label in Mexico by both men and women (who also use the term "lesbian") (see Lumsden 1991; Murray 1995; Prieur 1998). While the label is sometimes written as "gai" it is clear that it refers to a sexual identity, culture, and movement and is thus similar in many ways to the term "gay" as used in the United States. Lumsden (1991) explains this shift in identity constructions as a consequence of several political factors. The combination of urbanization/industrialization, along with the creation of *zonas de tolerancia,* in all probability provided the social spaces whereby sexual minorities could establish social networks and, at least to some degree, create "community."

This spatial segregation resulted in queer zones or ghettoes in some cities like Guadalajara and Puerto Vallarta.[5] In Puerto Vallarta, the south side of the city has become the de facto "gay side" with bars, hotels, and other establishments that cater to a gay male—especially tourist—clientele. It should also be stated, however, that as is the case in the United States, an entire city has also become identified as a "gay space." As previously mentioned, the city of Guadalajara itself has over time become known as the San Francisco of Mexico due to its gay and lesbian population. As one middle-aged gay man told me, "in Guadalajara all the men are either *mariachis* or *maricones* [fags]." However, the development of a gay and lesbian community in Guadalajara, along with the movement for gay rights, has been hotly contested by conservative forces in the community.

Guadalajara and Acapulco were common vacation destinations for gay men from Mexico City in the 1980s and early 1990s (Sanchez-Crispin and Lopez-Lopez 1997).[6] However, since that time, Puerto Vallarta has developed into Mexico's premier gay resort town as a sort of satellite gay space for its big sister (Guadalajara), much as Fire Island is to New York and Palm Springs is to Los Angeles.[7]

Another factor that has contributed to the development of queer tourism in Mexico is the slow but steady rise of a Mexican gay and lesbian rights movement. As mentioned in the previous chapter, Lumsden (1991) argues that the student movement in 1968 and the firing of a Sears department store employee can be understood as catalysts for challenging social oppression on the basis of sexual orientation in Mexico. Whether incidents like these were indeed the cause of the Mexican gay rights movement or not, what is clear is that the movement is not "new" to the Mexican political arena. Since the 1970s various gay and lesbian organizations have been created (and disbanded) throughout Mexico. Gay pride festivities are held in various Mexican cities and have become a tourist attraction in themselves. In fact, Cancún hosted the International Gay Pride Festival in 2001. These examples illustrate that a gay (and lesbian) identity exists in Mexico; and although it is not a clone of American constructions, there are many similarities.[8]

The rise of a gay identity is linked to the transnational ties of globalization between Mexico to the United States, in particular the gay United States. My interviews with Mexican men in Guadalajara and migrants in the Los Angeles area were particularly useful in shedding light on this matter. These transnational links gave rise to a sexual identity label in the 1980s (still used to a certain degree)—*internacional*. Carrier reported use of the *internacional* (international) label by the then "hipper" and younger homosexual men during his field research.[9] The label, which referred to men who were versatile in their sexual repertoire, obviously has transborder connotations. Clearly, then, Mexican sexualities are being transformed through transnational processes and linkages, including that of tourism.

Queer Tourism in Mexico

> The reason why a million or more American visitors have traveled to Mexico in the course of recent years, is that the average practical-minded person regards recreation travel from the angle of maximum returns at a minimum outlay of money and time. It is upon this purely practical consideration that Mexico makes its bid to the recreation-bent traveler.
>
> —Anonymous, "The Lure of Mexico"

While a growing body of literature has examined the impact of tourism and globalization on sexuality in the Pacific Rim (Truong 1990; Hall 1994a, 1994b), the way these phenomena are influencing Latin American countries has been largely ignored.[10] However, the fact that gay and lesbian tourism is a rapidly growing market in every part of the world—estimated at $17 billion (U.S.) dollars by the International Gay and Lesbian Travel Association (IGLTA)—demands greater attention.[11] With its proximity to the United States and the relatively low cost compared to other international sites, Mexico has become a desired destination for many gay and lesbian tourists. The recently created Tourist Promotion Board of Mexico plans to market "a number of product clubs featuring destinations and services *for certain types of people* like honeymooners, fishing buffs or nature lovers" (Guenette 2000, 42). Although the gay and lesbian market niche is not mentioned specifically by the government organization, there are signs of strategic growth, including a growing number of gay and lesbian travel companies with travel programs in Mexico and publications that cater to the gay and lesbian tourist in Mexico.

Although Mexico has long been a favored site for vacationing among Americans, the growing popularity of Mexico as a *gay and lesbian* tourist destination is due in large measure to the marketing efforts of the gay and lesbian tourist industry. Founded in 1983, the IGTLA is an international organization with member organizations throughout the world and growing representation in Latin America,[12] including Mexico. The development of gay and lesbian cruise companies, such as Atlantis, RSVP, and Olivia, have also contributed to making Mexico a popular destination.[13] In addition, there are a number of travel magazines and web sites that cater to gay and lesbian patrons, as do a growing number of gay and lesbian travel agencies that offer packages throughout Mexico. *The Ferrari Guides Gay Mexico* (Black 1997) lists more than forty businesses that offer travel arrangements throughout Mexico aimed at gay and lesbian clientele; not surprisingly, nearly all of these are based in the United States (mostly, but not exclusively, in major urban centers) (Córdova 1999). Among the numerous international travel guides for gay and lesbian tourists—including comprehensive guides by Spartacus, Ferrari, Odysseus, and Damron—are several that focus on travel information for the queer tourist in Mexico. There are three queer tourist guide books that focus exclusively on Mexico and for the most part target a male audience: *Gay Mexico: The Men of Mexico* (David 1998), *The Ferrari Guides Gay Mexico: The Definitive Guide to Gay and Lesbian Mexico* (Black 1997),[14] and *A Man's Guide to Mexico and Central America* (Córdova 1999). Each of the guides gives both general information useful to any tourist (i.e., money exchange information and maps) and information specific to the queer tourist (e.g., bath house locations and helpful Spanish phrases for meeting men).

All three guides provide city-by-city information. Señor Córdova's *Man's Guide* lists fourteen cities, Eduardo David's *Gay Mexico* has listings for twenty-five, and Richard Black's *Ferrari Guide* lists forty-three. While Mexico's urban centers (e.g., Mexico City, Guadalajara, and Monterey) and mainstream tourist destinations (i.e., Cancún, Acapulco, Los Cabos) are among the cities listed, the guides also list towns and cities that are more "off the beaten path," especially for the queer tourist. These include cities such as León in the state of Guanajuato (known as the shoe capital of the world) and the city of Oaxaca with its neighboring villages. The distinction between these sites and gay tourist sites is supposedly one of "authenticity." But while the travel guides forewarn gay tourists of the potential dangers of crossing into these native grounds, they are in reality tourist sites, too. Thus, "off the beaten path" does not necessarily mean that the sites are nontourist spaces but rather that they are more "mainstream," catering to a more "straight" clientele.

An examination of these guides and tourist services suggests that two "sides" of Mexico are most commonly represented: the "just like home" and the exotic. As Black (1997) explains in *The Ferrari Guides*, "For Americans, Mexico is close, yet foreign. For any traveler, it's different yet has many of the comforts of home. It offers something for everyone! You're in for a great time!" (14). While both the "just like home" and the exotic representations emphasize the homoerotic aspects of different sites in Mexico, one targets American tourists who want to vacation with all the gay comforts of home while the other seeks to attract those who seek an erotic adventure not to be found in any suburban American home life. Both speak to MacCannell's (1999 [1976]) insight that

> [t]he frontiers of world tourism are the same as the expansion of the modern consciousness with terminal destinations for each found throughout the colonial, ex-colonial, and future colonial world where raw materials for industry and exotic flora, fauna, and peoples are found in conglomeration. The tourist world has also been established *beyond* the frontiers of

existing society, or at least beyond the edges of the Third World. A *para-dise* is a traditional type of tourist community, a kind of last resort, which has as its defining characteristic its location not merely outside the physical borders of urban industrial society, but just beyond the border of the peasant and plantation society as well. (183)

Yet for queer tourism there also exists a "border" tension between the lure of an exotic "paradise" and the dangers of homophobia in foreign lands. Here, Mexico seems to represent a homosexual paradise free of the pressures of a modern "gay lifestyle," where sexuality exists in its "raw" form yet where the dangers of an uncivilized heterosexual authority also threaten.

Gay and lesbian cruises seem to target those more inclined to a mediated adventure where one can enjoy prefabricated representations of the exotic and always return to one's "home away from home" either aboard ship or in a hotel. The cruise destinations tend to be located either in the "Mexican Caribbean" on the east coast or in the Baja area on the west. Take, for instance, Atlantis's description of its services:

Atlantis vacations are designed for the way we enjoy ourselves today. We created the concept of an all-gay resort vacation and are the leaders in all-gay charters of first class resorts and cruise ships. All at exotic locations, exclusively ours for these special weeks, with an emphasis on friendship and camaraderie. Places where you can always be yourself and always have fun. That's the way we play.

The "home-away-from-home" approach to gay travel thus allows for the "best of both worlds" where one can "play" on exotic beaches but under controlled conditions. A new *zona de tolerancia* is born—a queer space that protects inhabitants from the threat of cultural mismatch, including homophobia. Thus, in this queer borderland, the tourist can enjoy Mexico's pleasures under a controlled environment free from the less "civilized" world *del otro lado* (on the other side) of tourist boundaries.

In comparison to the vacation cruise advertisements, gay guide books are more apt to give stereotypical representations of Mexican men. Consider David's (1998) description:

Many Mexican men are often breathtaking in their beauty. They are sensual and often unabashedly sexual. Proud to be male, aware of their physical nature, they are often ready to give of themselves and sometimes receive in return. . . .

The adventurous visitor may want to go farther afield in search of the men for whom Mexico is particularly famed: the butch *hombres* who would never walk into a place known to be gay, but who are ready to spring to attention when they catch a man's eye. These are men who must be pursued. (27–28)

This excerpt exemplifies a *colonial desire* that Robert Young (1995) defines as the dialectic of attraction and repulsion, to conquer (and be conquered by) the hypermasculine and sexually charged racial Other. The colonial message is reinforced in the guide books by advice on "rewarding" Mexican men for their services with gifts or money, suggesting that financial compensation for homosexual sex is a cultural norm.

Such representations are reminiscent of what is commonly referred to as "Spanish fantasy heritage" (see McWilliams 1948). At the end of the nineteenth century and in the first half of the twentieth century, the prevailing image of Mexicans (both in the United States and Mexico) was of "gay *caballeros*" and "dark and lovely *señoritas*" lazily dancing the night away under Spanish tile roofs. These representations were utilized to sell a romantic and exotic image of California and Mexico to tourists in the early decades of the twentieth century. Contemporary gay tourist images seem to either play up the "Latin lover" image or place greater emphasis on a bit rougher and more "savage" version of the gay *caballero*, both of which abound in gay travel guides. Compare, for instance, the cover images of the three travel guides.

The images on the covers of both Black's guide (figure 5.1) and Córdova's (figure 5.2) represent the "Latin lover" look, a light-complected (though tanned) young man in romantic settings, at least partially clothed and waiting to give the queer male tourist a *bienvenida* (a welcoming). The image on the cover of David's guide (figure 5.3) is a darker *mestizo* with facial hair in an ambiguous setting and framed suggestively (the reader is not sure of the model's state of dress). Not surprisingly, it is David's book that contains more information for the traveler looking for experiences "off the beaten path." Beyond the stereotypes of Latino masculinity, these images represent contradictions of internalized homophobia and the quest for the elusive "real" man among gay tourist themselves.

One of the ironies of this search is that as more gay male tourists look for these exotic places, virgin territory, off the beaten path of main-

Figure 5.1

Figure 5.2

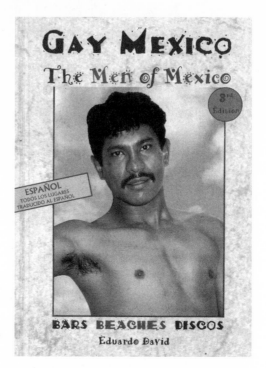

Figure 5.3

stream gay tourist sites, the sites become, in effect, conquered territory—
gay tourist spots. This type of "invasion" is complicated, of course, by
the tensions between a certain level of sexual liberation versus sexual
conquest. That is, as gay and lesbian tourists become more common to
an area, there is a certain level of normalization that occurs through visibility. However, it is not clear to what extent the opening of more legitimized queer space is a positive effect for Mexico's queer population and
to what extent this space is framed as "American."

The expansion of the gay and lesbian tourism industry in Mexico is
but one of the more visible manifestations of this queer manifest destiny.
As previously mentioned, other signs of this development are the gay
bars that now operate throughout Mexico, some with American-sound-
ing names like Relax (Acapulco), Blue City (Cancún), MN'MS (Ciudad
Juarez), and The Door (Mexico City). In each case, these Mexican gay
bars are located in sites commonly visited by foreign gay tourists. While
they are not technically or legally off-limits to queer Mexican nationals,

only those of at least a middle-class background and with more sophisti-
cated tastes who might mix better with tourists are commonly found in
such bars/discos. *Zonas de tolerancia,* yes, but within limits.

The question of how this tourism is influencing the lives and sexual
identities of Mexican men and women remains to be researched, but
Murray (1995; see also Black 1997) reports that the hospitality industry
is a common employer of Mexican gays and lesbians.[15] In addition, male
prostitution (as either an occupation or "part-time" activity) is obviously
linked to gay male tourism (Carrier 1995). And more recently, epidemi-
ologists have become more concerned with tourism and the spread of
HIV in the country. In the following section I explore these questions
more directly through the voices of Mexican men themselves.

Gay Caballeros and Phallic Dreams: Life in the Sexual Borderlands

> In . . . coordination of and responsibility for the diverse efforts of
> the nation, tourism has its place, a place that is characterized by
> its diversification, for it is indifferent to nothing and affects all, the
> local as much as the foreign. . . . And that does not refer only to
> foreign tourism, those visitors from afar who discover new realities,
> even as they offer them.
>
> —Héctor Manuel Romero, "Nada es indiferente al turismo"

Mexico's Gay *ambiente* has changed dramatically over the last decade.
What was once an underground world of private parties in the homes
of homosexual men has become a more public and therefore more visible phenomenon, as Santiago's observation (as noted in the previous
chapter) that "anybody can be gay now" illustrates. The commodification of Mexican gay spaces presents a complex set of factors in the lives
of queer Mexican men. The spaces created allowed for the development
of an identity and community that served as the foundation of the gay
and lesbian movement in Mexico. Queer tourists shape this space both
through their contact with Mexicans and through the creation of new
space to serve their needs. Contact provides an exchange of cultural and
political information around issues of queerness that has an impact on
men's lives.

Some men use this information as a rationale for migrating to the United States, which they construct as a more tolerant space/place. Armando is a 32-year-old man from Jalisco who lives in the Los Angeles area, where he works in HIV services. He is the oldest of eight children and moved to the United States in 1990. In 1995, he was living in Santa Ana after having moved from Los Angeles, where he had been living with his brother. At the time of the interview he was an undocumented immigrant. Armando learned about the United States through tourism, indirectly at first and later through his own experiences. In Mexico, Armando was a seminarian studying to be a priest. In the seminary he heard stories of gay life in the United States from friends (including other seminarians) who had visited the "north," and later he himself visited the United States for missionary exchange programs. It was after he was advised by a priest to move to the north, where he could live more openly as a gay man, that Armando migrated.

Lalo, a 33-year-old gay-identified man from Guadalajara, is a similar case. The fifth of nine children, Lalo comes from what he describes as a "very poor" class background. Lalo explained that after being rejected by his family for being gay, he moved to Puerto Vallarta for a time, where he worked in hotels. He explained that many of his coworkers were also gay and that they helped him get by to the extent of giving him an apartment in which to live. He migrated to Southern California on the advice of his friends in 1983. He is now a legal resident and lives in Fountain Valley. He explained,

> The people in the hotel would tell me "Go to the United States, it's beautiful, you make good money and there are a lot of homosexuals. You can hold [your lover's] hand and kiss in public and nothing happens." I thought it was an ideal world where homosexuals could be happy. [But I] learned that it wasn't true that homosexuals were free, that they can hold hands or that Americans liked Mexicans.

The reality that awaited Lalo was not a utopia but rather more of a nightmare. Soon after moving to the United States with the assistance of gay friends, he discovered not only that homophobia does exist in the United States but also that racism was a fact of life he would have to deal with, which is just one of the many tribulations and hardships that queer immigrants must face (see Luibhéid 1998). The fantasy of gay life in the United States reported to Lalo is a common one. As mentioned, in my interview with Santiago he referred to it as the *sueño fálico*, or "phallic dream," in which queer men in Mexico envision the United States as a sexual utopia, an erotic land of milk and honey. The irony, of course, is that many American gay tourists have a similar dream when they visit Mexico's gay resorts.

For those Mexican men who have the resources, travel to "gay-friendly" places is also an option, as in the case of Marcos discussed in the previous chapter. Another such case is that of Franco, who travels about once a year to the Los Angeles area to visit family. He and Angel, a gay cousin, always go to gay bars together and Franco admits to having a good time, but his real love is Cuba. With a grin he related, "The men in Cuba are fantastic. I always take some extra things like cologne and clothes. Cuban men will fuck you for a Nike baseball cap." Thus, like his American counterparts in Mexico who are tourists with expendable income, Franco seeks sexual conquest in exotic lands, in this case Cuba. The excerpt helps to highlight not only the diversity of Mexican male sexual experiences with tourism but also the importance of class in shaping the power relations of these experiences. Apparently, the phallic dream knows no borders.

But the road to the phallic dream that some Mexican men pursue is a two-way street, and the reality of racism in the United States is the slap that wakes them. Juan and Miguel, both in their midtwenties, are two Mexican men I met during my research in the Los Angeles area. They actually returned to Mexico in part because of the difficulty of living in the United States but also because of social and economic opportunities they felt existed in Mexico. Although Juan was a naturalized citizen of the United States, Miguel was an undocumented immigrant. On a return visit to the United States Juan explained,

> The situation for us here in the United States was just too difficult. The type of work that Miguel could find here, without papers, was very hard and did not pay well, and everything is so expensive too. We decided that it was better to go to Cancún and work with gay tourists there. I know English and I've learned a little French too. We have a very small apartment and it isn't always easy, but we are happy there.

Juan and Miguel chose to return to Mexico to pursue their dreams and a more comfortable life as gay men. That is, with some of the social and economic capital (although it was limited) they acquired in the United

States, Juan and Miguel were able to move to Cancún and begin anew in a better class position.

Some of the Mexican men whom I interviewed in the United States felt the same discomfort that Juan and Miguel expressed, but rather than return to Mexico to live, they vacation there. Julio, a Guadalajara native in his early forties, lives in Orange County, California. He migrated to the United States through a network of gay friends and soon after married a lesbian friend who is a U.S. citizen. Now a legal resident, he works as an accountant for most of the year and saves money so that he can return to Mexico for months at a time. Like his Mexican contemporaries, Julio also uses vacations and tourism as a strategy of escape, but from his American context.

> The men here are superficial and I haven't been able to meet someone that I can have a long-term relationship with. When I go to Mexico I visit my family and friends and I feel their warmth and love. I still have a lot of gay friends in Guadalajara and I always spend time in [Puerto] Vallarta too. I feel like I can be myself there and that people appreciate me for who I am.

The frustrations that Julio expressed to me were in reference to his experiences with American gay scenes in general, but he was also critical of gay Latino culture and norms in the United States. Julio feels that the affective connections and sense of community that he knows in Guadalajara are largely missing in the United States—even among gay Latinos. In addition, he feels that American gay culture, and American men in particular, are too superficial.

Mexican men's relationships with American men are not always contentious. Roberto is in his early forties and has resided in the United States since moving from Mexico City in 1996. The fourth of five children, he comes from a prestigious and well-to-do family in Nayarit, Mexico. Although never married, Roberto has a teenaged son who lives in Mexico with the son's mother. Roberto lives in Long Beach and works as an AIDS educator for a Latino community organization. Roberto explained to me that he was quite happy with his life in Mexico as a civil servant but that people had begun to gossip about his sexual orientation and he feared for his job security. Roberto had met a man from the United States who was vacationing in Mexico and had maintained a friendly relationship with the man. When the American suggested to

Roberto that he move to the United States to live with him in the Los Angeles area, Roberto took advantage of the opportunity and moved to L.A. Although he is no longer in a relationship with the American, they continue to be friends.

My own experience researching issues of sexuality and migration has taught me that Roberto's experience is a common one. Many men become involved in "binational relationships" (i.e., relationships where partners are of different nationalities). Such relationships are not recognized by U.S. immigration policy, which therefore does not allow for the legal migration of same-sex spouses. Despite the "illegitimacy" of these relationships for immigration purposes, gays and lesbians do migrate from foreign countries any way they can to be with their partners.

Although he is not sure when and how he got infected, Roberto's story also speaks to the issue of HIV/AIDS and its connection to queer tourism (see Haour-Knipe and Rector 1996; Clift and Carter 2000). It is impossible to determine to what extent queer tourism is responsible for the spread of HIV in Mexico, but it would be foolish to suggest that there is no connection. However, queer tourism does play another important role related to HIV/AIDS. Condoms, lubricants, medications, and literature on safer sex that foreign tourists bring to Mexico are also shared with Mexican men. It should also be noted that the gay Mexico travel guides mentioned here even suggest that their readers assist Mexican men in such a manner (David 1998, 70). That is, travel guides recommend that gay American men taking "plenty" of "lube and condoms" with them and leave any extras to Mexican "friends" they've met along the way.

As discussed previously, the image of the "gay *caballero*" marketed by gay travel guides is a fantasy that has very real implications for Mexican masculinities and sexualities. The frustration that many Mexican men feel over the racist macho stereotype that Americans have of them is a complaint that I heard time and again during my research. For instance, Javier is a bisexual man in his late twenties whom I met in Guadalajara. Javier is married and has two children but enjoys having sex with men. Javier bemoaned,

> I don't like to have sex with Americans. They always seem to want a sex machine. They want a big penis that screws them all night long. I don't have a big penis and I want someone who will hold me and kiss me. I don't want to be the *activo*, I just want a man to make love to me.

Throughout my interview with him, I was struck by the way in which Javier expressed his sexuality in a manner that was compatible with his masculine identity. Despite the fact that he admittedly enjoyed being *pasivo*, and contrary to much of the literature on the topic, he securely expressed a masculine nonhomosexual identity. As a married bisexual man, Javier has social privileges that many other men who have sex with men do not. His sense of sexual repression is based not in Mexican norms but in American ones. In Javier's experience, American tourists come to Mexico seeking a stereotype of Mexican masculinity that Javier cannot meet and yet it is a gendered performance that is demanded time and again by gay American tourists' search for the macho.

Conclusion

As I mentioned in the beginning of this chapter, borders are both real and imagined. In the Western queer imaginary Mexico and its men somehow seem to be locked in a spatio-temporal warp of macho desire. Mexico seems to represent a place fixed in time, where "real" men can be found. The stereotype of the Mexican macho is alive and well in the imagination of American tourists. However, far from being culturally stagnant, Mexico has undergone profound changes in the last several decades. These changes shape the everyday experiences of Mexican men and the meanings and identities of gender and sexuality. While anthropologists working in Mexico in the 1970s and '80s asserted that "gay" identities did not exist as we understand them in an American context, this is no longer the case in the twenty-first century. The boundaries of Mexican sexual identities are changing even as the spaces that produce them are remapped. The development of gay and lesbian tourism in the country is a key factor linked to these changes. The relationship between queer tourism and Mexican male sexualities is complex and multiply constituted, but in this chapter I have highlighted some of these dimensions, particularly as they are linked to a sexual political economy.

It should be clarified, however, that I am not arguing that modernization leads to one particular construction of sexuality or that gay and lesbian tourism creates a monolithic "gay" identity through globalization. On the contrary, what I am arguing against is any unidimensional or monolithic construction of Mexican sexualities. Indeed, the cultural-primacy model of Mexican male sexualities in many ways is also a monolith. Rather, my purpose in this chapter has been to point to some of the diversity of Mexican male sexualities that is shaped by a number of factors, including culture. By using a political-economic framework for understanding Mexican male sexualities, I assert that we might be able to better understand how Mexican men who have sex with men are differentially positioned in Mexico's *ambiente*. I have also argued that Mexico's *ambiente* is embedded not only in a nationalist development project but also in a global political economy. Although I have privileged the public sphere in my discussion, public and private spheres are neither clearly delineated nor mutually exclusive, especially in the realm of sexuality.

The geopolitical border that the United States and Mexico share is an often overlooked dimension in studies of Mexican and U.S. sexualities (epidemiological studies of HIV/AIDS being an exception). Historically, the Mexican border towns and "tolerance zones" have served as "safe spaces" wherein Americans could escape strict sexual mores and prying eyes in the United States. This early version of sexual tourism included space for homosexual activity that would gradually expand to other areas such as urban centers. These border zones and their linkages to a national development project are crucial to understanding the shifting boundaries of Mexican sexualities.

Mexico's modernization projects, including its industrialization and urbanization, have in part created the conditions for the development of commodified and more legitimized same-sex sexuality in urban centers. While space for same-sex sexuality is not necessarily "new," the greater visibility, legitimacy, and even identity basis of these spaces are. Queer communities such as those in Mexico City have been instrumental in the creation of a Mexican gay and lesbian movement. Such changes helped to establish the conditions that would allow the establishment of a formal queer tourist industry. In addition, as part of its strategy for national development, the Mexican government prioritized tourism with aspirations for economic growth and controlled urbanization, and one of the "side effects" of this strategy is that it also contributed to the development of queer tourism.

As I discussed, gay and lesbian tourism in Mexico has resulted in an expansion of commodified space, which has had the dual effect of creating sites in the country that are both sexually liberating and exploitative. In some instances, segregated spaces are actually created for gay and lesbian tourists through specialized cruises and/or resorts. In other instances, gay and lesbian tourists are encouraged to "mix with the natives" and in so doing transform queer Mexican space. These spaces both reproduce and rupture the racialized politics of the U.S./Mexican border. While creating spaces by which identities and community may form, commodification also brings with it exclusionary norms and practices. "Gay Mexico" is marketed to mostly foreign tourists through organizations such as the IGLTA and venues such as travel guides and web sites. Part of the "sell" to this market relies upon stereotypes of Mexican men with racist undertones and images and the idea that Mexican men are "for the taking," particularly in those areas deemed to be more authentic than the controlled spaces of queer resorts.

The commodification of Mexican gay space presents a complex set of factors in the lives of Mexican men. While gay and lesbian tourist markets do not exclude Mexican nationals, socioeconomic constraints often do. Thus for many Mexican men, contact with gay tourists may occur more regularly not through leisure activities but through their labor as service workers. Such spaces, however, have their own boundaries or borders, whereby someone such as Lalo who worked in the industry had no "real" contact with Americans until he migrated to the United States. However, sometimes native/tourist contact brings with it information that serves as incentive for some Mexican men to emigrate to other countries and for some men to form binational relationships through tourist contacts, too.[16] Roberto is a case in point. However, the experiences that Lalo and Roberto had with American gay tourists should not be read as simply different. Class differences between the two men no doubt shaped these trajectories.

Gays and lesbians in Mexico have responded to social regulation and oppression in a number of ways depending upon their social locations. These responses range from the creation of a subculture and communities to social protest. While Mexico's gay and lesbian movement does have a long history (although this is not often acknowledged in the literature), gay and lesbian tourism is also a factor in the shifting boundaries of space and place for queer Mexicans. The growing visibility of the gay and lesbian tourist market (including events such as the IGLTA conference in Cancún) and the dependence of both local and national economies on tourism, are important factors in the political environment for gays and lesbians in Mexico.

Tourism can also be a response to one's marginality. By traveling to other cities and countries some Mexican homosexual men are able to "escape" temporarily the constraints of their marginalized status. Again, social class is a key factor in determining the avenues by which the constraints of marginality might be maneuvered. Thus, while this chapter has focused on dimensions of American tourism to Mexico, the dynamics of Mexican queer tourism are not restricted to foreign tourists. Thus the tensions of sexual liberation/colonialism that arise with gay and lesbian tourism in Mexico are reproduced by Mexican upper-class men in other parts of the world as well.

Although the rise of gay and lesbian tourism in Mexico was not a planned outcome of the nation's tourist development project, it is an end result with important social and political reverberations. It is significant that those on the margins of Mexican society (*los otros*) and those on the margins of other nations, especially the United States (i.e., gays and lesbians) should come together under a nationalist project. However, as the border reminds us, and as I have argued here, life in these queer sexual borderlands has elements that are both liberating and oppressive. However, a central question remains: to what extent is the Mexican nationalist project willing to consciously embrace not only its gay and lesbian tourists but also, more importantly, its gay and lesbian citizens? The answer may ultimately lie not in the demands of Mexican gays and lesbians but rather in the demands of a queer market and the political economy of space.

6

A Place Called Home

Mexican Immigrant Men's Family Experiences

Fear of going home. And of not being taken in. We're afraid of being abandoned by the mother, the culture, la Raza, for being unacceptable, faulty, damaged. Most of us unconsciously believe that if we reveal this unacceptable aspect of the self our mother/culture/race will totally reject us. To avoid rejection, some of us conform to the values of the culture, push the unacceptable parts into the shadow. Which leaves only one fear—that we will be found out and that the Shadow-Beast will break out of its cage. Some of us take another route.

—Gloria Anzaldúa, *Borderlands/La Frontera*

Sometimes being queer feels like being an alien. Too many of the streets have no names, and there are not many friendly places to go. When you are living on the edges of things, the margins, "home" can be hard to find.

—Gordon Brent Ingram, et al., *Queers in Space*

Driving the Interstate 5 Freeway, near San Diego and the San Onofre border checkpoint, one sees large yellow signs graphically depicting a fleeing family (father leading, mother, and child, legs flailing behind). The almost surreal signs are meant to warn motorists of the danger of "illegal" immigrant families trying to cross the busy lanes. This image reveals not only the extreme risks that many immigrants are willing to take to get to the United States but also the way in which we imagine these immigrants. While most motorists probably do not think of a sexual message when they see the warning sign, it's there for us to see, if only we really look. The sign is symbolic at multiple levels: a nuclear family unit, heteronormative in definition, a threat to the racial social order by virtue of its reproductive potential. The sign is also symbolic of the current state of international migration studies: sexuality is an implicit part of migration that has been overlooked or ignored.

In this chapter I examine some of the ways in which sexuality, understood as a dimension of power, has shaped the lives, intimate relationships, and migratory processes of Mexican men who immigrate to the United States. More specifically, I utilize ethnographic data to examine how traditional family relations and alternative support systems such as "chosen families" (Weston 1991) influence migration among Mexican immigrant men who have sex with men (MSMs). The men whom I interviewed and introduce in this chapter had a variety of sexual identities both prior to and after migration. An important part of my research, therefore, is to examine from a queer materialist perspective dimensions that shape the social relations of families of origin and families of choice and thus, the intimate context by which identity itself is shaped. I argue for a theoretical move toward a queer political economy in order to understand the dynamics that shape "the sexuality of migration" and the fluidity of identities in a global context. In the first section of this chapter I briefly discuss how I conceptualize this theoretical framework. I then discuss the ways in which these theoretical concepts are grounded in the everyday experiences of Mexican immigrant men.

Among the Mexican men who have sex with men and migrate to the United States are those who, to quote Anzaldúa, have taken "another route" and identify as either homosexual or gay prior to migration or come to identify as such soon afterwards. Many of these men come to the United States seeking a "place" where they might have more opportunities to not only explore their sexuality more freely but also develop other aspects of themselves that are constrained by factors linked to homophobia and heteronormativity. But where exactly is this "place"? While at some levels the United States may be a more "open" society for gays and lesbians compared to Mexico, as Ingram declares in the above quotation, even here, "sometimes being queer feels like being an alien." Furthermore, racist and anti-immigrant sentiments create an environment that is far from hospitable. How then must gay Mexican immigrant "aliens" feel and how much more difficult must it be to find "home?"

Queer Mexican immigrants live in the borderlands, on the margins not only of mainstream "white" society and Latino communities but also of "mainstream" gay and lesbian communities, which Warner (1993) argues are generated by "Anglo-American identity politics." While Latino barrios and gay enclaves exist in the greater Los Angeles area, there are no "gay Latino" enclaves per se. That is, there is no identifiable geographical space that one might designate a gay Latino neighborhood. However, space is beginning to open up, and in this chapter I examine not only the geographical but also the sociopolitical dimensions in the formation of gay Latino communities in the greater Los Angeles area. These spatial dimensions are crucial in gay Mexican immigrants' attempts at adaptation and incorporation in the United States. I argue that the formation of gay Latino communities in Southern California is being driven by four distinct but intersecting factors: (1) demographic changes that include an increase in the area's Latino population, (2) the commodification of Latino sexuality, (3) the "institutionalization" or mainstreaming of both the gay and Chicano movements, and (4) HIV prevention programs that target the Latino community. While my focus is on the greater Los Angeles area, these factors are obviously more global in scope. In addition, while my main concern in this chapter is with communal space, in a more general sense, I am interested in lived spaces, including the household. For it is at the intersections of the global and the local, the personal and the social, where these queer borderlands are being formed.

A Sense of Space: The Borderlands

In order to understand the processes that are leading to the formation of a gay Latino *comunidad,* one must first understand the space in which this community is forming. The theoretical and analytical importance of space has recently been given greater attention not only by postmodern geographers but also by immigration scholars who focus on such issues as transnational community formations. Within each of these bodies of literature it has become clear that spatiality is more than physical location but also the site where social relations are formed and power is exercised—in essence, where social constraints and resistance is lived. Foucault referred to this sense of space as "heterotopia," a space that Soja (1996) has reimagined as "thirdspace," where "the simultaneity and interwoven complexity of the social, historical, and the spatial, their inseparability and interdependence" come together (3). Recently, queer and feminist scholars, working within this model of spatiality, have examined the gendered and sexualized dimensions of space (i.e., Rose 1993; Massey 1994; Bell and Valentine 1995). These scholars assert that the binary division of space into public and private realms is not as fixed as previously held. Furthermore, space has erotic dimensions linked to identities and their commodification. This space, which Ingram (1997) refers to as "queerscape," is envisioned as a "landscape of erotic alien(n) ations, ones that shift with demographics, social development, political economies, interventions of 'the state,' aesthetics, and—yes—desire" (31). Despite the fact that Ingram envisions the "queerscapes" as the products of multiple marginalities, most of this queer spatial literature focuses on desire, often at the expense of other dimensions, especially race.

While not necessarily theorizing space in the same ways as postmodern geographers do, migration scholarship considers space important. Whether it is in the form of the household, the enclave, or the global city, space is a dimension of analysis that is central to the study of immigration. For instance, migration scholars argue that social networks and modes of incorporation such as ethnic communities and economies are an important aspect of personal transition as they link migrants to social, cultural, familial, and economic resources.[1] While most studies have conceptualized social networks in terms of either familial relationships or men's labor networks, some scholars have demonstrated that alternative network arrangements exist, such as those of single women (Hondagneu-Sotelo 1994). Regardless of how these networks are arranged, they can only be produced by contacts and communications that eventually arise from shared space. Often these networks lead an immigrant to a "landing pad" household where resources for survival and adaptation might be shared (Chavez 1992). Similarly, ethnic economies and enclaves serve as means by which immigrants adapt to their new environments. But in the case of gay Latino/a immigrants one must ask where these "landing pads" for survival and adaptation might be. As previously mentioned, migration scholars have ignored the sexual dimensions of migration, including the ways in which sexuality influences migrant strategies. Thus, in this chapter I examine how race/ethnicity and sexuality shape spatiality among queer Latinos. I begin with the area's demographic context.

Various scholars have discussed what some have called the "browning" or "Latinization" of America, which refers to the increasing number of Latinos in the United States (see, for example, Stavans 1995; Fox 1996). Indeed, the proportion of the nation's "Hispanic" population has increased significantly since the creation of the category after the 1980 census.[2] In 1980, 6.5 percent of the U.S. population was of "Spanish ori-

gin." By 1996 the "Hispanic" population was 10.7 percent, and it is estimated to grow to 14.7 percent by the year 2020. Although the Hispanic
population is increasing in many states, it is geographically concentrated
in five states: Florida, Illinois, New York, Texas, and California (which
has the largest Hispanic population of any state). From 1990–1991 to
1993–1994, California's growth rate declined from 2.07 percent to 0.87
percent with a net loss due to the net migration of 212,000 "White"
residents from California between 1992 and 1994 alone. At the same
time the state's Hispanic population grew by a yearly average of 235,800
by "natural increase only"[3] (i.e., not including migration). By 2025, the
Bureau of the Census projects that Hispanics will comprise approximately one-quarter of the state's population while the non-Hispanic
white population will decline to less than half, at approximately 43 percent (U.S. Bureau of the Census 1994; State of California, Department of
Finance 1996a, 1996b).

According to 1990 census estimates, nearly half of California's population (49 percent, or 14.5 million people) lives in the Los Angeles Con-
solidated Metropolitan Statistical Area (CMSA), which includes Los
Angeles, Orange, Riverside, San Bernardino, and Ventura Counties. Los
Angeles County alone has a population of more than 9.6 million, 43.9
percent of which is Hispanic, while 22.9 percent of Orange County's
estimated 2.4 million population is Hispanic (U.S. Bureau of the Census 1993a, 1993b, 1994). The significant presence of Latinos in the Los
Angeles area is not new, of course. The region was part of Mexico's
territory prior to the U.S.-Mexican War, and in 1920 Los Angeles was
already referred to as "the American Capital of Mexico" (Oxnam 1970
[1920]). Latinos are residentially concentrated in six general areas in the
greater Los Angeles area. In these areas, Latinos comprise more than 60
percent of the population: the San Fernando Valley, Central Los Angeles
(centered around East Los Angeles/Boyle Heights), the San Gabriel Valley, Pomona, Wilmington/Long Beach, and Santa Ana.[4]

Determining the "gay and lesbian" population is a difficult if not an
impossible task. If we assume that 10 percent of the general population is
gay or lesbian, an estimate would stand at 1.4 million.[5] However, there are
ongoing debates as to what percentage of the population is gay or lesbian,
and it is not clear whether these estimates differ by gender, race/ethnicity,
and region. More important than these problematic statistics, and easier
to identify, are the spaces that have become identified with gay and lesbian communities. There are five major gay communities (or enclaves) in

the greater Los Angeles area: West Hollywood, Hollywood, Long Beach, Silverlake, and Laguna Beach. But gay organizations, bars, discos, and other businesses can be found throughout Southern California. In addition, both Venice Beach and Santa Monica also have sizeable gay and lesbian populations, but I do not consider them to be enclaves. The physical proximity of gay communities to Latino communities plays an important role in Latino marginalization and the larger politics of space.

During my research and fieldwork, it soon became clear that gay Latino immigrants' daily lives are in most ways tied more closely to the larger Latino community than to the larger gay one. Cultural similarities, including language, undoubtedly play a large role in this respect. But so, too, do the socioeconomic differences that segregate many gay Latino immigrants from other communities. Like most of their compatriots, gay Latino immigrants often work at jobs that are not only distant geographically from where they live but also distant socioculturally. Thus, Latino immigrant laborers often spend their paid working hours in spaces quite different from those to which they return home. "Home" in these instances often means the six Latino ethnic communities referred to above, with their own markets, theaters, and other gathering places that are in most instances heteronormative spaces. The Mexican immigrant men whom I came to know through my years of doing research and working with the gay Latino community did not live in any one particular area of the Los Angeles metropolis but did, without exception, live in areas that were either predominantly Latino or had a large percentage of Latinos in the vicinity.

Nearly all of the Mexican immigrant men I interviewed moved at least once after the time I met them and had reported moving several times since moving to the United States. But in each case, residential relocation remained within the general Los Angeles area. Most of the men I interviewed who identified as gay lived with other gay Latino men as roommates, even if they had a partner. Only four of the twenty men I formally interviewed lived with their families. Three identified as gay and one as bisexual. Of these, only two of the gay men were "out" to their family. The differences in the socioeconomic dimensions of these household arrangements seem to have a direct relationship to the men's sexual identities and lives. While different arrangements were made for sharing household resources, in each of these households information on jobs, social events, and general "gay" issues was shared among members of the household.

In one Santa Ana household, where five gay immigrant men lived, three were from Mexico and the other two were from Central America. Rent for the two-bedroom apartment was shared among the five men, as were costs for food. Household chores were also shared although cooking was usually done by only two of the men. This particular household was often the center of social events held either at the apartment or organized there and held elsewhere. Thus the household also became a social network "node" where gay Latino men were able to meet other gay Latino men. When the members of this household moved to separate locations, these established networks were used to set up new shared gay Latino households. While these households are far from what one might consider "stable," they are not unlike other Mexican immigrant households described in the migration literature (i.e., Chavez 1992). Perhaps more important than the longevity of these household arrangements are their very existence and the spaces they provide Mexican immigrant men to develop as gay men.

Clearly, sexuality plays an important role in shaping these "gay" household arrangements, but it should be understood that they provide a lens by which we can begin to question how sexuality shapes other household arrangements as well. Household arrangements where heterosexuality is the norm are no less influenced by sexuality; however, the power of these relations becomes invisible because of their normativity. The ways in which sexuality shapes immigrant household relations is all the more important because of their "landing pad" and adaptive functions.

For instance, in discussing his migration experience with me, Pepe, a 30-year-old immigrant from Michoacan, explained how he crossed the Mexican border with other "illegals" with the services of a "coyote" (a paid guide who assists undocumented immigrants cross the U.S.–Mexico border) who took them to a "safe house." As he explains,

> When we got to the place where they brought us, let me tell you, it was a room with mattresses thrown on the floor, a couch, and a very small restroom where the water didn't even work. So when everybody did their necessities, it all remained there, and there was a horrible smell. The windows were covered with paint or cardboard, I don't remember, but the thing was they didn't let us look outside. Everyone would place themselves wherever there was room, because the long mattresses were placed all over. So we were there and it was very uncomfortable.

But I'm going to tell you something that I have never told anyone but something I want to say. What happened was that there was a young man, well there were many, we were all men, he was about twenty-five and dark. I got to see him a little because there was a little bit of light. The room was almost dark, when you got up to go to the bathroom it was all the light you got. He had a medium stature and dark curly hair, that has always attracted me, well in short, I liked the young man. He was the one next to me, it was the only space left when we arrived and my brother was on the other side of the room. The room was almost dark but the young man saw me. I don't know what exactly happened but we ran into each other in the bathroom and I stared at him. I don't know if with the stare I told him that I liked him but he felt it. Then he would hold my hand and he would caress my body and we would embrace each other. My brother was there but I don't think he saw anything as you couldn't see from here to there. It was one experience I had that has always stayed with me.

Pepe and his brother would later join relatives in the Los Angeles area, but his story helps to reveal not only one way in which the "landing pad" space might be sexually charged (despite the literature, immigrants are not asexual) but also, more importantly, how heteronormativity operates within such a space. Argüelles and Rivero (1993) have already pointed to some of the ways in which women are subjected to sexual violence under similar conditions. Eventually, Pepe moved out on his own, and when we met he was sharing an apartment with a lesbian niece who was also an immigrant. This home, in turn, became a landing pad for at least one gay Mexican immigrant who stayed with Pepe and his niece for about a month until he found work and his own accommodations.

The sexual dimensions of the immigrant household and adaptation were reflected in a variety of ways in the lives of my informants. When I first met Manuel at a gay Latino men's social gathering, he identified as bisexual. HIV-positive and in good health, he lived with his family in Orange County. He was thirty years old and had moved to the United States in 1996. He is the third of eight children and grew up in Tlaquepaque, a town famous for its artisans and now considered part of the Guadalajara metro area. He was not working at the time of our first interview and his social life was constrained not only by his lack of income but also by the fact that he was not "out" to his family, who are Jehovah's Witnesses. Over the years of working with gay Latino men, I ran into Manuel from time to time and began to notice changes in his social "performance." Although when we met, Manuel had acknowledged that most of his sexual experiences had been with men, he asserted his bisexual identity and denied any possibility that he had contracted HIV from sex but instead assured me that he must have been exposed to the virus through his job as a nurse. Over time, however, Manuel's opinion on these matters changed. He soon began to identify as gay and to accept the possibility that he might have contracted HIV through sex. When we last spoke Manuel still had not come out to his family but the changes in his public expression may be attributed to his increased social interaction with gay-identified Latino men and the social pressure to "admit" one's "true" sexual orientation. As discussed in chapter 3, bisexuality in Mexico seems to have greater acceptance as a behavior and as an identity than in the United States. In this new social context, I myself witnessed on several occasions episodes of peer pressure in which Manuel was chided for not admitting his homosexuality. While he seems to have "submitted" to this pressure to a certain extent, Manuel's financial dependence on his family limits his ability to be an openly gay man, in a way that is more consistent with Almaguer's (1993) framework for understanding gay Latino identity.

Border Crossers: Family, Migration, and Identity

The immigrant men whom I interviewed for my research ranged in age from their early twenties to their early forties and lived in the greater Los Angeles area. I met these men during my research fieldwork from 1997 through December 1999 by making initial contacts through organizations, fliers, and friends and then using a snowball sampling technique to meet others. While each of these men's stories was in its own way unique, there were also similarities that became more evident as my research progressed.

Most of the men came from the Pacific states of Mexico, and approximately two-thirds came from the state of Jalisco. About half described their communities of origin as small cities or towns, with only a couple describing their origins as rural. Migration to larger cities (such as Guadalajara or border cities such as Tijuana) prior to migrating to the United States was also a common experience.[6] All the men included here were sixteen years old or older when they immigrated. Most came from lower-middle-class Mexican backgrounds[7] and had at least a high school education. Like many of their straight counterparts, many were undocumented. Only two of the interviwees were unemployed at the time of their interview; one man was unable to work due to health reasons related to AIDS/HIV, and the other was looking for work. Several of the men were actually holding down more than one job—one full-time and one part-time. The average annual income of the men was between twenty and twenty-five thousand dollars. Their fluency in English was relative to their time in the United States, but none of the men was completely fluent. The men interviewed reported that their daily lives were for the most part Spanish speaking. In addition, nearly all estimated that more than 75 percent of their social circles were Latino.

In the following pages I will introduce seven of the twenty men I interviewed formally. I selected these particular interviews as representative of the range of experiences shared with me. However, the interview excerpts I have included should not be considered representative of all Mexican immigrant men who have sex with men—the diversity of experiences is far greater than can be captured here. The men I have included identified as either bisexual or homosexual (gay) at the time of the interviews. In addition, I do not include the voice of transgendered Mexican immigrants, although some of the men do have experience with cross-dressing (although I do not mean to suggest that cross-dressing and transgender are the same). Yet the voices represented here do reveal the complexity of the sexuality of migration and the importance of including sexuality in our analysis. In addition to Lalo, Armando, Roberto, and Manuel, who were introduced in chapter 5, in this chapter I also highlight the experiences of Gabriel, Paco, and Carlos.

Gabriel is a 23-year-old undocumented immigrant who has lived in the Orange County area since the mid-1990s, where he works as a medical assistant. The fourth of six children, Gabriel moved to the United States from Nayarit, Mexico, in 1993 when he was eighteen. Gabriel is now living in Fullerton.

Paco, a native of La Piedad, Michoacan, is thirty years old and now lives in Tustin. Paco is the youngest of six children, four sisters and a brother. His father died three months after he was born, and he was raised by his mother and older siblings. Paco is a legal resident of the United States although he immigrated illegally in 1990.

Carlos migrated from Guadalajara in 1990 and was seeking political asylum in the United States on the basis of his sexual orientation. Because Carlos was an active member of the Democratic Revolutionary Party (PRD), an opposition party to Mexico's ruling Institutional Revolutionary Party (PRI), Carlos feared that he might be imprisoned or murdered if he returned to Mexico. He was living in Los Angeles at the time of our interview.

Family Life in Mexico

Social scientists have historically given great attention to the role of *la familia* in Latino culture. Scholarship often points to Latino "familism"—defined as the valuing and preservation of the family over individual concerns (Moore and Pachon 1985; Williams 1990) as the contentious source of both material and emotional support and patriarchal oppression. The stereotype is problematic for a number of reasons, not the least of which is the fact that the same argument could be made of most families regardless of their cultural context. Thus, in this section, while I discuss how the early family lives of Mexican immigrant MSMs influenced migratory processes, my aim is not to reproduce a cultural pathology of *la familia* but rather to examine the family as a site where normative constructions of gender and sexuality are reproduced and in which the dynamics of migration are materially embedded.

During my interviews, most of the men remembered their lives as children in Mexico fondly (all of the men came from households with more than one child). Yet even when memories of early family life were positive, the daily lessons of normative masculinity learned by these men often resulted in emotional conflicts. I asked them to share with me their memories of family life and educational experiences so that I could understand more fully the processes by which normative gender roles and sexuality are learned. Most early childhood memories were shared with smiles and consisted of generally carefree days: playing typical games and going to school. Most of the men also reported that they were good students who received awards for their scholarship and genuinely seemed to have enjoyed school. However, even men such as Paco, who reported that his childhood was "a great time . . . a very beautiful stage of my life," expressed a sense of inner conflict rooted in normative definitions of masculinity.

These conflicts were even more pronounced for men such as Lalo, whose memories of early life in Mexico were not good ones. As Lalo told me while recounting his childhood,

As a child I was very mischievous. I was sexually abused when I was seven by the neighbor, a man of forty. It was a childhood experience that affected me greatly. This person continued to abuse me, he would give me money, later I would go looking for him myself and I was like his "boyfriend" until I was nine. I knew what he was doing was wrong so I never told anyone.

Paternostro (1998) reports that child sexual abuse by a family member is a common phenomenon in Latin America (whether it is more prevalent than in other regions is debatable). In fact, Lalo was not the only man I interviewed who had been sexually abused as a child, but he was the most forthcoming about the experience.[8] Later in the interview he explained that he had also been abused by two older male cousins and that when he told his father about the abuse, his father's response was to rape him for being a "*maricón*" (fag).

None of the sexually abused men, including Lalo, remember connecting these experiences to homosexuality at the time of their occurrence, in part because they had no understanding of homosexuality. Lalo explained that although he had never heard the word "homosexual," words such as "*maricón*" and "*joto*" were commonly heard in his home. However, Lalo related these terms to effeminate men or *vestidas,* like the man in his neighborhood who dressed like a woman. Many informants related similar experiences. Carlos explained, "Across from us lived the town *maricón*. In every town there is the drunk and the *maricón*, and the *maricón* lived across the street." When he was a child, the question of what a *maricón* was remained somewhat of a mystery, although he knew it wasn't "good" to be a *maricón*. For example, Lalo explained how he came to understand what it meant to be a homosexual.

After about the age of twelve or thirteen there was a lot of sexual play among the boys of the *colonia*. We would masturbate one another. There were about twelve of us in the group and we would form a circle and masturbate one another. Later, couples would form and we would penetrate one another. Now they are all grown up and married but there was a lot of sexual play when we were kids. . . . There were some boys who would refuse to join us, saying, "that's for *maricones*" or "you're going to be a *joto* or a woman." It was then that I started to understand but I never thought that I was going to be like a woman.

Masculine discourse that devalues the feminine and equates homosexuality with femininity is, of course, not particular to Mexican culture (see Fellows 1996; Roscoe and Murray 1998). However, as Lalo explained, homosexuality and femininity are not popularly understood as synonymous. "Being a *joto* is to not be man. [It is] neither a man nor a woman, it is to be an abomination, a curse." Prieur's (1998) recent work on male-to-female transgendered residents of Mexico City supports Lalo's analysis and suggests that class perspectives are an important dimension of constructions of homosexuality. Thus, the relationship of homosexuality to the feminine is more complex than a synonymous equation implies. Homosexuality is not only the opposite of masculinity; it is a corruption of it, an unnatural form that by virtue of its transgression of the binary male/female order poses a threat that must be contained or controlled.

The liminal/marginal location of homosexuality, perhaps best understood as shaped by what Almaguer (1993) refers to as a sex/gender/power axis, is reproduced through messages in everyday life. Discussing his daily chores at home, Paco explained,

> My duties at home in particular, well, they were almost never designated to us. I liked very much to sweep, mop, wash the dishes, and when [my mother and sisters] would make cake I always liked to be there when they were preparing it. But, only when my mom and my sisters were there, because my brother would often be in the United States. I always liked to help my mom and my sisters, but when my brother would get there, I always had to hide or not do it because he would tell me "You are not a woman to be doing that, that's for the *maricones*." Then, since I was scared of him, I wouldn't do it anymore. But it was what I liked to do, up till now; I like cleaning very much and chores like that. I like to cook very much, I like to have everything clean—I've always liked that.

When I asked Paco to discuss the issue of "women's work" in more detail, he explained,

> In Mexico they say: "Oh, a homosexual person or a 'maricón' or a 'joto' are those persons that are dressed like women." They always have a little of that mentality. For example, there were times that a guy named Luis would pass by and he always left his nails long and his hair long like a woman. He had a bag, and he would put on women's pants or a woman's blouse, and he might have put on make-up but not a lot, but obviously he

would go around like a woman. Then all the people, well, they said things, but in my family one time I heard my mother call him, she would call them "frescos" [fresh], "there goes this 'fresco,'" "there goes that 'fresco,'" I would hear my mom say that. Then, I would get angry when I would hear that, because I would say: "Well, I am not like that, but I am attracted to young men."

Similarly to Paco, Armando expressed learning the same type of sex/gender message through child's play. Armando explained that he liked to play with paper dolls and more than anything liked to cut out the clothes, yet he hid when he did so. When I asked him why, Armando replied, "It's the only game I remember playing secretly. I knew my parents wouldn't like it. I thought it was perfectly normal, it was only bad because it was something that little girls do."

The struggle that Paco and Armando relate in attempting to negotiate the perceived contradictions of sex, gender, and sexual identities was a common theme of many of my interviews. Participants expressed a certain sense of isolation or "not belonging" and not wanting to disappoint their families. Even learning to emulate normative gender and sexual performances was not, in itself, sufficient to resolve these conflicts. For some men, these tensions were themselves catalysts for migration.

Leaving Home

One of the questions that I asked immigrant interviewees was what their top three reasons for immigrating were. After I analyzed the answers given, it became clear that sexuality was indeed influencing reasons for migration and that "family" dynamics were often linked to these reasons. However, understanding how sexuality actually influenced these decisions was not always as clear-cut as having people respond, "it was my sexuality"—although that sometimes happened. For example, Lalo told me, "Ninety percent of the reason I migrated was because of my sexuality." Such reasons obviously resonate with D'Emilio's (1993 [1983]) and Rubin's (1992 [1984]) models of rural-to-urban migration by gay men and women who are looking for a more urban atmosphere inclusive of gay life. Yet, in order to understand more fully how sexuality is linked to other socioeconomic dimensions, one must attempt to connect the micro with the meta and macro dimensions of life. That is to say, one cannot separate individual reasons for migration from the larger processes that shape people's everyday lives and perceived choices.

For example, all of the men I interviewed, in one form or another, gave financial reasons for migrating to the United States. And indeed, immigration scholars have traditionally placed a great deal of emphasis on economic reasons for migration, yet to a great degree their vision of the economic realm is extremely limited. Groups that are marginalized as sexual minorities are constrained by discrimination and prejudice that may limit their socioeconomic opportunities. For instance, even one of the people I interviewed in Mexico who owned his own pesticide and fertilizer business felt the constraints of heterosexism. Business networks, he explained, depend upon having the right image, which means a wife, children, and social events tied to church and school. Clearly, as a gay man he was outside this world. His class privilege and the fact the he is his own boss, however, permit him to remain in Mexico relatively free from economic pressures that drive others to migrate.

Thus, while men such as Lalo clearly migrate to escape a sense of sexual oppression, for others the decision to migrate to the United States is influenced by a combination of sexual liberation and economic opportunities. For example, Gabriel moved to the United States from Nayarit, Mexico, when he was eighteen but explained that he had begun to prepare himself for immigrating at sixteen. When I asked him why, he explained that he had two major reasons for coming to the United States:

> First, I wanted to get a better level of education. And the second reason was sexuality. I wanted to be able to define myself and have more freedom with respect to that. I wanted to come here to live, not to distance myself from my family but to hide what I already knew I had. I knew I was gay but I thought I might be able to change it. I needed to come here and speak to people, to learn more about it, because in Mexico it's still very taboo. There isn't so much liberation.

Gabriel's experience reveals how the tension of sexual desire versus "not wanting to distance" oneself from family may serve as a migratory "push." Yet while he clearly moved to the United States seeking a more liberal sexual environment, his doing so was also motivated by his perception that he had limited economic opportunities as a gay man in Mexico. Staying in Mexico might very well have meant either attempting to create a heteronormative family or dealing with social and economic discrimination as a gay man.

Sometimes homosexual relationships might have subtle influences, such as serving to establish or expand social networks, or they might have a more direct influence driving migration itself. Furthermore, as Roberto's sexual relationship and subsequent friendship with a U.S. tourist vacationing in Mexico illustrates, new transnational social bonds are created similar to the kinship networks that migration scholars argue facilitate migration. However, these networks are not blood based but, rather, based on affiliation and contribute to expanded transnational gay networks.

Finding Their Way Home

Adapting to life in the United States is difficult for any migrant, but for immigrants like Lalo who migrate to the United States expecting a gay utopia, the reality of life in the United States can be quite a shock. Indeed, Lalo had returned to Mexico for two years after first migrating to the United States because of his disillusionment, returning to the United States only when he realized that his prospects as a gay man were limited in Mexico. Thus, for Lalo, home was no longer Jalisco. In this section I focus on how sexuality might be related to a migrant's adaptation and incorporation. Specifically, I am concerned here with both kin networks and social location.

In her discussion of gay and lesbian kin relations, Kath Weston (1991) demonstrates how gays and lesbians construct "chosen" families based on shared affinities and relationships of both material and emotional support. Kinship (biological) plays a central role in migration as a means through which immigrants receive support and acquire important knowledge for survival and adaptation (see Chavez 1992). While the Mexican men I interviewed often utilized kinship networks to these ends, they also depended upon networks that were similar to those described by Weston. About half of the immigrants I spoke with utilized preexisting gay networks to migrate to the United States. Some men, like Lalo, migrated with the help of a gay compatriot already living in Los Angeles, or like Roberto, came with the help of a gay American. But even some of those who utilized kin networks for initial migration also used gay networks for meeting other gay Latino men, finding gay roommates, making job contacts, and acquiring other types of resources. The existence and use of these alternative networks depended to a large extent on how the men identified sexually, to what extent they were "out of the closet," and, to some extent, on their ability to speak English (and thus expand their networks into the mainstream gay world).

For instance, although Paco migrated and found his first job using kinship networks, he was soon able to develop a U.S.-based gay network as well.

> My second job was in a company where they made pools. I obtained that job through a [gay] friend, an American, who is the person, the third person that I have to thank about my legal status here in this country. He helped me get the job because it was the company of a friend of his. In the morning I would clean the offices and then I would go to the warehouse and take inventory or I would clean the warehouse or cut fiberglass, or things like that. And they paid me well at that time but I worked only a few hours. So after that, . . . they said "Oh, you clean so well," and they had some very beautiful houses, over in Laguna Beach. Sometimes I would stay over because I could not finish in the weekend. The owners of the company were gay. They would go to San Francisco, or wherever they were going, they always traveled on the weekend, they left me the key, "Here is the stereo and here is the television," and everything like that because I had to sleep over. Then I would go home when they returned on Sundays.

Ironically, Paco is one of the people who assured me that sexuality had not influenced his migratory experiences in the least. This excerpt, however, indicates the importance of gay social networks as an aid in his finding work. In addition, and as previously mentioned, Paco shares a home with a lesbian niece and has allowed other gay immigrants to stay with him temporarily until they are able to move on.

Carlos also made use of gay networks in a similar manner. When he migrated to the United States he first lived for two months in Watsonville, California, with a brother and then went to live in Milwaukee for two years with his two sisters, who are lesbians. He then moved to Los Angeles after meeting and starting a relationship with a gay man. Like Paco, Carlos revealed that his gay friends had helped him find work and even helped him out financially. "Because of my gay friends, I have never gone without," he said.

Both Paco's and Carlos's experiences also point to the fact that sexuality is an important dimension of immigrant household arrangements. As briefly discussed earlier, recent immigration literature has discussed the importance of household arrangements as "landing pads" for migrant adaptation (i.e., Chavez 1992, 1994); however, the sexual dimensions of these arrangements are missing from most analyses. For an individual who has migrated to the United States seeking a more liberal sexual environment, it makes little sense to live in a home constrained by heteronormative relations. While about half of the Mexican men I interviewed originally lived with family members when they migrated, most had formed alternative living arrangements as soon as possible. Lalo's living arrangement exemplifies this approach.

When I first met Lalo he was living in Santa Ana in an apartment that he shared with three other gay immigrant men. After our first meeting, Lalo moved twice and had a number of different roommates who were always gay Latino immigrant men. Sometimes the men, especially if they were recent immigrants, would stay only a short time until they found another place to live. It was clear that Lalo's home was a landing pad, but it was one where Latino men could be openly gay, support one another, and share information that was essential for adaptation. Although the men did not explicitly define these relations as "family," they did sometimes refer to each other affectionately as siblings (sometimes as "sisters" and sometimes as "brothers"). Regardless of how these relationships were labeled, it was clear that an alternative support system had been created. It is precisely in this type of living arrangement that many men discover the space that transforms the way they think about themselves and their sexual identities.

Migrating Identities

I asked the men I interviewed if they felt that they had changed at all since migrating to the United States. Nearly all of the men responded with a resounding yes. The changes they described generally centered around racial, gender, sexual, and class identities. Most of the men referred to a more liberal sexual environment as a reason for their transformations. Migrating to the United States was for many men one step in a series towards what might be called "a journey to the self."[9] For Gabriel, the desire to live in a place where he could develop his human potential as a gay man was a driving force in his decision to immigrate. He added,

> I have two names, Gabriel Luis, and my family calls me Luis. I've always said that Luis is the person who stayed in Mexico. Once I came here, Gabriel was born. Because, like I've told you, once I was here I defined myself sexually and I've changed a lot emotionally, more than anything emotionally, because I found myself.

This journey of self-discovery is intimately linked to resistance to the normative gender and sex regimes I have described earlier. The processes of resistance and self-discovery oftentimes begin at a young age. For example, most interviewees remembered first being aware of their attraction to boys or men in early childhood. Some remembered being attracted to the same sex as young as age four, but the majority of recollections were a bit later. Carlos remembered, "I was around eight years old. I could recognize the beauty of men. But from then on it was an issue of denial." The pressure to conform, or as Lalo described, "*la lucha de no querer ser gay*" (the struggle of not wanting to be gay) took a toll on most of the men I interviewed but perhaps was most eloquently described by Armando.

Armando explained that after around the fourth grade, he had been tormented by schoolmates, who would call him "*joto*" and "*maricón.*" He states,

> But I learned how to hide it better, so it wasn't noticeable. I no longer isolated myself, instead I would mix with the troublemakers at school so that their reputation would rub off on me and so no one would tell me anything anymore. A new student arrived who was even more obvious than me and to a certain extent he was my salvation. Everyone focused their attention on him and it was a load off of me. It gave me the opportunity to get closer to the other students and do everything that they did, to act like them, have girlfriends, and not be the "good boy" anymore—to take on the heterosexual role.

Armando would later join a seminary in an attempt to escape his sexual feelings and began to lift weights so that his appearance was more masculine. Eventually, however, he realized he needed to face who he "really" was.

I feel that I lost a lot of my essence as a homosexual during that time. I see it like that now. At that time I only wanted to be part of a group, to be accepted. It's horrible to feel marginalized, in a corner, abnormal. In my attempts to be like everyone else wanted me to be I lost much of my self.

Two months after migrating to the United States, seeking the freedom to be a gay man, he confessed to a cousin whom he was staying with that he was gay. She told him that she accepted and loved him as he was but that he needed to talk to his brothers. Armando told his brothers one by one and they all accepted his homosexuality (although it was by no means easy); he then decided to tell his widowed mother. At the time of our interview it had been five months since he had written his mother a five-page letter explaining his struggle to accept himself. A month later Armando's mother wrote him back asking forgiveness for taking so long to respond and assuring him that he would have her support and unconditional love. Armando has been able to successfully integrate his religious calling with his desire to be true to himself. He now works as an AIDS educator and program coordinator for an organization that serves gay Latino men.

Like Armando, other men who migrated to the United States also came out to their families and some found acceptance as well. In some of these men's cases it seems that the acceptance is in part tied to a reversal in family roles. Where once they were dependent upon their families for support, now their families are dependent upon them. Thus, while Almaguer (1993) has argued that economic interdependence stifles a gay identity from forming among Latino MSMs, my research reveals that it may actually facilitate familial acceptance. For instance, since migrating to the United States Lalo has also gained acceptance from the family who threw him out of the house. He explained to me that he has sent money to Mexico to have his mother's house repaired and to pay for his brother's tuition and that his family now respects him. Lalo related, "I'm much more secure now. I'm not afraid to say I'm a homosexual. I'm content being gay and I can help others. I'm stronger and have achieved a lot of things." Thus the transformation in economic roles and physical separation has allowed Lalo the opportunity to be both gay and accepted by his family.

There were, however, a couple of men I interviewed who were openly gay prior to migrating to the United States. In both cases these men had upperclass backgrounds. The difference that class makes in mitigating the effects of homophobia is significant and needs to be studied more closely. For example, when I asked Roberto about his son he laughed out loud and said,

Oh my son! My son was the product of an agreement. His mother knew that I was gay. My partner of ten years and I lived together [in Tepic, Nayarit] and she [my wife] lived in front of us. She knew of my relationship with Alejo and the three of us would go out to dance. In a small town, well, it was known that she was the friend of "the boys." We would go out to dance, she would come to our home to watch television, listen to music, or have a drink. Then one day she told me flat out that she wanted to have my baby. Then between the jokes I began to understand and between the jokes we ended up in bed. We had sex for two or three months and one day she called me and told me she was pregnant. I was twenty-three or twenty-four and was completely out of the closet with my family and I didn't care about anything.

Without a doubt, Roberto's class privilege allowed him to not "care about anything" as an openly gay man. In all probability it also shaped his gay social networks, which allowed him to migrate to the United States. In other words, his privileged position included having the economic means to migrate, not having to hide his sexuality from his family, and being able to seek support in the United States before migrating.

But for those men who do not have such economic privileges in Mexico, migrating to the United States does not necessarily afford them much in the way of financial benefits either. While there may be more space to be gay in the United States, migrating has its costs. For example, as Carlos lamented,

Being away from Mexico creates a strong nationalistic feeling with a lot of nostalgia. You begin to notice how different the system is here than in Mexico. An economic system that changes your life completely. A system where one forgets about other things that in Mexico were a priority. Here one lives life from the perspective of money. Working and making enough money to pay your bills is more important than having friends and doing what you like. In Mexico it's very different. It's more important to have friends. One lives less a slave to the clock. One forgets these things and becoming aware of that has made me very sad.

Discovering the virulence of racism in the United States seems to counterbalance any feelings of sexual liberation. I asked the men, in an open-ended manner, if they had ever experienced discrimination (without defining the type). Nearly all of the men responded in ways similar to Carlos:

"For being Latino, for not speaking English perfectly, for the color of my skin." The irony, of course, is that in their attempts to escape one form of bigotry, most of the Mexican men I interviewed discovered that not only had they not entirely escaped it but they now faced another. As Lalo said, "It wasn't true that homosexuals are free, that they can hold hands or that Americans like Mexicans." Under these circumstances the role of a support system becomes all the more important, and for queer Latino immigrant men this often means that new families must be created.

Building Family

I was naively surprised by the responses I received when I asked immigrant men about their future plans. I suppose that I had allowed myself to become so immersed in the migration literature that I was expecting to hear something more along the lines of "return to Mexico and start my own business." More common, however, were responses such as Paco's:

I want to be anywhere close to the person I love, to support me. If it's in Mexico, [it would be] a lot better because I would have my family and that person near me. But, more than anything, right now I worry a lot for my own person and for the partner who I think will be what I wait for in my life. And I see myself in a relationship with a lot of affection, and maybe by then, living with that person, together. And maybe even to get married.

In response to my next question—"So your plans for the future are to have partner?"—Paco answered,

A stable partner, be happy, and give them all my support, and I would help that person shine, succeed in anything I could help. I will try to do it all the time. If he accomplishes more than I have it will make me very happy because in that aspect I am not egotistical. And still more things that are positive; get more involved in helping people that need me, in every aspect. Be happy, make my partner happy, above all make myself happy, and my family, my friends, all the people that like me, and I like.

This type of response does not exclude dreams of material wealth and entrepreneurship, but it centers on and gives priority to affective dimensions—to building new families. The desires for stable relationships reflect not only the difficulty in maintaining such relationships in Mexico but also the isolation that these men feel in the United States. This isolation that gay Mexican immigrant men feel is due in some measure to language difficulties, but racial and class issues also play into it. For instance, Carlos explained to me that although he was in a relationship at the time of our interview he didn't see much of a future in it.

> I don't have many expectations for my relationship because my partner is not Latino. I think that, ideally, for a stable relationship I need to be with a Latino . . . someone who identifies as Latino. Someone intelligent and a little more cultured. Someone who has the capacity to go to an art or photography exhibit and enjoy it. Someone open-minded, open to learning from other cultures and who is financially independent.

The problem, of course, is that the social location of Mexican immigrant MSMs in the United States is a marginal one. Stability is not easily established and financial independence may take years to accomplish, if it is achieved at all. The problem is exacerbated by the fact that there are few public spaces where Latino gay men can openly meet one another. Thus, creating family or even a sense of community depends in no small part upon the ability of queer Latinos to build a new home with limited resources and external support.

"Who do you turn to for support?" I asked the men I interviewed. The standard response was, "family and friends." Yet it is clear from my discussions with these men, and the data presented here, that these relationships (whether biological or chosen) were sometimes strained, always evolving, and ultimately negotiated. A queer materialist analysis of the experiences of Mexican immigrant men who have sex with men reveals the ways in which dimensions of family, migration, and sexual identity intersect and are embedded within a political economy. Many of the men interviewed felt marginalized by heteronormative definitions of masculinity reproduced through and embodied in the traditional family. These norms, reproduced in daily activities since childhood, marginalize not only men with "feminine" characteristics but also those able to pass, who were instilled with a fear of discovery. Associations of femininity with homosexuality created a sense of confusion in some men, who although attracted to men did not identify as feminine. The economic liability that derived from not creating a heteronormative family unit as an adult also influenced the immigration process. These strict gender/

sex regimes were powerful enough to drive many men to migrate to the United States in search of a more liberal environment.

A queer political economy perspective of migration also aids in unveiling how sexuality has shaped processes and strategies for adaptation such as social networks and household arrangements. Alternative relations to biological families, which serve as systems of support, are created on the basis of sexual orientation. The members of these "chosen families" assist one another through the trials and tribulations of being queer Mexican immigrant men. Such assistance takes a variety of forms, including helping with migration itself, sharing knowledge and resources such as job information, and even sharing households.

New economic arrangements mean that some men find that they are empowered to "come out" to their biological families as gay men and maintain a level of acceptance and respect from their loved ones. Shared space is also an important dimension linked to the futures of these gay men. Faced with a sense of isolation and a deep desire to form the stable relationships that they were prevented from having in Mexico, these men found space to be the base for adaptation, community, and shared futures. Thus, for many men who have come to identify as gay, new family structures become a means by which dreams may be realized.

Although my focus has been on Mexican immigrant men, there are larger implications that need to be explored. When we understand sexuality as a dimension of power (that intersects with other dimensions such as race, gender, and class) in which certain groups are privileged over others, then these implications become more visible. For instance, Argüelles and Rivero (1993) argue that some immigrant women have migrated in order to flee violent and/or oppressive sexual relationships or marriage arrangements. Little research has been conducted on Latinas in general; far less exists on the intersections of migration and sexuality (regardless of sexual orientation). While it is clear that biological families reproduce normative constructions of gender and sexuality, the ways in which these norms and power relations influence different groups of people in terms of migration and identity are not understood.

Conclusion

In his essay on heterotopias, Foucault (1985) argued that "space is fundamental in any form of communal life; space is fundamental in any exercise of power" (252). In the preceding pages, I have demonstrated that for gay Latinos the "fundamentals" of community are largely missing and this lack has profound ramifications in terms of power. Gay Mexican men who migrate to the Los Angeles area seeking a "place" where they can develop as "gay men" soon discover that such places are difficult to find. This is due in part to the ways in which sexuality shapes space itself. The perceived lack of space where Mexican men can be "gay" is one of the reasons why these men tend to migrate in the first place (as discussed in chapter 4). Sexuality influences households, the very spaces that these immigrant men come to call home. And sexuality also shapes the spaces where Mexican gay men try to form communities. But sexuality is one of multiple axes that intersect and shape the spaces where these men live; race, gender, and class also shape these spaces (or the lack of them).

As we have seen in this chapter, experiences of sexism, racism, and homophobia described by the gay Latino men interviewed in this study resist flat cultural explanations. These men face many challenges in which they try to find a balance between the demands placed upon them as men and the factors that constrain their development. As gay Latinos, many of these men must face challenges that are exacerbated by a sense of isolation. The social isolation, or disconnectedness, that they experience is influenced by multiple and intersecting dimensions such as racism from mainstream and gay communities, homophobia outside and within the larger Latino community, limited accessibility (due to physical and social distance, as well as financial constraints) to gay community resources, and different legal migration statuses.

7

Entre Hombres/Between Men

Latino Masculinities and Homosexualities

While the mainstream lesbian and gay community has developed its own infrastructure of businesses, service organizations, and social clubs, these were not regularly utilized by the gay Latino immigrants I met. Communal spaces where gay and lesbian Latinos/as can mix and meet are few and far between (especially for women). The irony is that, as mentioned, mainstream gay and lesbian establishments (and even "cruising" sites)[1] are often either adjacent to or in Latino communities. Though it may be stating the obvious, the political economy of queer Latino space is shaped both by the larger political economics of sexualized and racialized space and by that which is more specific to queer Latinos. Thus, the dynamics that led to segregating marginal groups such as Latinos and queers from the mainstream and in effect created this neighbor/border situation are reproduced to marginalize queer Latinos from both communities. These new queer Latino spaces are shaped in large part by two political economic dimensions: the commodification of Latino sexuality and HIV funding.

While there are a number of possible places where gay Latino men might meet other gay Latino men,[2] the most common place mentioned by informants was gay bars and clubs. There are several bars and clubs that cater to gay Latinos in the greater Los Angeles area. Some, such as Arena in Hollywood, target a younger clientele with a "rave" type of atmosphere and a mix of Latin House, Rock en Español, and some more mainstream queer dance music. These types of clubs are perhaps best described as American gay bars with a Latin flavor; that is, they are very similar in most respects to mainstream gay clubs except that the majority of the patrons are Latino. The crowd, which is both native and immigrant Latino, tends to be in their twenties although it is not unusual to find men in their thirties and forties. In addition, there are bars that target more "traditional" Latino musical tastes and have a greater percentage of immigrant patrons. These clubs tend to play Latin music, such as Banda, Cumbias, and Latin Pop. In these spaces, Spanish is spoken almost exclusively. In addition, many "mainstream" gay bars now sponsor "Latin" nights on designated evenings. The bars use themes like "*Machismo*," supposedly in order to attract gay Latino customers but more probably to attract white patrons seeking Latino gay men. While one could argue that these establishments merely serve the demands of the market, the commodification of Latino sexuality (both straight and gay, male and female) is also shaping the creation of these spaces.

Beyond just serving a Latino market, these commodified spaces create the fantasy of the insatiable "hot" Latin sex machine. Figures 5.1, 5.2, and 5.3 illustrate how the male Latino body is exoticized and objectified to sell to both mainstream and Latino gay markets. While these images are obviously racialized (e.g., models with sarapes and big hot chiles), their portrayal of Latino men as belonging to the "lower" classes as manual laborers and gang members reproduces dominant views of Latino masculinity (the macho) that are often, if not always, attributed to "Latin culture." The lack of alternative types of spaces ensures that these commodified visions of Latino sexuality constrain the ways in which a gay Latino can envision himself at both a personal and a community level. Thus, despite being constructed as objects of desire, gay Latinos remain, in many respects, segregated from mainstream gay culture with few alternative spaces of their own.

While both gay and Latino communities have historically been segregated in spaces marginalized from the dominant white heterosexual community, they have also served as sites of resistance. Both the gay and Chicano/Latino movements have sprung from spatially segregated communities. Both movements have deep roots in their respective communities in the Los Angeles area and now play important roles in their contemporary formations. However, despite their important contributions, queer Latino concerns have for the most part been ignored by both of these movements. At both a national and a local level, mainstream gay and Chicano/Latino organizations have attempted to address these concerns with varying degrees of success (i.e., National Association for Chicana and Chicano Studies). In 1987, following the National March in Washington for Gay and Lesbian Rights, a group of Latina/o LGBT activists met and formed an organization that would eventually become the National Latina/o Lesbian, Gay, Bisexual, and Transgender Organization, or *LLEGÓ* as it is more commonly known. *LLEGÓ* played an

TABLE 7.1

LA Area Queer Latino Organizations *

Name	Location(s)	Description
Bienestar	East LA, Long Beach, Hollywood/Silverlake, Pomona, San Fernando Valley	HIV/AIDS Prevention and Services
Entre Hombres Program (Delhi Community Center)	Santa Ana	(MSM) HIV/AIDS Prevention and Services (Latino Services)
The Wall-*Las Memorias* Project	East Los Angeles	HIV/AIDS Prevention and Services
Hombre A Hombre & Jovenes in Action (AltaMed Health Services)	Los Angeles	(MSM) HIV/AIDS Prevention and Services
Gay and Lesbian Latinos *Unidos* (GLLU)	Hollywood	General (Social and Political)
Lesbianas Unidas	Alhambra	General (Social and Political)

* *Editors' update:* As of fall 2007, Bienestar has added five new sites (in El Monte/AHF, San Diego, South Los Angeles, San Bernardino, Van Nuys, and a specific La Casa LGBT) and seems to have discontinued or merged one (San Fernando Valley); the Delhi Community Center appears to continue to offer services to MSMs, as per the HIV Prevention Comprehensive Community Planning document for the years 2007–2010 (accessible on the web); The Wall-*Las Memorias* Project continues its HIV- related services, though no specific information on MSMs can be found on the web; AltaMed continues to list a *Hombre A Hombre* program, now with a specific youth component; Gay and Lesbian Latinos *Unidos* does not seem to be in existence; and *Lesbianas Unidas* is still listed as an active organization on the web.

important leadership role in the queer Latina/o community through its annual conferences, periodic programming, and small grant funding. In the past, the organization has sponsored programs specifically for Latino youth, lesbians, and transgendered people.[3]

There are several local organizations that serve queer Latino communities. Table 7.1 describes these organizations. Although this list is not inclusive of all Latino groups in the area, it is a fair representation of LGBT organizations that are Latina/o focused. Other organizations such as LGBT community centers in Los Angeles, Long Beach, and Orange County do have groups or services that are aimed at Latinas/os, but for the most part these are, like the majority of groups listed below, HIV/AIDS focused. For instance, the Center Orange County (which has the most Latino-inclusive programming of all the centers) lists five Latino programs under its auspices: *Encuentros, Entre Amigos, Hermosa y*

Protegida, Latina Lesbians, and Unicos. Of the five programs listed, only the Entre Amigos and Latina Lesbians groups are neither HIV focused nor HIV funded and are more social in nature.

Unfortunately, the Entre Amigos group no longer exists. A representative of the Center Orange County explained that the group disbanded in part due to problems with meeting consistently and the availability of newly funded HIV programs. *Encuentros* targets Latino MSMs who are not necessarily gay identified and is part of the Center's Latino AIDS Project. Unicos, which is also a part of the Latino AIDS Project, is an HIV prevention program that targets Latino day workers at the sites where they gather. From 1992 until 1998, the Center of Orange County utilized state HIV prevention funds to sponsor an annual event called "*Hermosa y Protegida* (Beautiful and Protected) Beauty Pageant," where transgendered Latinas compete for the crown of *Señorita Hermosa y Protegida*. According to event organizers, the winner is recognized as a leader in the community who helps promote HIV prevention to the transgender community. I served as a judge for the 1999 pageant and can testify to the important role that the event serves as a space for community building. However, the event does have a moralistic tone, and like the other programs, it emphasizes monogamy and self-control. My point here is not to diminish the importance of HIV/ AIDS prevention and services in the Latino community but rather to point to the fact that the politics of HIV/AIDS funding shapes not only the space that is available to queer Latinos but also the ways in which they imagine themselves as individuals and as a community. Within my research on gay Mexican immigrants, I have worked primarily with two of these organizations, Bienestar and Delhi Center's *Entre Hombres* program. For the rest of this chapter I will focus on my research with the latter of the two to examine how the sociopolitics of HIV shape this space.

The communal spaces that are beginning to form are shaped by a combination of influences, including demographic changes, social movement mainstreaming, market forces, and the institutionalization of HIV/ AIDS prevention. These dimensions provide both opportunities for growth and constraints upon the social relations and identities that are created in these new spaces. More spaces are definitely needed in order to provide environments where gay Latinos can come together and form communities of support.

Entre Hombres

On a cool May evening in the city of Santa Ana,[4] California, approximately fifty Latino men boarded a bus for a weekend-long retreat in the
Southern California mountain resort of Big Bear Lake. To the casual
onlooker, the congregation of men may have called attention to itself,
but the men themselves probably seemed nondescript in this predominantly Latino city. Yet this was not a usual gathering; these Latino men
were meeting to confront and discuss the challenges in their lives as
gay Latino men. This chapter utilizes data collected during two retreats,
or *encuentros* (encounters), organized by the *Entre Hombres* (Between
Men) program of Santa Ana's Delhi Center (a Latino community service organization). The weekend retreats at which my research was
conducted were held at a campground facility in the immediate area
surrounding the town of Big Bear, California, in November 1997 and
May 1998. These retreats were the third and fourth such events,[5] which
began in November 1996 for the purpose of exploring how issues of
masculinity, sexuality, HIV, and culture impact participants' lives as gay
Latino men.

Even though most of the *Entre Hombres* program participants are
immigrants, they too are by no means a homogenous group. While participants are predominantly from Mexico, which alone has numerous
regional differences, they also come from Colombia, Guatemala, Hon-
duras, Nicaragua, Peru, and Venezuela. Thus, despite the fact that these
men come together as gay Latino men, the *Entre Hombres* retreat organizers have learned that differences among the men is one of the first
obstacles to overcome.

For instance, during the May 1997 retreat, several exercises were
conducted that attempted to build a communal base. One exercise
had the participants answer descriptive questions about themselves on
butcher paper that was taped on the walls of the main meeting room.
Written entries included name, place of origin, sexual identity, whether
they were "out" or not, people they admired, and a motto. The majority mentioned either parents (particularly mothers) or religious figures
(such as the Pope) as people they admired, and the virtual dearth of
gay Latino role models couldn't be ignored. This became a point of
discussion that gave rise to the realization that gay Latinos, though not

absent from history, were invisible. Another exercise called on participants to list what they actually had in common. The exercise proved to be somewhat difficult even though the men had broken into six smaller groups. Participants in each of the groups would call out a topic until they found a characteristic that they all shared. Common responses were centered on hobbies or entertainment such as music, dancing, and sports, but they also included what can best be described as a shared need for intimacy, (i.e., looking for a relationship, love, and romance). What these responses have in common, of course, is that they all require, albeit at different levels, shared space. The men responded in a variety of ways such as with grunts, laughter, and sighs of frustration when an assumed similarity failed to be shared. One such characteristic that proved to be a "problem" was sexual identity.

The challenges that these men face as gay Latino men are multiple and complex. While these challenges include such dimensions as homophobia, racism, and poverty, these men are differentially constrained and have different means by which to resist these constraints depending upon their specific social locations and histories. To attempt to understand the lives and struggles of these men as gay Latino men is thus, in many ways, a constraint itself. I thus use the term "gay Latino men" with caution because the phrase implies a given unity or homogeneity that must be questioned.

While I believe that "culture" plays an important role in the lives and identities of gay Latino men, I contend that cultural arguments often obfuscate the structural power dimensions that shape the lives of men in marginalized social locations. It is not my intention to enter the ongoing anthropological debates about the problem of defining culture; neither is it my intent to reify culture, but rather, as it has been throughout the book, to critique the manner in which "culture" as a focal argument not only obscures other structural dimensions that shape Latino men's lives but also pathologizes our "culture." To borrow from Lila Abu-Lughod's (1991) conceptualization of this theme, in a phrase, I am "writing against culture."

Informed by such a framework, I examine how Latino men in the sociopolitical borderlands of Southern California negotiate and contest unequal power differentials of gender, sexuality, and race/ethnicity in their everyday lives. Integral to understanding these Latino men's lives as men is examining how their masculinity is shaped by structural dimensions.

Learning about Hombres Gay

The data for this chapter was collected at two weekend retreats sponsored by the Delhi Center. Eighty-four men participated in the retreats; there were thirty-one participants at the November retreat and fifty-three participants at the May event. Participants were between the ages of twenty and forty-eight (median age 29.8) and were predominantly Spanish-speaking immigrants. Thus, while some English is spoken at the retreats, they are for the most part held in Spanish. Ethnographic methods such as field notes, participant-observation, and focus groups were used during the two events. I conducted in-depth personal interviews with ten of the participants and additional interviews with retreat organizers (mostly in Spanish) at other times and locations lasting between forty-five minutes and three hours. In addition, an evaluation survey that was given before and after the May event was also analyzed for descriptive-type variables (rather than evaluation, which is not the focus of this study).

The data derived from these retreats is not meant to be representative of gay Latinos, nor even gay Latino immigrants. The men who participate in the program are men who are to varying degrees open to going on a weekend retreat with other men to talk about HIV and sexuality issues. They vary as well in terms of "closetedness." Some are what might be considered very "out," but the majority are coming to terms with their same-sex attraction. The men, therefore, have a variety of labels that they use to define their sexuality. My use of terms like "gay," "queer," and "homosexual" is imposed unless noted otherwise. For that matter, even the label "Latino" is imposed, as many men identify by their nationalities.

In addition, there are two methodological components that need further explanation. The first is my use of the term "focus groups." The retreat program included exercises in which the men gathered either in small groups or in a single group to discuss such issues as personal and community challenges, what they had in common, and HIV. The groups were facilitated either by Dr. Damian Goldvarg, a psychologist and retreat coordinator, or by one of five cofacilitators who assisted with the event. My role was mostly that of an observer although I did facilitate several exercises. Through each of these group discussions that I refer to as focus groups, I took notes and recorded the discussions on a standard cassette recorder. Another exercise that was helpful in gathering data about the men was an exercise in which participants decorated a sheet of butcher paper approximately fourteen by twenty-four inches in diameter with markers and a Polaroid picture of themselves and provided the following information: name, age, place of birth, occupation, if they considered themselves in or out of the "closet," the label they used for their sexual identity, if they were in a relationship, and the names of three people whom they admired. Each of these methodological components served to provide insights into the issues that influence their lives as *hombres gay* (gay men).

The retreats served as an ideal ethnographic site at which to conduct this research, for several reasons. As I will elaborate in a later section of this chapter, gay Latino men, particularly in the Orange County area, have limited social spaces and resources that allow them to interact as gay Latino men. The retreats, therefore, provide an alternative, albeit temporary, site at which gay Latino men can "be themselves" and freely discuss issues that concern them. Methodologically, the rationale for the site also resonates with Harry Brod's (1994) suggestion that "researchers attempt to integrate men's standpoints into gender studies in at least three ways: (a) by focusing on men's emotions, (b) by studying men in groups, and (c) by placing men's experiences in structural context" (55).

The *Entre Hombres* retreats allow for the exploration of such an approach in that they provide a site where men gather to discuss the emotional, psychological, and structural dimensions that are part of their everyday lives. However, the site alone is insufficient to move towards Brod's methodological suggestions. As Brod (1994) and Hodagneu-Sotelo and Messner (1994) assert, analyses must be informed by a structural feminist approach (rather than a cultural one) if we are to understand the intersecting axes that cross the social locations of "gay Latino men." In this chapter I examine these intersecting dimensions in the lives of men and as they relate to masculinity. Discussions of class, race, sexuality, and cultural issues should therefore be understood as being intimately linked to masculinity and not separate from it.

The Mission

According to a pamphlet distributed at the 1998 *Encuentro Entre Hombres* (EEH) retreat, the program's mission is to "improve the quality of life of the gay, bisexual, and transgendered Latino community. Creating spaces for self understanding, integration, and social well being; starting from our human values." The mission statement is reflective of the way in which the Delhi Center, a Latino-staffed organization, envisions its role in the larger Latino community. As program coordinator Luis Lopez states,

> The agency [Delhi Center] really looks at developing the leadership ca-
> pabilities of the individuals it serves so they can provide their own op-
> portunities and advocate for their own issues and really be involved in
> their communities. So, we're not concerned so much with the provision of
> service as we are with persons—person skills, volunteerism, and leadership
> development.

This ideology seems particularly useful in dealing with a "community" that is in many ways difficult to define. As previously mentioned, while gay communities or enclaves exist in most, if not all, major urban areas, they are shaped by a "mainstream" culture that is predominantly a gay, white, male, middle-class culture. There are no gay Latino "enclaves."[6] In the words of Luis Lopez, the gay Latino community is

> not a geographically defined area . . . there are social networks in place,
> people know people, there hasn't been a whole lot in terms of formal or-
> ganized efforts. It's starting. In the last couple of years since the onset of
> prevention work, in the county, it's started but it's never been there before.
> What's been in place has been informal social networks of people that just
> know who's gay and where you meet and those type of informal networks.
> Which are in my mind not any less valid, but for whatever reasons they
> haven't addressed issues like HIV in an organized way, or issues of social
> isolation, that a community needs to address for its collective well-being.

Whether the roots of queer Latino communities in the United States trace back to a time prior to the HIV/AIDS epidemic is debatable; but it is clear that HIV/AIDS has had a tremendous influence on queer Latino social space. As an "imagined community"[7] (Anderson 1983; Chavez 1994) that lacks geographic specificity and is marginal to the mainstream gay community, queer Latino communities have in many ways been con-structed out of the necessity to confront the threat of HIV/AIDS. Partici-pants are recruited through social networks and outreach programs at local bars that cater to gay Latino men and other sites where Latino men who have sex with men congregate. These sites and networks are not confined to geopolitical boundaries. Thus while the program targets gay Latino men in the Orange County area, in this fourth retreat approximately 28 percent of participants came from other parts of the Southern California area, including Los Angeles, Riverside, and San Bernadino Counties.[8] Events sponsored by the *Entre Hombres* program, such as the weekend retreats, are aimed at HIV education and prevention among this high-risk group, but such programming must juggle the understood needs of the population that Delhi serves with the expectations and constraints placed upon them by funding agencies.

> I firmly believe you can't address some of these issues, prevention of HIV, without addressing all the cofactors, all the other issues involved with gay Latino men. I think with Latino gay men you really have to address some of the self-esteem issues, some of the mental health issues, some of the disconnectedness, the marginalization, the alienation that some of these individuals feel. . . . Funders have a hard time with that, they want to see that we're preventing HIV, period, and for them, it's difficult to conceive of it as something that's going to include coming out to my family, 'cause that's not HIV prevention, of belonging to a strong and healthy gay community, 'cause that's not HIV prevention, that's a political agenda, all these other issues which are very real and very impacting.

As Lopez eloquently illustrates, "disconnectedness" is more than a client problem. Funding agencies, such as the county and state that fund the *Entre Hombres* program, regulate programming through an institutional discourse that is based in part on academic studies of "gay Latino men." Such discourse reproduces "relations of ruling" by either ignoring the social locations of Latinos altogether or masking them in the terminology of culture. The end result is that programs such as *Entre Hombres* must either coach their programs in the language of regulatory and funding agencies (learn the language) or take the risk of alternative programming on their own.

The *Entre Hombres* program walks a fine line trying to negotiate the requirements of regulatory agencies with their own understandings of their clients' needs. Events therefore combine the two demands in an attempt to find a balance, however precarious. Programs like the retreat commonly mix HIV prevention techniques with leadership training and community building. Furthermore, the organization's events are attended by both HIV-negative and HIV-positive individuals in order to deconstruct sexual myths at an interpersonal level. The events also include cultural components that seem to help the clients feel that they are in a supportive environment. The inclusion of a spiritual dimension in the programs is one such cultural component. It is not unusual for events to open and/or close with a candle lighting ceremony in which the men form a circle and reaffirm, through prayer, the gift of life as well as a gay existence. Culture, in this instance, is utilized in a somewhat subversive way to open up supportive spaces for queer Latino men.

Although cultural affinities are partly responsible for bringing these men together, the social isolation that Lopez describes cannot be attributed to cultural differences between mainstream and Latino communities alone (i.e., cultural isolation in a mainstream "Anglo" culture). While many HIV programs that target gay populations are based on the generalized research of gay white men, a few programs attempt to address the special needs of minority communities such as gay Latino men. One such program that attempts to address HIV prevention in alternative terms is the Hermanos de Luna y Sol program in San Francisco's Mission Health Center. The program is designed in part after research conducted by Rafael Díaz (1998) of the Center for AIDS Prevention Studies (CAPS) at the University of California, San Francisco, and is described in his book *Latino Gay Men and HIV: Culture, Sexuality, and Risk Behavior.* While Díaz's scholarship is much needed and to be commended, his sociocultural paradigm falls into the same cultural analysis discourse trap that much of the literature on Latino men falls into. Discussing the problem of gay Latino men's "limited ability to self-regulate sexual activity" Díaz (1998) argues,

> Limitations in the ability to self-regulate sexuality, however, should not be understood as the result of a personal deficit, but rather as the natural outcome of socialization within a culture that promotes sexual silence about homosexual activity from the interpersonal, affective, and rational lives of gay men at the same time that it undermines perceptions of sexual control; and breeds fatalism. The causes for the sexual self-regulatory problems observed in Latino gay men can be found within the context of our socialization into a homophobic-machista culture, coupled with harsh experiences of poverty and racism as members of an ethnic minority group in the U.S. (150)

By giving primacy to a "homophobic-machista culture" and subordinating "the experiences of poverty and racism" to it, Díaz's argument cloaks the structural dimensions of homophobia and sexism. Lest we forget, gay Latino men's experiences of homophobia and sexism are not bound to their Latino communities. I do not mean to imply that homophobia and sexism do not exist in Latino communities; they obviously do, but in which communities do they not exist? If we understand the homophobia and sexism that Latino gay men face as a "cultural problem," are we not then caught in a discourse that "others" Latino gay men and minimizes how homophobia, sexism, and racism are linked and tied to a dominant "culture?"

When directly asked what they felt were the personal challenges in their lives, the men listed the following: (1) coming out of the closet, (2) preparing oneself to be in a relationship, (3) maintaining a relationship, (4) being more assertive, and (5) dealing with loneliness and depression. These challenges point less to the homophobia of Latino culture specifically than they do to a sense of isolation and a need for intimacy. Culture is obviously a component of these challenges, but the homophobia, sexism, racism, and poverty that many of these men face are shaped by structural dimensions beyond "Latino culture."

For instance, while the literature on Latino male homosexuality asserts that sexual identity is dependent on the active or passive role of the actors, only one of the participants of the November and May retreats referred to himself as *activo* and none identified as *pasivo* when they were asked, "How do you classify your sexual identity?"[9] Only one of the participants identified as "straight." Sixty-four percent of the November group and 26 percent of the May group identified as either gay or gay Latino; 4 percent of the November group and 56 percent of the May group used the term "homosexual"; and 28 percent of the November group and 13 percent of the May group had an ambiguous answer such as "excellent" or "normal." While one could interpret such ambiguous answers as a cultural resistance to identifying as gay, one could also interpret such responses as individual resistance to use *any* label, or simply as indicating that the question was not understood. During my interviews with some of the participants, I asked them about their sexual identities and why they had chosen particular labels; the majority of respondents explained that "homosexual" and "gay" were interchangeable terms for them, and one of the respondents who had given an ambiguous answer explained that he wasn't quite sure which label to use since he had sex with both men and women. When asked directly about the labels of *"activo"/"pasivo,"* most of the men I spoke with, either in interviews or informally, explained that the terms were somewhat archaic, especially as identity labels, and that one might ask a prospective sexual partner what "they liked" but that they expected a partner in a committed relationship to be more versatile in his sexual repertoire.

Sexual identity and its relationship to structural dimensions arose within my interviews as well. In this respect, Almaguer's assertions of gay Chicano identity seem most relevant. Almaguer argues that because Chicano gay men are located in a subordinate racial position, they are more dependent upon familial relationships for their survival than Anglo gay men—a "gay" identity is therefore constrained from development. The argument is conceptually linked to D'Emilio's (1993 [1983]) assertions, which link sexual identity to capitalist development, the lessened dependence on family, and the migration of homosexuals to urban gay communities in San Francisco, Los Angeles, Chicago, and New York after World War II. Thus, economic dependence upon family members may constrain the development of a gay identity, but the reverse may happen as well.

Rafael is a 29-year-old Mexican immigrant born in Mexico City but raised in the state of Michoacan. He moved to the United States in 1991 to join family members and help his infirm mother financially. Eventually he brought his mother, who is separated but not divorced from his father, to the United States to live with him. At the time of my interview with him, Rafael was working three "jobs," two of which were paid positions while the other was volunteer work with an AIDS services organization. Despite the fact that Rafael has two jobs, his annual income is only about twenty-six thousand dollars. Rafael describes his family situation in the following way:

> My siblings think of me as their father because for a very long time I've given them the confidence to speak to me about anything. They all care for me a great deal, my mother cares for me a lot too. She knows that I'm gay. She doesn't completely like it, but she accepts it. She's very Catholic and at times we have our little problems because she thinks that God doesn't permit my lifestyle. She won't talk to me openly about the issues but she loves me for my support of the family. My sisters all know about me and I can speak openly with them but not my mother. I think that with time, you know, I'm her son and she loves me. Then with time, if God permits, she will accept me. I don't blame her.

Rafael's story exemplifies the complexity of sexual identity among gay Latinos. While he uses the term "Latino gay" for self-identification, the "coming out" process has been constrained at a certain level by his family obligations. Yet, Rafael is "out" to his family and tries to maintain a balance between his individual needs and a sense of respect for the family. Although these identity issues may seem at a superficial level to be cultural constructs, they are also influenced by social and economic dimensions. Rafael's economic situation seems to parallel those of *travesti* in Mexico City as reported by Prieur (1998), wherein family members became dependent upon the income of a "queer" family member and thus, to some extent, were forced to accept the family member's queerness. Yet, Rafael is an undocumented immigrant, which places social as well as economic constraints on his "lifestyle" as a gay man. Rafael explains,

> This is where I really opened up to the experience of being gay, [and] to my dreams of finding someone who cares for me and understands me and I him. I think I've changed a lot, over there I didn't express who I was in Mexico. It wasn't so easy, people wouldn't accept me. Even more so because I lived with my sisters and I was worried about scandals that arise when people talk. . . . I've learned to live differently, that life isn't necessarily tragic.

Rafael's words suggest that, although he didn't explicitly move to the United States because of his sexual orientation, his sexual identity and perspective as a gay man have been transformed by the move. This is due in part to greater economic opportunities that have transformed his relationship with his family and his ability to assert his right to live his life a gay man and to meet others like him.

Some of the Encuentro participants shared with the group that they had in fact migrated to the United States in order to find a place where they could more openly express their sexuality. Armando, for instance, is a 32-year-old Mexican national born in the state of Jalisco, where he spent eight years in a seminary studying to be a priest. Three years ago, after much inner turmoil and reflection over his suppressed homosexuality, he spoke to his religious mentor about his feelings. His mentor, a Catholic Mexican priest, advised him to accept himself as God had created him and not hide in shadows of the Church but leave it to discover himself. He accepted the advice and decided to move to the United States. Armando's knowledge of gay life in the United States was based on a combination of conversations with gay friends who lived in the States and his frequent visits here as a missionary. As he explains,

> I decided to come out of the closet, to accept my homosexuality and whatever comes with it. . . . [I came to the United States] because I feel as if the environment here, with respect to the services, the way that it is more open to homosexuals, there are more roads open to us, more forms of help.

Armando's coming-out story reveals the contradictions in the narrative that the literature constructs of a pervasively homophobic and sexist culture. Although Armando migrated to the United States because he felt that the environment was a better place than Mexico to be gay, it was a Mexican priest who advised him to do so. This illustrates one of many contradictions of gay life in Mexico. As in other countries, including the United States, in Mexico there are contested spaces of queer resistance and visibility in the streets, in politics, and in the media while antigay forces of the Right try to repress them. I am not trying to suggest with this narrative that Armando's story is representative of the Latino experience. On the contrary, what I am trying to suggest is that the "Latino experience" is far more complex than a universalizing notion can capture.

Like Armando, Eduardo is also an immigrant from the state of Jalisco. But Eduardo's story is a different one. Eduardo is forty-two years old and from the city of Guadalajara, which has a large gay and lesbian population. In expressing his observations of the May retreat, Eduardo says,

> I noticed many people expressed frustration and discrimination in childhood and there's a lot of self-policing because of social norms. I found that many people felt the frustration of trying to be their true selves. Some try to leave, to escape. In my case, I don't think it has affected me as much. I am who [I] am, and I like being who I am. I've had people in my life to support me. If I had the choice to be a man, woman, or a gay man, I'd choose to be gay. We have to be who we are.

However, the "choice" to be gay may be easier for Eduardo to make than for others. Eduardo's background is a middle-class one. In Mexico he worked as an accountant and as a performer. He has a job in the United States as an accountant but is thinking of returning to Guadalajara where he can perhaps be "himself" to a greater degree than he can in the United States. In Eduardo's case, his social class allows him more freedoms in Mexico than some of his queer contemporaries. These free-doms are in many ways constrained in the United States due not so much to homophobia (although that too is part of it) as to the effects of racism and a different class status in the United States.

The stereotypes of Latino culture, discursively produced in academic texts, "scientific" research, and HIV/AIDS policies and programs, are both accepted and challenged at the ground level. While gay Latino partici-pants may accept the stance that "machismo" is a barrier for Latinos, they also resist totalizing applications. In one exercise, retreat director Damian Goldvarg raised the issue of the social norms of crying for Latino men. As he expressed, "We are all taught that it's not appropriate for men to cry, aren't we?" The dissenting voices of several participants' objections to the statement rang out through the meeting room. A few minutes later, when the group was discussing the issue of homophobia in Latino "culture," one participant announced, "In my case, my uncle, my father's only brother, is gay. My parents raised us using him as an example, not to copy him or be like him, but to teach us that we have to be ourselves." The sentiment was reinforced by another participant who stated, "I also had a positive gay role model, my uncle on my mother's side—the only male. He went to college in Argentina and we all knew he was gay. Above all, he was a role model of a positive human being who was gay."

Such responses, which in reality shouldn't come as a surprise, contra-dict the stereotypes that arise from the one-dimensionality of cultural arguments in the literature on Latino masculinity. Again, the point here is not to argue that these examples are the "rule" but rather that Latino masculinity and sexuality issues are much more complex and contradic-tory than the dominant construction or "rule" allows for. Most the men did, for instance, discuss the personal contradictions they felt of being attracted to men and not believing (nor wanting to believe) that they themselves fit the feminine homosexual stereotype.

Besides the men who had role models who were different from dom-inant stereotypes, there were also several men who were in fact more stereotypically gay. These individuals made the social regulation or self-policing of gender dynamic more evident. Throughout the events, it was evident that many of the men were consciously trying to behave and dress in accordance with a masculine gender performance. Yet two exer-cises in particular challenged these concepts. The first took place during one of the day's spiritual sessions when the facilitator spoke of the need to get in touch with one's feminine side, to accept it and embrace it as part of one's uniqueness. Subsequently, I overheard several of the men discussing the fear they had of "letting their feathers show" (i.e., letting down their guard and revealing their feminine side).

The second event was held on the Saturday night of each weekend retreat. At this event, a "drag show" is held and some of the more masculine men are selected from the group (as well as volunteers) and then made up in complete drag. A Miss Big Bear is then selected from the performers, who compete for the award through events that include lip-synching and answering a question provided by a panel of judges (who are also retreat participants). On the Sunday mornings after the shows, many of the participants commented on a sense of liberation they felt at either directly participating in the drag show or witnessing it. This is not to suggest that the participants suddenly became in touch with an essentialized feminine side. It does, however, point to the restrictions that these men feel in terms of normative definitions of gender performance: a gender performance that is driven not just by cultural factors but also by socioeconomic ones.

Most of the men work in jobs that are physically demanding and/ or pay minimum-level wages; this means that their everyday displays of gender are shaped by class/labor dimensions and that maintaining these jobs depends upon a traditional gender performance. In an attempt to get participants to understand that they had common concerns, retreat organizers created an exercise in which each of the men was given either a pink, a blue, or a purple inflated balloon that represented different types of gay men (feminine, masculine, and HIV infected). The participants were then instructed to toss the inflated balloons in the air and keep them from hitting the ground; if they did hit the ground they were to be left there. After a few minutes the men were instructed to stop. With various balloons lying on the ground, they were told that without unity, without teamwork, gay Latino men would, like the balloons, fall; but together, even in a diverse community, all could be supported.

The exercise seemed to have a profound effect on the men as they began to intermingle more and talk more openly about their experiences. Participants began to share stories of an extremely personal nature, such as past sexual abuse, substance abuse, and HIV infection. As one participant put it,

It's difficult to talk about many of these things. We've all been affected by them and yet even in this retreat many of us are afraid to speak openly. We carry these problems with us and they affect those around us. To overcome them we need to speak openly about them.

Another participant added,

We all have our problems from childhood but we reach an age where we need to be who we are. Society influences us, and yes, I think many of us leave our countries to be who we are but we don't owe society anything. We all have to support ourselves, society doesn't do it. We don't need to please society, we are all the same, *maricas, jotos, putas,* and we need to support each other.

These points seemed to really be driven home by the Miss Big Bear drag contest. Although the contest was meant to be all in fun, some of these same contestants seemed to take their gender transformations quite seriously and attempted to be as feminine as they possibly could. The next day, two of them confessed that they had discovered both a new respect for the skills of the *vestidas* and a sense of their own feminine sides. This is not to suggest (in a Butlerian sense) that these men were suddenly liberated from their gender regimes by the drag performance (which in some ways is problematic itself), but the exercise does indeed seem to aid in a sense of empathy and community building.

Conclusion: Barriers and Bridges between Men

In their article "Theorizing Unities and Differences between Men and between Masculinities," Hearn and Collinson (1994) argue against a uniform notion of masculinity and argue for an acknowledgment of diversity wherein one "not only consider[s] diversity but also interrelations and contradictions" (110). In the preceding sections of this chapter I have attempted to demonstrate that not only do cultural arguments in the literature on gay Latino men serve to create a discourse of difference but also such explanations mask the structural dimensions that shape gay Latino men's lives.

The "othering" that the cultural discourse produces is made more visible in a review of Rafael Díaz's (1998) book *Latino Gay Men and HIV: Culture, Sexuality, and Risk Behavior,* by the editor of the *Journal of Homosexuality,* which states that safer sex guidelines for gay Latino men "must be embodied in an understanding of subjective meanings of their sexual unions within a culture that is pervasively homophobic and sexist."[10] The discursive implication is that Latino culture is deviant or deficient relative to the unspoken hegemonic norm and that interventions, *cultural interventions,* are necessary to correct the problem. Is an "Americanization" program then the solution? To what extent is the dominant American culture not "pervasively homophobic and sexist," or for that matter racist?

Alternatively, by examining homophobia and sexism as structural issues, as are poverty and racism, can we better understand how the social locations of gay Latino men relate to social inequalities, including their higher risk for HIV infection? Díaz (1998) and other scholars have made some important inroads in this regard by examining structural issues of poverty and racism. For instance, scholars argue that the combination of increased migration between Mexico and the United States, in conjunction with a resistance to discussing homosexuality in an informed manner, has contributed to the prevalence of AIDS among "gay" Mexican men (Alonso and Koreck 1993; Wilson 1995). While homophobia and sexism are probably linked to resistance to discussing homosexuality, such resistance may also be linked to social class, education, and the availability of HIV literature in Spanish; furthermore, the social locations of Mexican men in a global economy that induces migration should not be downplayed.

By representing Latino culture as static, monolithic, and exotic (if not primitive), cultural arguments fail to give an accurate analysis even on a purely cultural level. The lack of research on Latino sexuality, and the tendency for scholars to attribute Latino differences to cultural influences calls for new research that investigates Latina/o sexuality within a political economy framework that examines the multiple and intersecting dimensions of gender, race/ethnicity, culture, class, and migration. What is needed is a move towards a "political economy of identity" that examines the multiple sites of power with historic specificity at the same time as it unveils commonalities across *intersecting* dimensions of power. By examining the interrelatedness of power differentials across groups we can not only achieve a better understanding of the margins but also bring the margins to the center of men's studies (see, for example, Rotundo 1994). Incorporating these multiple and intersecting dimensions is by no means an easy task, but when the complexities of "gay Latino men's" lives are attenuated to cultural reductionist arguments, we are not only "misdiagnosing" the problem through cultural pathologization but also reproducing the very inequalities that we strive to address.

8

Toward a Queer Political Economy of Sexuality

Places, Spaces, and Shifting Identities

> A boundary is not that at which something stops but, as the Greeks recognised, the boundary is that from which something begins its essential unfolding. That is why the concept is that of Horismos, that is, the horizon, the boundary.
>
> —Martin Heidegger, *Basic Writing*

When I began to formulate my research in 1995, I knew from personal experience (as I imagine most queer people do) that sexuality was linked to migration. But how? In the approximately four years that I have been working on this topic, speaking to immigrants, familiarizing myself with their issues, and critically reading the relevant transdisciplinary literatures, that first seemingly simple question has multiplied into hundreds of complex ones. I do not pretend to have "the" answer to this complex web of intersecting questions and issues relating to what I have come to call "the sexuality of migration," but this framework does offer an important first step. Also, it must be noted that my use of the singular in "the sexuality of migration" rather than the plural "sexualities" is done consciously. I do not mean to suggest a singular experience, but rather I am emphasizing sexuality as a dimension of power with a variety of lived experiences and manifestations.

In the preceding pages I offered a theoretical framework, a queer political economy of migration, by which the social, political economic, historical, and spatial dimensions of sexuality and migration could be brought to the fore and analyzed. In this final chapter, I summarize my arguments and findings by reexamining the research questions that I posed in the introductory chapter. I will then discuss some of the theoretical and political implications of my work for future research.

Five research questions were presented in the first chapter of this book: (1) How is Mexican migration to the United States influenced by sexuality? (2) Do gay Mexican male migrants have alternative reasons for migration and modes of incorporation, as a result of their sexual orientation, than those posed by the current research on migration? (3) How do gay Mexican immigrants adapt to, negotiate, and resist the constraints of their marginalization (in terms of their sexual orientation, gender, race/ethnicity, class, and legal status)? (4) How is sexual identity among gay Mexican men shaped by sociostructural and migratory factors? (5) What is the relationship of sexual identity to gender identity and definitions of masculinity? I now turn to each of these questions, respectively, in order to summarize my findings.

How is Mexican migration to the United States influenced by sexuality? This is the central question of my research that is linked to, and answered in part by, the other research questions. As an approach to understanding the issues posed by this question I have proposed a theoretical framework that I refer to as a queer political economy of migration. I have argued that through the queer material standpoint we may understand sexuality as a dimension of relations of power (as are race, class, and gender) whereby those sexualities that fall outside of the socially prescribed "heteronormativity" (such as homosexuality) may be understood as marginal and stigmatized.

Understanding sexuality from a queer materialist perspective is especially important for an analysis of Mexican MSM immigration for two primary reasons. First, Mexican migrants comprise the largest contemporary immigrant group to the United States, yet the sexual dimensions of this migration have been largely ignored. Analyzing Mexican migration from a queer materialist standpoint allows us to examine more closely how the historical, social, and spatial dimensions of sexuality shape identities and migratory variables such as social networks and household arrangements.

Second, understanding sexuality from a queer materialist perspective is also important because previous research on Latino sexualities has given primacy to cultural constructions of homosexuality. These cultural reductivist analyses are often ahistorical and ignore the effects of capitalism and its global expansion. While gay and lesbian studies scholars have argued that capitalist development, urbanization, and weakened family ties led to the migration of "homosexually inclined" men and women to the major urban centers of the United States and the formation of a "gay" identity and community (D'Emilio 1993 [1983]; Rubin 1992 [1984]), the argument has not been expanded to examine the implications of globalization. Migration to the United States serves a similar purpose for Mexican men who are either "marked" by the stigma of homosexuality or fear it. While studies of homosexuality in Mexico (Carrier 1995; Murray 1995) suggest that only men who assume "passive" sexual behavior or men who adopt an "*internacional*" identity are stigmatized by the larger society, it is clear from the voices of Mexican immigrant men that even those who are able to hide their desire are impacted by this stigmatization to the point that some flee it. Men who may pass as straight in Mexico but who have "homosexual inclinations" may be more prone to assume a "gay" identity in the separation of social and familial constraints.

Do gay Mexican male migrants have alternative reasons for migration and modes of incorporation, as a result of their sexual orientation, than those posed by the current research on migration? My research points to the fact that sexuality does indeed influence processes of migration. While some men explicitly mention sexuality as a reason for migration, a queer political economic perspective reveals other ways in which sexuality influences migration as well. The sexual political economy of Mexico shapes the lives of Mexican men differently, intersecting with other dimensions such as class and gender. Mexican MSMs may not migrate, despite the stigmatization of homosexuality, for a variety of reasons. Three general themes, which arose from my fieldwork in Mexico, suggest that Mexican men who are relatively well-to-do and are able to maintain either bisexual or gay lives with minimal social costs are less likely to migrate. In addition, strong emotional and/or material ties to Mexico may either prevent migration or diminish the desire to migrate. Some men who expressed a desire to migrate had not been able to successfully do so because they do not have support systems in the United States (particularly gay ones) to assist them with migration.

Among the reasons given for migration by Mexican MSM immigrants (other than "sexual liberation") were as follows: discrimination and other forms of economic marginalization of queers in Mexico meant that their socioeconomic opportunities were limited; they had formed gay social relations that either facilitated or were the purpose of migration; and the very survival of some men is threatened by staying in

Mexico. My research also points to the ways in which gay immigrants have created their own alternative social networks to assist in migration and incorporation. These social networks are utilized to find employment, find roommates, and build new support systems of friends and lovers. Gay communities, economies, and networks that have developed as alternatives to the mainstream may serve as support mechanisms to migration and incorporation at both points of origin and points of destination. In the case of gay Mexican migrants, gay social networks formed in Mexico may be utilized to facilitate migration to the United States, as well as finding housing and employment in the city of destination.

How do gay Mexican immigrants adapt to, negotiate, and resist the constraints of their marginalization (in terms of their sexual orientation, gender, race/ethnicity, class, and legal status)? Mexican MSM immigrants are a diverse group with different constraints and opportunities for "incorporation"; class, legal status, English-language proficiency, duration in the United States, and premigration experiences shape both identities and the means by which men are able to adapt to their new surroundings. First and foremost, migration itself should be understood as a means of resistance.

Men who are stigmatized because of their homosexuality may utilize alternative support systems and networks not only locally but also transnationally through international migration. American gay communities and economies may serve as alternative modes of incorporation for gay Mexican immigrant men, but predominantly white gay communities are also sites of racial and class discrimination. Communal space and resources, therefore, become essential mechanisms of gay immigrants' chances for incorporation.

How is sexual identity among "gay" Mexican men shaped by sociostructural and migratory factors? Identities are socially constructed meanings that are dependent upon social location for interpretation. Social location includes not only geographical space but also social, cultural, and historical factors. As mentioned above, gay identities are social constructions shaped by the social relations of capitalist development and the intersecting influences of race, class, and gender.

What is the relationship of sexual identity to gender identity and definitions of masculinity? Almaguer's conceptualization of Latin America's gender/sex/power system is useful in understanding the relationship between gender and sexuality. However, the cultural primacy argument he posits lends itself to a reproduction of normalizing discourses by which Latino masculinity and sexuality are products of an "Other" culture backwards and deviant from that of the Western norm. Furthermore, the primacy of culture in Almaguer's conceptualization of the gender/sex/power axis in many ways masks other important structural dimensions. The relationship should be understood as intersecting with multiple dimensions of power, including race and class, and not simply as culturally derived. Such a reformulation allows us to better examine the complexities of Latino masculinities and sexualities in their multiplicities and sheds light on how these constructions differ, for instance, between a 30-something college-educated gay Chicano man, a 20-year-old queer *cholo*,[1] and a 40-year-old Mexican immigrant man who has sex with men.

How do sexual identities travel through Mexican tourism and circular migration? Borders are both material and symbolic, both real and imagined. The gay tourist industry constructs the Mexican man through a trope of machismo that shapes the desire of gay tourists and feeds the construction of commodified spaces in places like Mexico City. The queer materialist perspective brings into sharp relief how these constructions are fundamental to nationalist development as well as global political economic projects. The resultant queer sexual borderlands are simultaneously liberalizing and oppressive.

Each chapter has illustrated one aspect of these research questions, and ways of addressing them based on the empirical data from the research. There are, however, some political and theoretical aspects that are also emergent, and to which I turn attention to now.

Implications

The implications of the research that I have presented here may be best discussed as two distinct yet interrelated areas—the theoretical and the political. One of the contributions of postcolonial and postmodern theory (including Queer Theory) is that identity is no longer understood as something inherently fixed and stable. Rather, identity is understood as mutable and plural—that is, the subject is the intersection of multiple identities (race/ethnicity, gender, sexuality, and so forth) that change and have salience at different moments in time and place. Given the dramatic sociospatial changes that immigrants experience, their sexual identities cannot therefore be assumed stable. Iain Chambers (1994) explains that "identity is formed on the move" (25). The effects of migration upon the sexual identities of Mexican immigrant MSMs are ultimately linked to their emotional and material relationships to their biological families and the degree to which they have been able to resolve the normative sexuality and gender conflicts that fed their desire to migrate.

In chapter 1, I explained that a goal of my study was to contribute to queer migration studies by exposing how migration research and literature is framed by heteronormative assumptions that deny the existence of nonheterosexual subjects and cloak the ways in which sexuality influences migratory processes. I also stressed that I wanted to produce an intersectional analysis of the sexual dimensions of migration and avoid an additive or reductive approach. To adopt a queer standpoint means more than adding gays and lesbians as migrant groups; it means understanding sexuality as a dimension of power and interrogating the means by which it operates even within academic discourse. As Chambers (1994) asserts,

> The multiple representations and voices of the once excluded, of women, of black peoples, of discriminated sexualities, in contemporary culture, history and society, for example, do not simply exist in creating a space for them, of widening academic disciplines, political institutions, and adopting a pluralist gaze. It lies rather in reworking the very sense of history, culture, society and language that had previously excluded or silenced such voices.

Thus, my research and theoretical framework have the potential to inform not only sexuality studies but also the migration literature as well. To aid in illustrating this potential, I here briefly examine how sexual power relations are embedded in two cases that have previously been studied by immigration scholars.

The first case is that of the Mariel exodus to Miami in 1980. In their discussion of these events in *City on the Edge: The Transformation of Miami* (1993), Portes and Stepick argue that the negative reception that Marielitos received from quarters of both Anglo and coethnic communities was shaped by racial, class, and ideological differences. However, there were also some important sexual dimensions that were overlooked. Within their own text, Portes and Stepick cite first Fidel Castro as saying, "Those that are leaving from Mariel are the scum of the country—antisocials, homosexuals, drug addicts, and gamblers, who are welcome to leave Cuba if any country will have them" (qtd. in Portes and Stepick 1993, 21). The authors then reference the *Miami Herald* of May 1, 1980, which quotes a "'high-ranking U.S. official surveying the *sullen, seedy looking* contingent that arrived aboard the *Ocean Queen* [who] said privately: "just look at that bunch. Awfully funny that there are no women and children in the group. Something tells me we have a bunch of criminals here"'" (qtd. in Portes and Stepick 1993, 24). Portes and Stepick also cite a *Miami Herald* article of July 7, 1980, claiming "that over twenty thousand homosexual Cuban refugees await sponsors" (out of a total of 114,000 Mariel refugees reported to have arrived by June 30, or approximately 17.5 percent) (qtd. in Portes and Stepick 1993, 26). What these references point to is the fact that sexuality did indeed play an important role in shaping the type of reception that Marielitos received. The issue is not what percentage of refugees were actually homosexual, but rather, that a discourse of sexual deviance was used, in addition to race, class, and ideological factors,[2] to portray the immigrants as undesirable.

My argument for theoretically integrating sexuality into migration scholarship should not be read as merely including "gays" in our research. My assertion is that sexuality, understood as a dimension of power relations embedded in a political economy, shapes migratory processes. The second case of Latina immigrant domestic workers helps to better illustrate this point.

In her book *Gendered Transitions: Mexican Experiences of Immigration*, Pierrette Hondangeu-Sotelo (1994) mentions at least two areas where sexuality is an important factor in the lives of Mexican women. The first is that of marital infidelity by immigrant husbands, which, along with informal polygamous relationships, is declining in acceptance due to cultural changes, including the growing acceptance of divorce and the financial burden of supporting more than one family unit. Hondagneu-Sotelo argues that a double standard has traditionally allowed immigrant men more sexual freedom while subjecting women to the moral scrutiny and policing of neighbors and family. In addition, Hondagneu-Sotelo asserts that some women may choose live-in domestic work due to sexual power relations:

> These women choose live-in work because it lessened the risks they would be exposed to as women and undocumented immigrants. Compounding the dangers faced by an "illegal" presence in the country, a young unmarried woman unaccompanied by family or kin is easy prey for those who might take advantage of her sexuality. (1994, 131)

While each of these examples clearly reveals gendered dimensions of migratory experiences, it is important to analyze sexuality as a separate (though interrelated) dimension. In each of these examples, gender norms regulate the relative position of women to men but sexuality is the mechanism of control.

The implications of understanding the sexuality of migration are not just theoretical; there are political implications as well. There are several political or public policy–oriented implications of this research. Perhaps the most important of these is exposing the ways in which U.S. immigration policy discriminates against not only gays and lesbians but any form of relationship not considered "legitimate." A second issue raised is that of how HIV/AIDS funding and services are impacting queer Latino community formation. For instance, in their article entitled "Gender/Sexual Orientation Violence and Transnational Migration: Conversations with Some Latinas We Think We Know," Argüelles and Rivero (1993) argue that migration is a strategy used by women to resist sexual abuse and/or "heterosexist oppression" and that migration studies need to theorize the role of sexuality and sexual violence in transnational migration. This includes examining how sexual repression and inequalities are linked to migration and how the experience of migration is influenced by sexualities.

In addition, we need to investigate how sexual politics such as state policies and social norms of contraception and reproduction influence migratory processes. And while HIV and other STDs among migrants have been studied, this research has been largely epidemiological and has not analyzed how globalization and the sexual political economy may influence the spread and treatment of these diseases. For example, greater attention needs to be given to how tourism and other forms of international travel may be transforming social norms, communities, and identities in communities around the world.

The main point is that sexuality is an important dimension of the political economy of migration that has been largely ignored. This book represents a move towards unraveling the complex and various ways in which sexuality shapes the social relations of migration and how identity is in turn shaped by political economy (including that of class, space, and family). Future research may either expand the ideas presented here, or take issue with them; in either case, a dialogue has begun.

Editors' Conclusion

Nancy A. Naples and Salvador Vidal-Ortiz

In this concluding chapter, we consider Lionel Cantú's contributions to the growing field of gender, sexuality, and migration studies and highlight new theoretical and empirical developments. We focus on the avenues of investigation that are most directly linked to Cantú's theoretical and empirical work and close with an assessment of what questions remain and how Cantú's work provides a foundation for subsequent inquiry.

As mentioned in our introductory chapter, Cantú was one of the first to contribute to this new field of inquiry. Scholarship has developed in a number of important directions that have deepened our understanding of the intersection of immigration and sexuality.[1] It is no longer necessary to argue that these areas of investigation need to be brought into conversation with one another. In addition to the book edited by Luibhéid and Cantú (2005), the collection that most directly demonstrates the rich new field is *Passing Lines: Sexuality and Immigration* (Epps, Valens, and González 2005). In the editors' words, this interdisciplinary collection "pushes at the shrine of national heteronormativity, and proposes, in the process, a more supple, assertive, and just appreciation of the intricacies of humanity and democracy" (38).

This new scholarship has contributed to a wide-ranging discussion of sexuality in the context of immigration, globalization, and "queer diasporas" (see Patton and Sánchez-Eppler 2000; Manalasan 2006). The North (or the West) has been decentered in several important studies.[2] This scholarship offers "new 'articulations' of same-sex desire" (Leap and Boellstorff 2004), processes of "transculturation" (Peña 2004), and postcolonial sexual formations and contestations (Peña 2007a). Analysis of the border and borderlands has also deepened into a new framework called "border theory." This scholarship speaks to one of the many theoretical developments anticipated in *The Sexuality of Migration*.

Theorizing the Border and Borderlands

In addition to Cantú's most fundamental contribution, which is to place the fields of sexuality and immigration into conversation with one another, he offers several specific interventions that are especially noteworthy in light of subsequent research and analysis. For example, he analyzes the state as influential in developing the frameworks of deviance through which gay immigrants are read as deserving or nondeserving of entry (see, for example, Luibhéid 2005; Coll 2005). Recent literature addresses how officials and interviewers "read" gay asylum applicants and make determinations based on constructions of the authentic "gay" or "lesbian" immigrant (Luibhéid 2005). These assessments intersect with gendered constructions of sexuality and "overt" sexual identification.[3]

Other scholars foreground, not the gender performance of sexuality, per se, but the problematic boundary setting of legal-illegal status and the construction of the border between the United States and Mexico in relation to the identity and culture of Mexican immigrants (Bosniak 2006; Yamamoto 2007; Vila 2000, 2003, 2005). Gloria Anzaldúa (1987), offers a dynamic vision of a borderland that she defines as "a vague and undetermined place created by the emotional residue of an unnatural boundary. It is in a constant state of transition. The prohibited and forbidden are its inhabitants" (3).

While the goal of border studies has been to explicate how borderlands offer those who dwell within them a different vantage point, Pablo Vila (2003) expresses concern that "[t]his approach not only homogenizes distinctive experiences but also homogenizes borders" (308)—and, we would add, following Cantú, homogenizes cultural identities as well. Cantú's vision of the borderlands retains Anzaldúa's insight that borderlands "both protect and violate life" (Connolly 1995, 163). Cantú also demonstrates that, it is also important to recognize the symbolic meaning of the boundary crossing for border crossers as well as for those who police borders (see Naples forthcoming; Suárez-Orozco 2005; and Epps 2001).

An area of scholarship that has been especially productive for challenging conceptualizations of borders, genders, and law is found in the research on transgender and transsexual people (see, for example, Currah 2006; King 2003). Paisley Currah (2006) illustrates this challenge in his essay "Gender Pluralisms under the Transgender Umbrella," which offers an analysis of the "extraordinary diversity of cross-gender practices, identities, and beliefs about gender within gender nonconforming communities." He argues for the value of organizing through the frame of "gender expression" rather than more fixed identity categories (5). He recommends social movement strategies that will "'dis-establish' gender from the state by ending the state's authority to police the relation between one's legal sex assigned at birth, one's gender identity, and one's gender expression" (24).

Around the time of his death, Cantú was beginning to articulate the borders (and linkages) between gender and sexuality in theoretically productive ways (for recent illustrations of similar productive analyses, see Howe, Zaraysky, and Loretzen 2008; Peña 2007b; Sears 2008; Subero 2008). For instance, while Cantú used "transgendered gay man" to refer to one case (Hernández-Montiel), and in other instances of his research mentioned the variance in gender presentation of the field informants (born in Mexico and the United States), he did not directly engage the complexity of transgender experiences in his writing until 2001. In a 2001 review essay on *Mema's House* (Prieur 1998) and *Travesti* (Kulick 1998), Cantú (2001b) discussed the multiple (and sometimes conflicting) meanings of gender expression, transvestism, and transsexuality. Cantú was on a theoretical path to empirically demonstrate the complicated relationship between, on the one hand, gender and sexuality in homosexual and transgendered contexts, and on the other hand, migration and trans experience. His analyses of border crossings include the one between so-called gender identity and sexuality that is also evident in recent cultural portrayals of transgender individuals, such as in the graphic testimonial *Sexile/Sexilio*, by Jaime Cortéz (2004).

The Shifting Politics of Latino Masculinities and Sexualities

Cantú's empirical investigation illustrates the multiple masculinities and sexualities that are evident in Mexico and elsewhere. He challenges the reductive and stereotypical constructions of Mexican men and sexuality that was dominant in the literature as recently as the 1990s. Cantú offers an important analysis of the complexity of sexual expression and constructions of masculinity by Mexican men who have sex with men living on both sides of the Mexican border. Contemporary scholarship further complicates the analysis of Mexican heterosexual identity and sexuality to demonstrate, among other things, how Mexican masculinities, femininities, and sexualities are impacted by religion, cultural attributes, and migration but not in any linear fashion.[4]

Cantú's critique of the limits of the *activo/pasivo* framework and his assessment of the liminality of Chicano/Mexican/Latino family in the United States has been incorporated into contemporary scholarship on Mexican sexuality (Guzmán 2006; see also González-López and Vidal-Ortiz 2008). Scholars who have utilized the *activo/pasivo* framework in the past have recently argued that this old model, which attached stigma to the penetrated and/or flamboyant homosexual, is no longer as relevant for the contemporary performance of Latino same-sex sexuality (Lancaster 2005). In his recent study of homosexualities and culture, Lancaster notes how the terms "homology" (fusing the sexual activity of men who have sex with other men with a homosexual identity, often attached to the United States) and "heterology" (discussing not just the sexual actors, but the acts themselves in relation to stigma, gendered interpretations, and cultural backgrounds, linked regularly to Latin American countries) cannot be inherently attributed to one or the other culture. Furthermore, as Guzmán (1997) and Kulick (1998) point out, some men engaged in same-sex sexuality might not view their sexuality through the lens of same-sex desire. Gender identity and what it means to be a man or a woman must also be interrogated and cannot be assumed to be static, based on biological sex. For example, Chant and Craske (2003) find that many Latino men who have sex with men and play the penetrative (or so-called active role) will not deny their homosexuality (see also Manalasan 2006; Mirandé 1997; Prieur 1998).

In the now-classic study of masculinities, Connell (1995) demonstrates how hegemonic masculinity is indeed a contested, albeit central, type of masculinity. For Cantú, the homogenization of all Latino masculinities into a singular masculinity was problematic, yet also productive as it served to challenge the hegemonic masculinity reified by more mainstream scholarship. In other words, constructing a masculine Latino sexuality and opposing it to a dominant non-Latino sexuality opens up a space for the discussion of the multiplicities of masculinities. The presumed excessive or non-normative (Latino) masculinity adds to the notions of masculinities, shadowing hegemonic ones but serving as a referent to them (in much the same way as femininity and masculinity have been used to define what each other is not). The normative and the marginal thus become mutually constitutive of each other, at the same time that the Latino masculinities are collapsed into one.

Through his analysis of working-, middle-, and upper-class Mexican men living in Mexico, as well as immigrant Mexican men in the United States, Cantú demonstrates the need for analyses of masculinities along the axes of nationality, gender identity and presentation, migration choices, and other more traditional axes of power such as race, class, and gender. Furthering such critique would require looking at research on the situational experience of men from various national backgrounds, socioeconomic positions, migration experiences, gender presentations, and color and/or indigenous/African heritage.

Globalization, Sexuality, and Power

Recent scholarship on globalization and queer identities has helped us theorize links between the local (often heterogeneous) processes of identity formation and naming, on the one hand, and a presumed global homogeneity on the other (see, for example, Wright 2005). While globalization increases the circulation of gay identities both discursively and through migration and gay tourism, it also makes visible the diversity of sexualities and contradictory spaces for the expression of same-sex desire.[5] Jon Binnie (2004) and Dennis Altman (2001) both elucidate the complex relationship between queer identities in different contexts, although others scholars like Gayatri Gopinath (2005) argue that these discussions of globalization and gay citizenship tend to erase other situational markers such as race.

A number of books have emerged over the last decade that are written by non-Western and immigrant scholars and draw attention to the limits of Western framing of sexual citizenship and sexualities.[6] This work offers a rich counterpoint to the reductive approaches to the globalization of sexualities that presume an unquestioned incorporation of a Western-derived gay identity. Furthermore, as Cantú vividly demonstrates, gay identities are multiple even in the West.

When Cantú began his research in the late 1990s, few scholars had explored the sexuality of immigrant women (Espín 1997, 1999). Gopinath (2005) critiques the Western-centric view of sexuality that masks racial, ethnic, national, and cultural differences. Like Cantú, in her book *Impossible Desires: Queer Diasporas and South Asian Public Cultures,* she weaves together different theoretical strands to demonstrate the gaps in each. For example, she analyzes the processes by which queer female subjectivity is erased through "patriarchal and heternormative nationalist and diasporic discourses, but also . . . [by] some gay male and liberal feminist framings of diaspora," as Romit Dasgupta (2006) explains in his review of *Impossible Dreams*.

Katie King (2002) also speaks to the invisibility of lesbians in her essay in *Queer Globalizations: Citizenship and the Afterlife of Colonialism* (Cruz-Malave and Manalansan 2002). She offers a powerful critique of the process by which identity constructions serve to reinforce the power of dominant groups who are able to define and stabilize identity categories. She also speaks to another theme that runs through Cantú's analysis, namely, that even when the same terms are used in different contexts, they can have very different meanings. As she explains,

> Both "lesbian" and "feminist" have local and global meanings for particular nationalisms and challenges to nationalisms by women. Using them as global terms is a political act. Refusing them as global terms is also a political act. No uses are neutral and purely descriptive, although some users intend them to be and long for such possible categories. (34–35)

King addresses the construction of "new gay identities" that depend on the power of certain "locals" to travel physically or via the internet (41). In contrast to the efforts to construct and stabilize gay identities, she argues for an approach that links "layers of locals and globals, emphasizing that they are relative and relational" (40). She offers the construct "lesbianisms in multinational reception" to indicate "that the term is plural and various, that there are many kinds of receptions of the term, that such receptions are not inextricable from its traveling possibilities" (43).

Not surprisingly, the new work on globalization and queer identities also points to the importance of cyberspace for facilitating the transnational construction of queer communities. Wakeford (2002) analyzes "new technologies and 'cyber-queer' research" and highlights the significance of class in determining who can access new technologies. Neoliberalism and class privilege also form central components in Binnie's analysis (2004) of how "the respectable, responsible gay or lesbian living in a so-called family of choice is prompted as a responsible consumer, as opposed to the dangerous queer whose desires cannot be so easily commodified" (17; see also Hennessy 2000).

Cantú's analysis of gay tourism also speaks to the powerful inequalities that travel across space and place and shape local experiences. Neocolonial and orientalist discourses of the "Other" are eroticized and sold for consumption by those with the resources to travel. Cantú's critique of gay tourist guides that promote certain locales as meeting sites of diverse cultures, different groups of men, distinctive sexualities, emphasizes how same-sex desire and gender expression are mediated by the economic inequalities of globalization and the globalization of gay identities.

Some of the most provocative scholarship found in the new literature on globalization and sexuality is shaped through the lens of "diaspora," as illustrated by the collection of essays edited by Cindy Patton and Benigno Sánchez-Eppler (2000). The editors' insightful analysis of identity as "a highly mobile cluster of claims to self that appear and transmogrify in and of place" (4) offers a fruitful way to consider the politics of identity. They further clarify that "place is also a mobile imaginary, a form of desire" (4). This formulation further explicates some of what Cantú found in his interviews with Mexican men who have sex with men who immigrated to the United States. Like Cantú, Patton and Sánchez-Eppler (2000) caution against the "drift of discourse" in some queer theoretical writing on queer diasporas that fails to take into account the "'real people' who might also inhabit the discursively fantasized space" (10). In the following quotation, we are reminded of Cantú's opening discussion of his discovery of an Orange County Latino gay bar following his move from San Antonio, Texas, to Irvine, California: "Dislocated bodies may refind their native discourses when they get 'there,' as if they have 'discovered' that the Other elsewhere is 'naturally' the same" (10).

Leaving Home/Finding Home: Negotiating Homeplace

It seems fitting to conclude with a focus on family. Cantú drew great strength from his own family of origin and developed extended family or fictive kin wherever he settled and whenever he traveled. However, as mentioned in our introduction, he also recognized that families were powerful sites for the production and surveillance of heteronormativity. Much of the new scholarship on sexuality, immigration, and family also makes this point. Furthermore, as Cantú demonstrates, families are much too complex and diverse for this tendency to overshadow the complicated ways in which constructions of family and familial experiences intersect with controlling logics such as capitalism and nationalism. Miranda Joseph (2002a) argues in her contribution to *Queer Globalizations* that "family plays a particularly central role in legitimating the localities to be included in capitalism" (89). She points out that "discourses of sexuality and kinship actually operate together to produce white European national bourgeoisies in relation to raced colonial others" (90). They also serve as sites of resistance to these logics (hooks 1990).

Not surprisingly, many queer studies scholars, like Joseph, question the focus on same-sex marriage that has taken a central place in LGBTQ social movement organizations, especially in the United States. Linking concern for the normative assumptions of what constitutes the deserving citizen that is often associated with claims for same-sex marriage with the focus on consumption that is often linked with the expansion of "economic recognition and consumptuary opportunities" (Pellegrini 2002), many scholars find the growing visibility of gay and lesbian subjects in the media and as targets for consumption to be "a fulfillment" of rights "that can only disappoint" (135). However, as Pellegrini asks, "might these consuming subjects also queer capitalism?" (135). Regardless of the possibility that capitalism can be queered, the recognition of same-sex relationships offers material benefits for many who cannot afford to purchase medical insurance and legal assistance for the drafting of wills and other documents to protect their partners. Recognition of same-sex marriage has particular significance for binational couples who cannot sponsor their partners for immigration. In this case, it is clear that a queer materialist framework offers a particularly important vantage point through which to view the relationship between the symbolic and material, which are mutually reinforcing as well as in tension as the dynamics of race, class, gender, nation, and sexuality are brought into view.

Concluding Remarks

We end much the way we started—by honoring the important insights Cantú offered us, but with much regret that he was unable to carry his project forward. Further development and explication of a queer materialist epistemology are left to others. Fortunately, he has left his mark on a new field that will continue to flourish. It is all the richer for the work he did and for his commitment to bridging the gap between theory and practice, sexuality and immigration studies, and the personal and the political.

Afterword

Dissertation Liberation Army

Scholarship emerges from a community process, and often that process is invisible. Lionel Cantú was a founding member of the Dissertation Liberation Army (DLA), a dissertation support group of graduate students at the University of California, Irvine. Lionel's influence on the group was profound, and the group provided him with a safe place to develop his ideas. We thought that this introduction, together with thoughts from each of the DLA members—Chrisy Moutsatsos, Ester Hernandez, Clare Weber, Vivian Price, Jose Alamillo, Jocelyn Pacleb, and Leslie Bunnage—was appropriate to include as an afterword to the book version of Lionel's dissertation. We saw Lionel's writing mature over several years, as he presented us with chapter drafts and chapter outlines and shared with us struggles regarding interview methods and the frustrations of dealing with border politics, homophobia, and racism. It was sometime in the mid-1990s that the idea for a dissertation support group emerged. Several of us in the social sciences were starting to write our dissertation proposals, or were taking our orals, and felt somewhat isolated. It was Lionel and Chrisy who initially thought that a support group was a good idea, and our first meeting was at Chrisy's house—she made it so comfortable for us in her apartment with tea, food, and her strange cat that would act affectionately and then bite us.

Calling the group the Dissertation Liberation Army was a playful and ironic gesture, yet reflected our desire to liberate our minds and work from the conformity of our academic disciplines. The ground rules evolved, as did the composition of the group. The idea was to provide a space in which each one of us could present our work in progress, be it an idea, an outline, a chapter, whatever, just something that would push us to produce and nudge our ideas forward and allow us to get feedback in nonjudgmental form. The last concept was the one that was most difficult. We were all teaching assistants who were used to coaxing our students towards embracing certain ideas from the assigned readings, and it wasn't easy to find ways to react to each other's work without expressing suggestions about how the writer "should" proceed. And wasn't that what we wanted? A reviewer's advice? A sympathetic reader's remarks? It took a while to find ways to talk to each other in a way that was helpful to the person being critiqued without being overbearing. We learned to offer each other the kind of comments we thought would be the most helpful: comments about organization, examination of arguments, application of theory, etc. Finding the ways to nurture each other's voice and intellectual vision became increasingly rewarding.

Over the years that we met, we grew to include a diverse group of scholars who took each other's work and styles seriously. Lionel encouraged us to "cross borders" in research, teaching, and everyday life. Lionel helped create a nurturing space in which we could freely express our frustration with graduate school and its isolating effects, especially during the dissertation writing process, and after we had done much whining and complaining, encouraged us to critique each other's work with big hearts.

Lionel was passionate about his scholarship and the meaning of his work to the gay community, to communities of color, and to academia, and this commitment inspired us and helped elevate all of our work. Lionel shared not only chapters of his dissertation but also drafts of his grant proposals, his dissertation outline, his job talk, and his job cover letters, and they served as a model that we all used. His intellectual leadership was instrumental in keeping the group disciplined and focused, but the group was more than a scholarly support group, and Lionel had a hand in that, too. We would often start off a session just going around the circle so that we all had a chance to check in with one another and understand what was going on in our lives. Our meetings became more than a forum for sharing ideas. We built trust and friendships, brought food to share with each other, and grew closer. It was clear from the beginning that his work was groundbreaking, and we are so proud and grateful to Nancy Naples, Salvador Vidal-Ortiz, and the Lionel Cantú Working Group for making it possible for us to see it come out in print. Our personal statements follow.

Chrisy Moutsatsos

Having just completed my fieldwork in the summer of 1997 and being faced with the daunting and lonely task of writing a dissertation, I was eagerly looking for a group of committed and kind people with whom to share my work and anxieties. It was only natural that I would first approach Lionel with this idea; he and I belonged to the same cohort, and over the years we had become close friends, sharing the same views regarding our place in academia and the rest of the world. I could not have asked for a better group than the DLA. It is not possible in the short space allowed to fully elaborate on the positive influence Lionel and the rest of the DLA members have had on me professionally and personally. Nor is it possible to reflect on the terrible void Lionel's early departure has left in my life. With his help, and that of the others in this fine group, I was able to make sense of my data, shape it into comprehensible paragraphs, and finally produce a completed manuscript. Our weekly DLA meetings taught me how to give constructive feedback, as well as how to receive it. Our group was also important for my professionalization process. In this regard, all the members of the group, but especially Lionel, who was already on his professional track, were key in prompting me to be unafraid to put my work out there. Our regular meetings also became a social space where casual friendships developed into strong lifelong bonds. Lionel's playful take on things—especially those having to do with sex—always spiced up things and gave us a reason to laugh. I like to believe that his kindness, insightfulness, and exuberance is with us whenever the rest of us meet in the DLA tradition to discuss our work and cultivate our relationships.

Ester Hernandez

It is quite a difficult task for me to provide a brief account of how the DLA helped me to complete my work, to make myself accountable for my own professional development, and to maintain my own personal life in balance. DLA member support, expectations, and enthusiasm gently forced us to produce material for review on deadlines. While being mindful of the "work-in-progress" nature of our effort, we endeavored to give each other constructive feedback every step of the way. The group benefited me by providing models of leadership, pedagogies, and solidarities. As a Latina woman crossing the borders and boundaries of academia, I had much in common with Lionel on a personal level and in our professional interest in immigration research. He was instrumental in bringing together the mix of members that made up the DLA.

While our group continued after Lionel completed his Ph.D. and became an assistant professor at UC Santa Cruz, his presence and contribution to the group was greatly missed. Ultimately, we collectively lost a lifelong friend and colleague. For me, the imprint of his friendship and his collegial style remains. *Pax.*

Clare Weber

I started the DLA when I was pregnant. Lionel loved to joke about the size of my abdomen. My child is now five years old. Lionel and all the members of the group were happy for me when I gave birth. They were patient on the occasions when I brought my baby to the group and attempted to give feedback on someone's piece in spite of the sleep deprivation that comes with caring for a baby. For this I am grateful. I greatly admired Lionel Cantú. He was a sociologist capable of integrating studies of immigration, race/ethnicity, gender, sexuality, and political economy. He was able to communicate complex ideas in ways that were clear and accessible. He saw sociology as a political endeavor and worked to include underrepresented people in the discipline. He did this with a big heart and great jokes. It was the combination of his brilliant mind and his loving spirit that made Lionel the person whom everyone wanted to know and be close to. The DLA still meets and we always remember to think hard, be political, tell good jokes (especially about sex), share harmless gossip, and take care of each other. It is probably the best way to honor Lionel, our colleague. *Presente.*

Vivian Price

Lionel was a wonderful, down-to-earth person with a brilliant mind, a compassionate heart, and an uncanny ability to succeed while maintaining his integrity. I particularly appreciated the risks he assumed being an out gay scholar and an activist in community groups as well as in the academy, and he helped open the space for me and for others to follow his example. His role in the DLA was pivotal in developing the model of a group that could sustain a deep commitment by its members to support one another personally and intellectually. I miss his intensity, his zest for life, his zany humor, and sharing in his excitement for what would come next.

Jose Alamillo

Lionel was a great mentor, colleague, and *compañero*. He introduced me to the DLA at a time when I had completed my community research and needed to write and share my findings with others to make better sense of my dissertation. As my office mate in the Chicano/Latino Studies Program, Lionel always impressed me by his ability to mentor undergraduate students as his good reputation quickly spread across campus and all kinds of students sought him out for guidance and advice. His leadership on student issues was also demonstrated when he mobilized support among graduate students and faculty members to make the Chicano/Latino Studies Program more accountable to the needs of undergraduate students. Many of our conversations centered on Chicano/a academics' larger social responsibility to not only research but advocate on behalf of underprivileged Chicano-a/Latino-a communities, especially the most marginalized within the community. As a gay Chicano activist, Lionel was committed to educating the Latino/a community on gay and lesbian issues, whether by frequently voicing his opinion on Spanish-language news broadcasts, by testifying as an expert witness on court cases, or by conducting AIDS prevention workshops. His pathbreaking and innovative research on sexuality and migration, his cheerleader-like ability to inspire colleagues, including myself, and his unwavering commitment to improving the lives of all Latinos and Latinas will never be forgotten.

Jocelyn Pacleb

I joined the DLA at a difficult time in my graduate school experience. I saw my colleagues passing their comprehensive exams and moving on to the research and writing stage of the dissertation. I felt stuck in the pre–comprehensive exam stage and I seriously considered dropping out of graduate school. What held me back from quitting was the fact that there were few graduate students of color at UC Irvine. I was fortunate to have friends such as Lionel Cantú and Jose M. Alamillo, who actively sought out ways to connect with graduate students from different academic disciplines to create scholarly and social spaces. In the late 1990s, I joined the DLA and found a wonderful and supportive group. The members came from diverse backgrounds, and we all actively shared strategies to demystify the graduate school experience, and later the job search process. Lionel in many ways led us through this unfamiliar terrain. He became a role model and he unselfishly shared his expertise on race, class, gender, immigration, and sexuality, as well as information on fellowships and grants. Though Lionel is no longer physically with us, he continues to be a part of us. We celebrate him in our meetings when we laugh, joke, and eat, and in the quiet pauses that occur when something reminds us of him.

Leslie Bunnage

As the last addition to the DLA, I benefited tremendously from Lionel's legacy. What initially struck me about this group was that it was about building community despite the ridiculous obstacles provided by the graduate school environment. There is nothing automatic about graduate students supporting each other. I strongly believe that for many graduate students, our academic training often encourages competition and individualism, and this becomes a crucial part of our socialization as academics. Also, we have been taught to separate our thought processes, our intellectual work, and our academic identities from our political environment. As with Lionel's own scholarship and practice, the group he coformed helped to combat some of the isolation and depoliticization of the academy. The DLA was not composed of the straight male and pale graduate students that often navigate their way through the academy with ease. After I had experienced a few harried years in graduate school, the DLA provided me with much needed political and academic oxygen. By creating this group, and shaping it in the ways that he did, Lionel punctured a hole in the strange collegial practices that teach us both that we should not turn to each other and that we should separate our political and academic lives. I am now part of a group, the Dissertation Guerilla Girls, inspired by the DLA. Using the DLA as our model, another generation of graduate students benefits from the contributions, influence, and memory of Lionel Cantú.

Notes

EDITORS' INTRODUCTION

1. See, for example, Almaguer 1993; Espín 1999; de Genova and Zayas 2003; Hondagneu-Sotelo 2003; Nagel 2003; Nakano Glenn 2004; Rodríguez 2003; Gonzalez-Lopez 2005; Luibhéid and Cantú 2005; Guzmán 2006.

2. See, for example, Argüelles and Rivero 1993; Carrier 1995; Herdt 1997.

3. The concept of *positionality* foregrounds the way social actors can strategically "use their positional perspective as a place from where values are interpreted and constructed rather than as a locus of an already determined set of values" (Alcoff 1988, 434).

4. Sedgwick 1990; Butler 1990, 1993; de Lauretis 1991; Warner 1993.

5. Harding 1991; Smith 1987, 1990a, 1990b.

6. See Anzaldúa 1987; Collins 1991; Moya 1997; Sandoval 2002.

7. See, for example, Duberman, Vicinus, and Chauncey 1990; Rodríguez 2003.

8. See, for example, Hammonds's (1994) response to de Lauretis's (1991) discussion of "queer" studies.

9. In a recent collection on *Queer Globalizations*, Miranda Joseph (2002a) also highlights the importance of the family for its "central role in legitimating the localities to be included in capitalism." She explains that "[t]he task of promoting kinship as the legitimating basis for local and communal economic units while keeping it flexible and expansive is a delicate one, resulting in rather ambivalent and contradictory articulations of the global/localization literature" (89).

10. See also the introduction to the *Social Text* issue: "What's Queer about Queer Studies Now?" (Eng, Halberstam, and Muñoz 2005); and Patton and Sánchez-Eppler 2000.

11. See, for example, Carrillo (2002); Hirsch (2003); and Quiroga (2000).

CHAPTER 1

1. See Jagose 1996; Foucault 1990 [1978]; Butler 1990, 1993; Evans 1993; Seidman 1996.

2. By "Latino" I mean those nationalities and groups that have been under the Spanish realm of influence; I am not including groups that have had other colonial cultural influences such as the Portuguese in Brazil. The

"*hispano*"/"*luso*" distinction ["*hispano*" to reference Spanish origins, "*luso*" to reference Portuguese origins] is commonly used, although many researchers group the two together as one cultural monolith.

3. California governor Davis requested mediation to settle an appeal of Proposition 187 in June 1999. The mediation resulted in an agreement on July 29, 1999, which concluded that "no child in the state of California will be deprived of an education or stripped of health care due to their place of birth" (American Civil Liberties Union 1999). The agreement also affirmed "that the state cannot regulate immigration law, a function that the U.S. Constitution clearly assigns to the federal government" (ibid.).

4. Cousins and Hussain 1984; Foucault 1990 [1978]; Martin 1988.

5. See also Gluckman 1997; and Seidman 1996.

6. While recent debates between social constructionists and essentialists have heated up with genetic research, I assume that sexuality is more complex than the either/or debates allow for. I therefore focus on the social aspects of sexuality (i.e., the social constructionist perspective). The constructionist argument has also been made from a cultural perspective. In his classic study of the Sambia of New Guinea, anthropologist Gilbert Herdt (1994 [1981]) examined the cultural meanings of homosexuality and masculinity in a nonindustrial society and demonstrated, through his examination of "boy-inseminating rituals," that meanings of homosexuality and norms of gender are not universal but, rather, are culturally constructed.

7. Broadly, the study of "homosexuality" may be broken into two theoretical frames that are today the center of much debate: (1) essentialist and (2) social-constructionist approaches. Essentialist constructions of sexual identity are biologically and psychologically based; their basic premise is that sexuality is a predisposed trait (Allgeier and Allgeier 1988; Burr 1993). While essentialist studies of sexuality offer insights into the genetic, hormonal, and cognitive influences of sexual identity, they offer a limited understanding of the complex nature of sexuality (Altman 1987). Such studies have been critiqued by some feminist, minority, and queer scholars for their universalizing analyses, their tendency to define difference as deviance or pathology, their ahistorical treatment of sexuality, and their tendency to see sexual identity as a fixed characteristic (Altman 1987; Weeks 1993). In light of these critiques and the given focus of my research project, I assume that sexuality is a continuum of expression that has some biological and psychological base but that is greatly influenced by social, cultural, and economic factors. I will therefore focus my discussion here within the social-constructionist debates.

8. For example, Murray (1996) reports that Latino gay men had an earlier median age of first homosexual experience (15.0), had an earlier median age of "coming out" (21.0), and were more likely to stay with someone they knew (35.7) compared to White, Black, and Asian respondents.

9. Unfortunately, Murray (1995) uses the terms "migrant," "immigrant," and "émigré" interchangeably.

10. Wood (1982) attempts to reconcile these differences by focusing on the household as a unit of analysis that bridges micro- and macro-economic concerns. But the household analysis has its limitations as well, including a bias towards the individual actor that obscures some of the macro-level dimensions of migration, such as the role of the state and sociocultural influences. In addition, a focus on the "household" *exclusively* tends to conceal dimensions of the transnational or binational household and other adaptive strategies by assuming (in at least some of the literature) a nuclear household configuration with one "head" and fully shared resources—that a "household" has a "choice" is a problem of reification as well.

11. Douglas Massey et al. (1993) categorize various theories of international migration into five conceptual frames: neoclassical economics, the new economics of labor migration, segmented labor market theory, social capital theory, and world systems theory.

12. Ghatak, Levine, and Price 1996; Massey et al. 1993.

13. World systems theory, originally formulated by Wallerstein (1974) and Frank (1978) to explain "national 'development'" with reference to "an aggressively expanding Europe-centered 'world-system'" (Chase-Dunn 1999, 166; see also Chase-Dunn 1998a, 1998b).

14. Dependency scholars argued that the industrial nations of the core (such as the United States and Europe) kept peripheral nations (e.g., countries in Latin America) that produced primary products for export in a state of perpetual poverty and therefore dependent on core nations.

15. Key elements of the ghetto according to Wirth are institutional concentration (gathering places and commercial establishments), culture area (culture of a group dominates a geographic space), social isolation (segregation), and residential concentration (as cited in Levine 1979).

16. Murray (1996) also refers to a liminal phase for gay migrants to San Francisco that he defines as the first phase of settlement.

17. Foucault 1990 [1978]; Cousins and Hussain 1984; Martin 1988.

18. Particularly a "postmodern" form of drag referred to as "genderfuck."

19. Case (1993) makes a similar argument for the subversive potential of the butch/femme resignification of gender performance.

20. EDITORS' NOTE: Symbolic interactionism is an approach initiated by George Herbert Mead and subsequently developed by Herbert Blumer to account for the ways in which meaning is created through interaction (Prus 1996).

CHAPTER 2

1. As reproduced in *Lesbians, Gay Men, and the Law*, edited by William B. Rubenstein (1993).

2. Citizenship is analyzed and discussed in this context from a Western sociohistorical construction of the category.

3. In his historical analysis Marshall (1964 [1950]) proposes that citizenship consists of three elements: (1) the civil—individual rights such as freedom of speech, which he asserts emerged in the eighteenth century; (2) the political—the right of franchise and access to community decision making, which he links to the nineteenth-century struggles of the working class; and (3) the social, which he ties to the institutions of education and social services or welfare and which he places historically in the twentieth century.

4. EDITORS' NOTE: Of course we have seen an increase in surveillance and changes in the mission and work scope of the INS after September 11, 2001. Most significant is the insertion of the immigration and naturalization services, now called Immigration and Customs Enforcement (ICE), under the newly formed Department of Homeland Security. This department includes the following divisions: Border and Transportation Security; Emergency Preparedness and Response; Science and Technology; Information Analysis and Infrastructure Protection; and Management. Citizen and Immigration Services is now one of the components within the department. This is the stated objective of the component:

> Through the U.S. Citizenship and Immigration Services (USCIS), DHS continues the tradition of welcoming immigrants into the country by administering services such as immigrant and nonimmigrant sponsorship; adjustment of status; work authorization and other permits; naturalization of qualified applicants for U.S. citizenship; and asylum or refugee processing. Immigration enforcement, which is the responsibility of the Directorate of Border and Transportation Security, includes preventing aliens from entering the country unlawfully, detecting and removing those who are living in the U.S. unlawfully, and preventing terrorists and other criminal aliens from entering or residing in the United States. The Department makes certain that America continues to welcome visitors and those who seek opportunity within our shores while excluding terrorists and their supporters. (see http://www.dhs.gov/dhspublic/display?theme=57)

5. EDITORS' NOTE: Fordism refers to the industrial mass production strate-gies instituted by Henry Ford and other industrialists of the early twentieth century that replaced craft-based modes of production and was based on the production of standard items marketed on a mass scale. Post-Fordism is char-acterized by increased internationalization of capital accumulation and produc-tion, flexible markets and consumption patterns, a mobile labor pool, and the decline in the welfare state (see Harvey 1990).

6. The purpose and responsibilities of the agency would be further specified in 1952, a watershed year for immigration, and then again in 1990 (Calavita 1992).

7. There are the nineteen categories that allow the legitimate entry of desir-able "aliens," as follows: Gov. Official (A Visa), Visitor (B Visa), Transit (C Visa), Crewmen (D Visa), Treaty Trader (E Visa), Student (F Visa), International Organization (G Visa), Temporary Worker (H Visa), Foreign Media (I Visa), Exchange Visitor (J Visa), Fiancé of U.S. Citzen (K Visa), Intra-Company Trans-feree (L Visa), Vocational Student (M Visa), Parent or Child of Int. Organization (N Visa), Alien with Extraordinary Ability (O Visa), Performer, Athlete, Enter-tainer (P Visa), Int. Cultural Exchange Program (Q Visa), Religious Worker (R Visa), Alien Working in Cooperative Research & Development (S Visa).

8. While homosexuality is no longer grounds for exclusion, the following reasons are still used by the INS: invalid documentation, health-related reasons, economic reasons (i.e., poverty), criminal or moral grounds (including illiteracy, mental incompetence, draft evasion) and the belief of an INS official that the visa holder intends to violate the terms of the visa (i.e., stay in the country for a period longer than permitted).

CHAPTER 3

1. EDITORS' NOTE: The use of the phrase "transgendered gay man" in the text of the court's decision in 2000 contributed to shifting understanding of transgender and transsexual identities that included attention to transgender expression (that is, an expression that exceeds traditional gendered behavior, typically associated with sex and congruency with sex: that is, male masculini-ties and female femininities) and earlier formulations of transsexuality (as in the expression of noncongruency between a person's sex—as defined by genitalia— and alterations to the body to "match" a person's body to her/his desired gender identity). As the chapter illustrates, in the *Hernandez-Montiel* case, the feminin-ity of the asylum applicant was taken into account, with the court assuming the applicant's sexual and gender identity to be that not of a transsexual but of a homosexual. See Valentine (2007) for more on the development of the trans-gender category and its relationship to transsexuality. For recent scholarship

addressing the intersection of gender (as in this case, gender effeminacy), sexuality, and migration, see Peña (2005, 2007b).

2. Randazzo (2005) provides an excellent discussion of this history with greater detail.

3. There are other organizations that are also concerned with queer immigration but not as a main concern; such organizations include Amnesty International, the Human Rights Campaign Fund, the Lambda Legal Defense and Education Fund, and the Freedom to Marry Coalition.

4. EDITORS' NOTE: Julie Dorf stepped down as executive director in 2000. Surina Khan then led the organization until 2002. Paula Ettelbrick came on board as the new executive director in 2002 and supervised IGLHRC's move from San Francisco to New York City in 2004.

5. EDITORS' NOTE: Lavi Soloway was the national coordinator when Lionel Cantú conducted his research. As this book goes to press (2009), the executive director of Immigration Equality is Rachel B. Tiven.

CHAPTER 4

1. Wockner (1997b) reports 225 participants in the parade, with approximately half being from the United States.

2. The Wall-Las Memorias Project is a Latino AIDS organization.

3. Commonly referred to as *"bugas"* by queer Mexicans.

4. *"De ambiente"* is a Spanish phrase that literally translates as "of the ambience" and in gay jargon is code for "queer" (as translated by Murray and Dynes in Murray 1995). An alternative, although less literal translation, might be the phrase "in the life," which has a similar history and meaning in the United States. Lumsden (1991) reports that the term has taken on an expanded meaning in Mexico City to incorporate what is popularly called an "alternative" atmosphere in the United States today. It can refer to anything from a crowd of mixed sexual orientation to just a nonmainstream environment.

5. In fact, during my research in Mexico, both radio and newspapers reported that bisexuality among Mexican men was a "social problem" due to its prevalence and its assumed link to the spread of HIV. Other scholars have reported on the prevalence of bisexuality, including Carrier (1995). See Prieur (1998) and Murray (1995) for discussions of the acceptance/stigmatization of bisexuality in Mexico.

6. Gender is understood here as the "complex of social meanings that is attached to biological sex" (Kimmel and Messner 1995).

7. Social science scholars have argued that Latino machismo is a symptom of a traditional culture and "an inferiority complex based on the mentality of a conquered people" (i.e., Spain's conquest of Mexico) (Baca Zinn 1991, 34).

8. Unfortunately, the *Journal of Hispanic Behavioral and Social Sciences* has published many articles that make what Baca Zinn (1991) and I would call "cultural-deficit" arguments (see, for example, Casas, Wagenheim, Banchero, and Mendoza-Romero 1994).

9. These categories are often treated as mutually exclusive.

10. Lewis's (1959) "Culture of Poverty" thesis, which blamed Latino culture for Latino poverty, serves as a prime example of such a "cultural" analysis. In a similar vein, "machismo" is a racialized marker of gender oppression, a "culture of masculinity," which is read as a pathological cultural trait. The structural dimensions of sexism thus get displaced under the racist subterfuge of "machismo."

11. See Lancaster 1992; Almaguer 1993; Carrier 1995; Murray 1995.

12. EDITORS' NOTE: The Bracero program was an arrangement for Mexican farm laborers to come to the United States and work on the land. Over four million Mexicans came to the United States under such programs (Calavita 1992; Acuña 1972).

13. EDITORS' NOTE: CTCA (California Trade and Commerce Agency) was established in 1993 to promote economic development, create jobs, and retain businesses in California. As of this writing, the editors have not been able to locate the full reference for this citation. However, we note that in 2006, China surpassed Mexico as the second-largest U.S. trading partner (Drajem 2008).

14. For a brief period from 1980 to 1988, there was a decrease in the urbanization rate and an actual reversal that may have been a consequence of both the 1982 crisis and growing urban problems, particularly in Mexico City, which suffered a devastating earthquake in 1985 (Central Intelligence Agency 1990).

15. 1995 estimates (Central Intelligence Agency 1998).

16. Http://www.sedesol.gob.mx/desuryvi/desurb/p100c.htm.

17. For more on this topic, see Nolan and Nolan (1988) and Clancy (1999).

18. "*Mayates*" is a term used in Mexico to refer to men who act as sexual penetrators or insertors in a same-sex sexual relationship. *Mayates* are often contrasted with homosexually identified men, who are presumed to be the penetrated partners in same-sex sexual relations.

19. In comparison, twenty-three U.S. states had sodomy laws on the books in 1999. [EDITORS' NOTE: All sodomy laws were overturned by the Supreme Court in 2003.]

20. The term "*joto*" may loosely be translated as "faggot." While the term's etymology is unclear, Buffington (1997) argues that the term is derived from "Cell Block J" ("*jota*" in Spanish), which refers to the location in the federal penitentiary in Mexico City where prison authorities attempted to isolate overtly homosexual inmates.

21. One such party held in Mexico City in 1901 was raided by the police and forty-one upper-class homosexual men were arrested. "41" has since become a code word for homosexuals in Mexico (see Lumsden 1991).

22. While my focus here has been Mexican MSMs, clearly globalization is influencing sexualities more generally as well.

1. The web site has text in both English and Spanish. Interestingly, however, the messages are completely different. The text in English is extremely erotic; in Spanish, however, the discourse focuses on national treasures and seems to target tourism within Mexico (http://www.mexico-travel.com).

2. It is important here to note that the focus on this literature is both the label and the identity "gay." There are numerous historical and contemporary terms for homosexuality in Spanish; see Murray and Dynes (1995).

3. Although, to my knowledge, there are no statistics on the countries of origin of gay and lesbian Mexican tourists, one may assume (given the marketing tactics of the industry and Mexican tourism statistics) that their demographics reflect those of tourists in general, i.e., a majority are from the United States.

4. This phenomenon seems consistent with Chauncey's discussion of homosexuality in pre–World War II New York, where marginal (racially segregated) areas became havens for different types of "deviance," including homosexuality, and a sort of playground for the more well-to-do. However, it is not clear how prevalent the *zonas* were in areas other than border towns and the urban center of Mexico City.

5. To my knowledge, there does not exist any literature on the demographics of this community. However, traditional Mexican culture makes it easier for unmarried men (as opposed to women) to live apart from their families, and both economic conditions and the growing popularity of the area are also factors that affect the demographics of its residents.

6. Sanchez-Crispin and Lopez-Lopez (1997) also argue that the liberalization of Acapulco for gays and lesbians was due to its popularity among international gay and lesbian tourists.

7. The satellite space status of Puerto Vallarta is supported by the fact that many (if not all) bars in Guadalajara carry the Puerto Vallarta gay paper/flyer with all its ads and a map.

8. Even in the United States, the "gay" label fails to capture the numerous experiences and identities that are commonly grouped under it.

9. This terminology is reportedly also used by lesbians.

10. The Caribbean, particularly Cuba, is one area that is beginning to be studied. See, for instance, Davidson (1996) and Lumsden (1996).

11. International Gay and Lesbian Travel Association, 2000, http://www. iglta.com. Tourism Industry Intelligence estimated the global market at $10 bil-

lion (U.S.) dollars in 1994 (as reported in Holcomb and Luongo 1996), and an industry survey by Community Marketing (2008) estimates the American gay and lesbian market alone to be worth more than $64.5 billion.

12. The IGLTA is represented in Argentina, Brazil, Chile, Bolivia, Venezuela, Colombia, Ecuador, Panama, and Costa Rica as well.

13. While Atlantis and RSVP advertise as open to both men and women, their main market seems to be men, while Olivia targets a lesbian clientele.

14. While the *Ferarri Guide* does have some information for women, the guide is aimed mostly at men. This is due in part, no doubt, to the greater visibility of gay men as opposed to lesbians in Mexico.

15. Madsen Camacho (2000), who has conducted research on the Mexican tourist industry in Huatulco, Mexico, reports that businesses in the hospitality industry, particularly hotels, often desire gay men as workers due to their perceptions that gay men have a "higher" cultural aesthetic and more cultural capital, which serves the hospitality industry's needs (personal communication).

16. These dynamics are also transforming queer space in Los Angeles; thus my argument is not unilateral.

CHAPTER 6

1. Chavez 1992; Portes and Borocz 1989; Portes and Rumbaut 1990; Portes 1995.

2. Prior to 1980 "Spanish Origin" was the label used to capture the characteristics of those now referred to as of "Hispanic Origin." The term "Hispanic" is meant to refer to people whose ancestry is from Spanish-speaking countries.

3. "Natural increase" is a demographic term that refers to the excess of births over deaths and does not include migration in its calculation.

4. For a map of Latino residential concentration in the greater Los Angeles Area see William Bowen's Geographical Survey—Digital Atlas of California at http://130.166.124.2/CApage1.html.

5. There have been a number of attempts to estimate the homosexual population. Perhaps the most famous is that of Kinsey and his associates, who estimated that 10 percent of the male population was "exclusively" homosexual (compared to 2–6 percent of females). "Ten percent" has become a sort of rallying cry for the gay and lesbian community despite the facts that other estimates have varied widely and that Kinsey's original estimate may well have been historically specific. For a summary of other estimates see Singer and Deschamps 1994, 9–12.

6. This urban migration generally occurred during the participants' childhood and was not a common experience of their adult life.

7. Distinguishing social class was a difficult task in large part because the Mexican middle class is quickly disappearing from the country's socioeconomic

landscape and also because of the international relativity of social class defini-tions. My measure of class is, therefore, informant defined and takes into account the men's educational and career backgrounds as well as those of their parents.

8. For ethical reasons, I did not pressure any of my interviewees to discuss traumatic experiences in more detail than they were comfortable with. I had informed all of them prior to the interview that if there were questions with which they felt uncomfortable, they could choose not to answer them and/or to end the interview at any time they so wished.

9. I do not mean to imply that there is some essential or "true" sexual nature that awaits "discovery"; rather, I utilize the term as a means to convey infor-mants' expressed understandings of their sexual journeys.

CHAPTER 7

1. Cruising sites are places where people seek others for sex, in this case men who are looking, or cruising, for other men to have sex with. Such sites might be found anywhere but are commonly found in parks, adult bookstores, and public bathrooms.

2. Cyberspace is beginning to function as an alternative "space" for such needs, but access is limited by material resources and the fact that a majority of this media, such as *Quo Vadis* (*QV*) magazine, is written mostly in English.

3. EDITORS' NOTE: Unfortunately *LLEGÓ*, the national organization that provided seed funding and technical assistance to many of these organizations, closed its doors in 2004.

4. Santa Ana is the county seat of Orange County, California, a 782-square-mile area located in Southern California between Los Angeles, Riverside, and San Diego Counties. With 2,410,556 inhabitants counted in the 1990 Census, Orange County is the fifth largest county in the nation and the fifth fastest growing county in the state. Although Orange County's population remains less diverse than that of other metropolitan areas in California, such as Los Angeles or San Francisco, the ethnic composition of the county has changed dramati-cally since 1980—most notably in the proportion of those in the Asian/Pacific Islander and Hispanic categories. In 1990, approximately 23 percent of Orange County identified as "Hispanic" (U.S. Bureau of the Census, 1990 PUMS file).

5. Retreats have been held during the months of May and November each year since its inception.

6. In this respect it is important to note that gay enclaves in many urban areas have historical roots that arise from marginal areas, which have often been either African American or Latino neighborhoods. Thus, many contempo-rary gay enclaves not only border Latino neighborhoods but also, due to gen-trification, force Latinos out of these spaces. The social relations that arise from

such dynamics as well as the way queer Latinos are positioned within them is a subject that to my knowledge has yet to be studied.

7. While Anderson (1983) uses the concept of "imagined community" in terms of the nation, the concept may also apply to those who form communities within and marginal to the nation, such as Chavez's (1994) application of the concept among undocumented Latino immigrants.

8. To what extent educational information from the retreat reaches beyond even these boundaries is unclear, but given the transnational social networks that many of the men maintain, it seems almost certain that some information is transmitted via these networks.

9. *¿Cómo calificas tu identidad sexual?*

10. The review referenced here is by John De Cecco, and was published on the back cover of Díaz's book (1998 edition).

CHAPTER 8

1. "*Cholo*" refers to people of Mexican mixed heritage (male: *cholo*; female: *chola*). It is generally used to reference contemporary dress codes and hair styles seen in urban spaces that are associated with Mexican gang members (or the equivalent of Chicano gangsters).

2. The linkage of "homosexuality" to leftist ideologies is, of course, not new and was a common strategy during the Red Scare of the 1950s.

EDITORS' CONCLUSION

1. See, for example, Ahmadi 2003; Donato, Gabaccia, Holdaway, Manalasan, and Pessar 2006; Epps, Valens, and Johnson González 2005; Mahler and Pessar 2006.

2. See, for example, Arnfred 2005; Boellstorff 2005, 2007; Massad 2002; McLelland and Dasgupta 2005.

3. Miller 2005; Peña 2005; also see Granhag, Strömwall, and Hartwig 2005.

4. González-López 2005; Hirsch 2003; Zavella 1997, 2003; Zavella and Castañeda 2005.

5. See Gibson-Graham (1996) and Sassen (1988). Recent analyses and discussions of queer or gay tourism include books by Johnston (2005); Luongo (2004, 2007); Markwell and Waitt (2006), and the special issue of GLQ: A Journal of Lesbian and Gay Studies, edited by Paur (2002), which includes Cantú's article on queer tourism that forms the basis for chapter 5.

6. Dasgupta 2006; see, for example, Eng 2001; Gopinath 2005; Manalansan 2003; Shah 2001; and Muñoz 1999.

References

Abu-Lughod, L. 1991. "Writing against Culture." Pp. 137–62 in *Recapturing Anthropology: Working in the Present*, edited by Richard G. Fox. Santa Fe, NM: School of American Research Press.

ACLU (American Civil Liberties Union). 1999. "CA's Anti-Immigrant Proposition 187 Is Voided, Ending State's Five-Year Battle with ACLU, Rights Groups" (http://www.aclu.org/ ImmigrantsRights/ImmigrantsRights. cfm?ID=8635&c=22). Retrieved: July 29, 1999.

———. 2000. "ACLU Lauds Appeals Court Ruling Granting Asylum for Gay Man Persecuted for Sexual Orientation." *ACLU Press Release* (http://www. aclu.org/ news). Retrieved: August 25, 2000.

Acosta, Katie. 2005. "Invisible Immigrants: The Experiences of Gays and Lesbians from Latin America." Unpublished master's thesis. Storrs, CT: University of Connecticut.

———. 2008. "Lesbians in the Borderlands: Shifting Identities and Imagined Communities." *Gender & Society* 22:639–659.

Acuña, Rodolfo. 1972. *Occupied America: The Chicano's Struggle toward Liberation*. New York: Harper & Row.

Ahmad, Muneer. 2002. "Homeland Insecurities: Racial Violence the Day after September 11." *Social Text* 72: 101–15.

Ahmadi, Nader. 2003. "Migration Challenges View on Sexuality." *Ethnic and Racial Studies* 26(4): 684–706.

Alcoff, Linda. 1988. "Cultural Feminism versus Post-Structuralism: The Identity Crisis in Feminist Theory." *Signs: Journal of Women in Culture and Society* 13(3): 405–36.

Allgeier, Albert, and Elizabeth R. Allgeier. 1988. *Sexual Interactions*. Lexington, MA: Heath.

Almaguer, Tomás. 1993. "Chicano Men: A Cartography of Homosexual Identity and Behavior." Pp. 255–73 in *The Lesbian and Gay Studies Reader*, edited by Henry Abelove, Michèle Aina Barale, and David M. Halperin. New York: Routledge.

———. 1994. *Racial Fault Lines: The Historical Origins of White Supremacy in California*. Berkeley: University of California Press.

Alonso, Ana María, and María Teresa Koreck. 1993. "Silences: 'Hispanics,' AIDS, and Sexual Practices." Pp. 110–28 in *The Lesbian and Gay Studies Reader*, edited by Henry Abelove, Michèle Aina Barale, and David M. Halperin. New York: Routledge.

Altman, Dennis. 1987. *Which Homosexuality? Essays from the International Scientific Conference on Lesbian and Gay Studies.* London: GMP.

———. 2001. *Global Sex.* Chicago: University of Chicago Press.

Anderson, Benedict. 1983. *Imagined Communities: Reflections on the Origins and Spread of Nationalism.* London: Verso.

Anonymous. Circa 1940. "The Lure of Mexico." P. 3 in *Mexico: That Far Away Land Nearby.* Mexico, DF: Mexican Tourist Association (travel brochure).

Anzaldúa, Gloria. 1987. *Borderlands/La Frontera: The New Mestiza.* San Francisco: Aunt Lute.

Arellano, Esquiroz. 1996. "Recipe for Growth." *Travel Agent* 279 (April 22): 8.

Argüelles, Lourdes, and Anne M. Rivero. 1993. "Gender/Sexual Orientation Violence and Transnational Migration: Conversations with Some Latinas We Think We Know." *Urban Anthropology* 22(3–4): 259–76.

Arnfred, Sgine, ed. 2005. *Rethinking Sexualities in Africa.* Uppsala, Sweden: Nordiska Afrikainstitutet/Nordic Africa Institute.

Baca Zinn, Maxine. 1991. "Chicano Men and Masculinity." Pp. 33–41 in *Men's Lives,* edited by Michael Kimmel and Michael Messner. Boston: Allyn and Bacon.

Bach, Robert L. 1978. "Mexican Immigration and the American State." *International Migration Review* 12: 536–58.

Ballard, Roger. 1987. "The Political Economy of Migration: Pakistan, Britain, and the Middle East." Pp. 17–41 in *Migrants, Workers, and the Social Order,* edited by Jeremy Eades. New York: Tavistock.

Bean, Frank D., Harley L. Browning, and W. Parker Frisbie. 1984. "The Sociodemographic Characteristics of Mexican Immigrant Status Groups: Implications for Studying Undocumented Mexicans." *International Migration Review* 18: 673–91.

Bell, David. 1995. *Mapping Desire: Geographies of Sexualities.* New York: Routledge.

Bell, David, and Gill Valentine, eds. 1993. *Mapping Desire: Geographies of Sexualities.* London and New York: Routledge.

Bennett, James R. 1996. "Materialist Queer Theory: A Working Bibliography." Pp. 381–92 in *The Material Queer,* edited by Donald Morton. Boulder, CO: Westview Press.

Bergesen, Albert. 1980. "Modeling Long Waves of Crisis in the World System." Pp. 73–92 in *Crises in the World System,* edited by Albert Bergesen. Beverly Hill, CA: Sage.

Bergmann, Emilie L., and Paul Julian Smith, eds. 1995.*¿Entiedes? Queer Readings, Hispanic Writings.* Durham, NC: Duke University Press.

Berlant, Lauren Gail. 1997. *The Queen of America Goes to Washington City: Essays on Sex and Citizenship.* Durham, NC: Duke University Press.

Bernstein, Mary, and Renate Reimann, eds. 2001. *Queer Families, Queer Politics: Challenging Culture and State.* New York: Columbia University Press.

Bhabha, Homi K. 1990. "The Other Question: Difference, Discrimination, and the Discourse of Colonialism." Pp. 71–88 in *Out There: Marginalization and Contemporary Cultures,* edited by Russell Ferguson, Martha Gever, Trinh Minh-ha, and Cornel West. New York: New Museum of Contemporary Art & MIT Press.

Binnie, Jon. 2004. *The Globalizaton of Sexuality.* London: Sage.

Bishop, George D., Albert Alva, Lionel Cantú, and Telecia K. Rittiman. 1991. "Responses to People with AIDS: Fear of Contagion or Stigma?" *Journal of Applied Social Psychology* 21(23): 1877–88.

Black, Richard. 1997. *The Ferrari Guides Gay Mexico: The Definitive Guide to Gay and Lesbian Mexico.* Phoenix, AZ: Ferrari Guides.

Blomström, Magnus, and Björn Hettne. 1984. *Development Theory in Transition: The Dependency Debate and Beyond, Third World Responses.* Boston: Zed Press.

Blumer, Herbert. 1986. *Symbolic Interactionism: Perspective and Method.* Berkeley: University of California Press.

Bock, Gisela, and Susan James, eds. 1992. *Beyond Equality and Difference: Citizenship, Feminist Politics, and Female Subjectivity.* New York: Routledge.

Boellstorff, Tom. 2005. *The Gay Archipelago: Sexuality and Nation in Indonesia.* Princeton, NJ: Princeton University Press.

———. 2007. *A Coincidence of Desires: Anthropology, Queer Studies, Indonesia.* Durham, NC: Duke University Press.

Bonilla, Frank. 1989. "Migrants, Citizenship, and Social Pacts." *Radical America* 23(1): 81–89.

Borker, Susan R. 1987. "Sex Roles and Labor Force Participation." Pp. 181–91 in *Current Conceptions of Sex Roles and Sex Typing: Theory and Research,* edited by D. Bruce Carter. New York: Praeger.

Bosniak, Linda. 2006. *The Citizen and the Alien.* Princeton, NJ: Princeton University Press.

Boutilier v. Immigration and Naturalization Service (INS). 1967. 387 U.S. 118, 123, Certiorari to the United States Court of Appeals for the Second Circuit. No. 440, Argued March 14, 1967. Decided May 22, 1967.

Boykin, Keith. 2005. *Beyond the Down Low: Sex, Lies, and Denial in Black America.* New York: Carroll and Graf.

Brod, Harry. 1994. "Some Thoughts on Some Histories of Some Masculinities: Jews and Other Others." Pp. 82–96 in *Theorizing Masculinities,* edited by Harry Brod and Michael Kaufman. Thousand Oaks, CA: Sage.

Brod, Harry, and Michael Kaufman, eds. 1994. *Theorizing Masculinities.* Thousand Oaks, CA: Sage.

Buffington, Rob. 1997. "Los Jotos: Contested Visions of Homosexuality in Modern Mexico." Pp. 118–32 in *Sex and Sexuality in Latin America*, edited by Daniel Balderston and Donna J. Guy. New York: New York University Press.

Burr, Chandler. 1993. "Homosexuality and Biology." *Atlantic Monthly* 271(3): 47–65.

Butler, Judith. 1990. *Gender Trouble: Feminism and the Subversion of Identity.* New York: Routledge.

———. 1991. "Imitation and Gender Insubordination." Pp. 13–31 in *Inside/ Out: Lesbian Theories, Gay Theories*, edited by Diana Fuss. New York: Routledge.

———. 1993. *Bodies That Matter: On The Discursive Limits of "Sex."* New York: Routledge.

———. 1994. "More Gender Trouble: Feminism Meets Queer Theory." *Differences: A Journal of Feminist Cultural Studies* 6(2/3): 1–26.

Butler, Judith, and Joan W. Scott. 1992. *Feminists Theorize the Political.* New York: Routledge.

Calavita, Kitty. 1992. *Inside the State: The Bracero Program, Immigration, and the I.N.S.* New York: Routledge.

Calhoun, Craig, ed. 1994. *Social Theory and the Politics of Identity.* Cambridge, MA: Blackwell.

Cantú, Lionel. 1995. "The Peripheralization of Rural America: A Case Study of Latino Migrants in America's Heartland." *Sociological Perspectives* 38(3): 399–414.

———. 1996. "Latino Poverty and Immigration in California and Orange County: An Analysis of Household Income in the 1990 Census." Center for Research on Latinos in a Global Society, Working Paper No. 1. Irvine: University of California.

———. 1999. "Border Crossings: Mexican Men and the Sexuality of Migration." Ph.D. dissertation, University of California, Irvine.

———. 2000. "Entre Hombres/Between Men: Latino Masculinities and Homosexualities." Pp. 224–46 in *Gay Masculinities*, edited by Peter Nardi. Thousand Oaks, CA: Sage.

———. 2001a. "A Place Called Home: A Queer Political Economy of Mexican Immigrant Men's Family Experiences. Pp. 112–36 in *Queer Families, Queer Politics: Challenging Culture and the State*, edited by Mary Bernstein and Renate Reimann. New York: Columbia University Press.

———. 2001b. "Review Essay: Máscaras: *Gender Performance and Sexuality in Latin America.*" *Qualitative Sociology* 24(1): 117–21.

———. 2002. "*De Ambiente*: Queer Tourism and the Shifting Boundaries of Mexican Male Sexualities." *GLQ: A Journal of Lesbian and Gay Studies* 8(1): 141–68.

Cantú, Lionel, with Eithne Luibhéid and Alexandra Minna Stern. 2005. "Well-Founded Fear: Political Asylum and the Boundaries of Sexual Identity in the U.S./Mexican Borderlands." Pp. 61–74 in *Queer Migrations: Sexuality, U.S. Citizenship, and Border Crossings*, edited by Eithne Luibhéid and Lionel Cantú. Minneapolis: University of Minnesota Press.

Caporaso, James A. 1981. "Industrialization in the Periphery: The Evolving Global Division of Labor." *International Studies Quarterly* 25(3): 347–84.

Carrier, Joseph. 1995. *De Los Otros: Intimacy and Homosexuality among Mexican Men*. New York: Columbia University Press.

Carrigan, Tim, Bob Connell, and John Lee. 1987. "Hard and Heavy: Toward a New Sociology of Masculinity." Pp. 139–92 in *Beyond Patriarchy: Essays by Men on Pleasure, Power, and Change*, edited by Michael Kaufman. Toronto: Oxford University Press.

Carrillo, Hector. 2002. *The Night Is Young: Sexuality in Mexico in the Time of AIDS*. Chicago: University of Chicago Press.

Casas, Manuel, B. R. Wagenheim, R. Banchero, and J. Mendoza-Romero. 1994 "Hispanic Masculinity: Myth or Psychological Schema Meriting Clinical Consideration." *Hispanic Journal of Behavioral Sciences* 16: 315–31.

Case, Sue-Ellen. 1991. "Tracking the Vampire." *Differences* 3(2): 1–20.

———. 1993. "Toward a Butch-Femme Aesthetic." Pp. 294–306 in *The Lesbian and Gay Studies Reader*, edited by Henry Abelove, Michèle Aina Barale, and David Halperin. New York: Routledge.

Castells, Manuel. 1997. *The Power of Identity*. Cambridge, MA: Blackwell.

Castill, Vasquez. 2004. *Land Privatization in Mexico: Urbanization, Formation of Regions, and Globalization in Ejidos*. New York: Routledge.

Castillo, E. Eduardo. 2006. "Mexico City Approves Gay Civil Unions." *Associated Press*, November 9.

Cathcart, Rebecca. 2008. "Boy's Killing, Labeled a Hate Crime, Stuns a Town." *New York Times*, February 23.

Central Intelligence Agency. 1982. *The World Factbook*. Washington, DC: Government Printing Office.

———. 1984. *The World Factbook*. Washington, DC: Government Printing Office.

———. 1990. *The World Factbook*. Washington, DC: Government Printing Office.

———. 1994. *The World Factbook*. Washington, DC: Government Printing Office.

———. 1998. *The World Factbook*. Washington, DC: Government Printing Office.

Chambers, Iain. 1994. *Migrancy, Culture, Identity*. New York: Routledge.

Chant, Sylvia, with Nikki Craske. 2003. *Gender in Latin America*. New Brunswick, NJ: Rutgers University Press.

Chapin, Jessica. 1998. "Closing America's 'Back Door.'" *GLQ: A Journal of Lesbian and Gay Studies* 4(3): 403–22.

Chase-Dunn, Christopher. 1998a. *Global Formation: Structures of the World-Economy*. 2d ed. Lanham, MD: Rowman & Littlefield.

———. 1998b. "Globalization and the Postcolonial World: The New Political Economy of Development." *Journal of Asian Studies* 57(3): 805–6.

———. 1999. "Globalization: A World-Systems Perspective." *Journal of World-Systems Research* 5(2): 165–85.

Chase-Dunn, Christopher, and T. D. Hall. 1999. "World-Systems in North America: Networks, Rise and Fall and Pulsations of Trade in Stateless Systems." *American Indian Culture and Research Journal* 22(1): 23–72.

Chauncey, George. 1994. *Gay New York: Gender, Urban Culture, and the Making of the Gay Male World, 1890–1940.* New York: Basic Books.

Chavez, Leo. 1992. *Shadowed Lives: Undocumented Immigrants in American Society.* San Diego, CA: Harcourt Brace Jovanovich College.

———. 1994. "The Power of the Imagined Community: The Settlement of Undocumented Mexicans and Central Americans in the United States." *American Anthropologist* 96(1): 52–73.

Chodorow, Nancy. 1978. *The Reproduction of Mothering.* Berkeley: University of California Press.

———. 1994. *Femininities, Masculinities, Sexualities: Freud and Beyond.* Lexington: University Press of Kentucky.

Clancy, Michael J. 1999. "Tourism and Development: Evidence from Mexico." *Annals of Tourism Research* 26(1): 1–20.

Clark, Danae. 1993. "Commodity Lesbianism." Pp. 186–201 in *The Lesbian and Gay Studies Reader*, edited by Henry Abelove, Michèle Aina Barale, and David M. Halperin. New York: Routledge.

Clarke, Paul Barry. 1994. *Citizenship.* London: Pluto Press.

Clifford, James. 1988. *The Predicament of Culture: Twentieth-Century Ethnography, Literature, and Art.* Cambridge, MA: Harvard University Press.

Clift, Stephen, and Simon Carter, eds. 2000. *Tourism and Sex: Culture, Commerce, and Coercion.* London: Pinter Press.

Codina, G. Edward, and Frank F. Montalvo. 1994. "Chicano Phenotype and Depression." *Hispanic Journal of Behavioral Sciences* 16: 296–306.

Cohen, Robin. 1987. *The New Helots: Migrants in the International Division of Labor.* Aldershot, UK: Avebury.

Coll, Kathleen M. 2005. "'Yo No Estoy Perdida': Immigrant Women (re)locating Citizenship." Pp. 389–410 in *Passing Lines: Sexuality and Immigration*, edited by Brad Epps, Keja Valens, and bill Johnson Gonzáles. Cambridge, MA: Harvard University Press.

Collins, Patricia Hills. 1991. "Learning from the Outsider Within: The Sociological Significance of Black Feminist Thought." Pp. 35–39 in *Beyond Methodology*, edited by Mary Margaret Fonow and Judith A. Cook. Bloomington: Indiana University Press.

Coltrane, Scott, and Elsa O. Valdez. 1993. "Reluctant Compliance: Work-Family Role Allocation in Dual Earner Chicano Families." Pp. 151–75 in *Men, Work, and Family*, edited by Jane C. Hood. Newbury Park, CA: Sage.

Community Marketing. 2008. *LGBT Tourism Demographic Profile*. (http://mark8ing.com/mkt_tdp.htm). Retrieved: November 17, 2008.

Connell, R. W. 1995. *Masculinities*. Berkeley: University of California Press.

Connolly, William E. 1995. *The Ethos of Pluralization*. Minneapolis: University of Minnesota Press.

Córdova, Señor. 1999. *A Man's Guide to Mexico and Central America*. Beverly Hills, CA: Centurion Press.

Cornelius, Wayne A. 2002. "Ambivalent Reception: Mass Public Responses to the 'New' Latino Immigration to the United States." Pp. 165–89 in *Latinos: Remaking America*, edited by Marcelo M. Suarez-Orozco and Mariela M. Paez. Berkeley: University of California Press.

Cortéz, Jaime. 2004. *Sexile/Sexilio*. The Institute for Gay Men's Health (AIDS Project Los Angeles and Gay Men's Health Crisis). For document access in English, see http://apla.org/publications/sexile/Sexile_web. pdf. For Spanish access, see http://apla. org/espanol/ sexilio/Sexilio_web.pdf. Retrieved: May 31, 2008.

Cousins, Mark, and Athar Hussain. 1984. *Michel Foucault*. New York: Macmillan.

Cruz-Malavé, Arnaldo, and Martin F. Manalansan, eds. 2002. *Queer Globalizations: Citizenship and the Afterlife of Colonialism*. New York: New York University Press.

Currah, Paisley. 2006. "Gender Pluralisms under the Transgender Umbrella." Pp. 3–31 in *Transgender Rights*, edited by Paisley Currah, Richard M. Juang, and Shannon Price Minter. Minneapolis: University of Minnesota Press.

Currah, Paisley, Richard M. Juang, and Shannon Price Minter, eds. 2006. *Transgender Rights*. Minneapolis: University of Minnesota Press.

Curtis, J., and D. Arreola. 1991. "Zonas de Tolerancia on the Northern Mexico Border." *Geographical Review* 81(3): 333–47.

Dasgupta, Romit. 2006. Review of Gayatri Gopinath, *Impossible Desires: Queer Diasporas and South Asian Public Cultures. Intersections: Gender, History, and Culture in the Asian Context* 14 (November) (http://intersections.anu. edu.au/issue14/dasgupta_review.htm). Retrieved: June 3, 2008.

David, Eduardo. 1998. *Gay Mexico: The Men of Mexico*. Oakland, CA: Floating Lotus Press.

Davidson, Julia. 1996. "Sex Tourism in Cuba." *Race and Class* 8(1): 39–49.

Decena, Carlos U. 2004. *Queering the Heights: Dominican Transnational Identities and Male Homosexuality in New York City*. Unpublished dissertation, American Studies, New York University.

de Lauretis, Teresa. 1991. "Queer Theory: Lesbian and Gay Sexualities: An Introduction." *Differences: A Journal of Feminist Cultural Studies* 3(2): iii–xviii.

———. 1994. *The Practice of Love: Lesbian Sexuality and Perverse Desire.* Bloomington: Indiana University Press.

D'Emilio, John. 1993 [1983]. "Capitalism and Gay Identity." Pp. 132–34 in *Cases and Materials on Sexual Orientation and the Law: Lesbians, Gay Men, and the Law*, edited by William B. Rubenstein, Carlos A. Ball, and Jane S. Schacter. New York: New Press.

Díaz, Rafael. 1998. *Latino Gay Men and HIV: Culture, Sexuality, and Risk Behavior.* New York: Routledge.

Donato, Katharine M., Donna Gabaccia, Jennifer Holdaway, Martin Manalasan IV, and Patricia R. Pessar. 2006. "A Glass Half Full? Gender in Migration Studies." *International Migration Review* 40(1): 3–26.

Donovan, Josephine. 1992. *Feminist Theory.* New York: Continuum.

Dorf, Julie. 1998. Executive Director, International Gay and Lesbian Human Rights Commission (IGHLRC). Personal Interview.

Duberman, Martin, Marcha Vicinus, and George Chauncey. 1990. *Hidden from History: Reclaiming the Gay and Lesbian Past.* New York: Plume.

Dusek, Jerome B. 1987. "Sex Roles and Adjustment." Pp. 211–22 in *Current Conceptions of Sex Roles and Sex Typing: Theory and Research*, edited by D. Bruce Carter. New York: Praeger.

Dolan, Maura. 2008. "California Supreme Court Overturns Gay Marriage Ban." Los Angeles Times, May 16 (http:// www.latimes.com/news/local/la-me-gay-marriage16-2008may16,0,6182317.story).

Drajem, Mark. 2006. "China Becomes Second-Largest U.S. Trade Partner (Update 1)" (http:www.bloomberg. com/apps/news?pid=20601086&refer=news &sid=aFCMVe9aVeco). Retrieved: June 8, 2008.

Eades, Jeremy. 1987. *Migrants, Workers, and the Social Order.* New York: Tavistock.

Eng, David L. 2001. *Racial Castration: Managing Masculinity in Asian America.* Durham, NC: Duke University Press.

Eng, David L., Judith Halberstam, and José Esteban Muñoz. 2005. "Introduction: What's Queer about Queer Studies Now?" *Social Text* 23(304): 1–17.

Engels, Frederick. 1993 [1942]. *The Origin of the Family, Private Porperty, and the State.* New York: International.

Epps, Brad. 2001. "Passing Lines: Immigration and the Performance of American Identities." Pp. 92–134 in *Passing: Identity and Interpretation in Sexuality, Race, and Religion*, edited by Maria Carla Sánchez and Linda Schlossberg. New York: New York University Press.

———. 2005. "Intimate Conduct, Public Practice, and the Bounds of Citizenship: In the Wake of *Lawrence v. Texas.*" Pp. 189–236 in *Passing Lines: Sexuality and Immigration*, edited by Brad Epps, Keja Valens, and Bill Johnson Gonzáles. Cambridge, MA: Harvard University Press.

Epps, Brad, Keja Valens, and Bill Johnson González, eds. 2005. *Passing Lines: Sexuality and Immigration*. Cambridge, MA: Harvard University Press.

Erickson, Pamela I. 2001. "Negotiation of First Sexual Intercourse among Latina Adolescent Mothers." Pp. 97–107 in *Speaking of Sexuality: Interdisciplinary Readings*, edited by J. Kenneth Davidson Jr. and Nelwyn B. Moore. Los Angeles: Roxbury.

Escobar, Augustin, M. Gonzalez, and B. Roberts. "Migration, Labour Markets, and the International Economy: Jalisco, Mexico, and the United States." Pp. 42–64 in *Migrants, Workers, and the Social Order*, edited by Jeremy Eades. New York: Tavistock.

Espín, Olivia M. 1997. *Latina Realities: Essays on Healing, Migration, and Sexuality*. Boulder, CO: Westview Press.

———. 1999. *Women Crossing Boundaries: A Psychology of Immigration and Transformations of Sexuality*. New York: Routledge.

Evans, David T. 1993. *Sexual Citizenship: The Material Construction of Sexualities*. New York: Routledge.

Evans, Peter B. 1979. "Beyond Center and Periphery: A Comment on the Contribution of the World System Approach to the Study of Development." *Sociological Inquiry* 49: 15–20.

Fagot, Beverly I., and Mary D. Leinbach. 1987. "Socialization of Sex Roles within the Family." Pp. 89–100 in *Current Conceptions of Sex Roles and Sex Typing: Theory and Research*, edited by D. Bruce Carter. New York: Praeger.

Fairbairn, Bill. 2005. "Gay Rights Are Human Rights: Gay Asylum Seekers in Canada." Pp. 237–54 in *Passing Lines: Sexuality and Immigration*. Cambridge, MA: Harvard University Press.

Fellows, Wiliam D. 1996. *Farm Boys: Lives of Gay Men from the Rural Midwest*. Madison: University of Wisconsin Press.

Ferguson, Roderick A. 2004. *Aberrations in Black: Toward a Queer of-Color Critique*. Minneapolis: University of Minnesota Press.

Fernández-Kelly, M. Patricia, and Anna M. Garcia. 1989. "Informalization at the Core: Hispanic Women, Homework, and the Advanced Capitalist State." Pp. 247–64 in *The Informal Economy: Studies in Advanced and Less Developed Countries*, edited by Alejandro Portes, Manuel Castells, and Lauren Benton. Baltimore, MD: Johns Hopkins University Press.

Fine, Gary Alan. 1993. "The Sad Demise, Mysterious Disappearance, and Glorious Triumph of Symbolic Interactionism." *Annual Review of Sociology* 19: 61–87.

Foucault, Michel. 1972. *The Archaeology of Knowledge and the Discourse on Language*. New York: Harper & Row.

———. 1985. *The Foucault Reader*, edited by Paul Rabinow. New York: Pantheon.

———. 1990 [1978]. *The History of Sexuality: An Introduction*. New York: Pantheon.

Fox, Geoffrey E. 1996. *Hispanic Nation: Culture, Politics, and the Constructing of Identity*. New York: Carol.

Frank, Andre Gunder. 1978. *World Accumulation, 1492–1789*. New York: Monthly Review Press.

Frank, Andre Gunder, and Barry K. Gills. 1993. *The World System: Five Hundred Years or Five Thousand?* London: Routledge.

Garnets, Linda D., and Douglas C. Kimmel. 1993. *Psychological Perspectives on Lesbian and Gay Male Experiences*. New York: Columbia University Press.

Genova, Nick de, and Ana Ramos Zayas. 2003. *Latino Crossings: Mexicans, Puerto Ricans, and the Politics of Race and Citizenship*. New York: Taylor and Frances.

Ghatak, Subrata, Paul Levine, and Stephen Price. 1996. "Migration Theories and Evidence: An Assessment." *Journal of Economic Surveys* 10(2): 159–98.

Gibson-Graham, J. K. 1996. "Queering Globalization." Pp. 239–75 in *Post-Colonial, Queer: Theoretical Interventions*, edited by J. C. Haley. Albany: State University of New York Press.

Gilroy, Paul. 1992. "Cultural Studies and Ethnic Absolutism." Pp. 187–98 in *Cultural Studies,* edited by Lawrence Grossberg, Cary Nelson, and Paula Treichler. New York: Routledge.

Gluckman, Amy. 1997. *Homo Economics: Capitalism, Community, and Lesbian and Gay Life*. New York: Routledge.

Goffman, Erving. 1959. *The Presentation of Self in Everyday Life*. New York: Doubleday.

González-López, Gloria. 2000. "Beyond the Bed Sheets, beyond the Borders: Mexican Immigrant Women and Their Sex Lives." Ph.D. dissertation, University of Southern California, Los Angeles, CA.

———. 2005. *Erotic Journeys: Mexican Immigrants and Their Sex Lives*. Berkeley: University of California Press.

González-López, Gloria, and Salvador Vidal-Ortiz. 2008. "Latinas and Latinos, Sexuality, and Society: A Critical Sociological Perspective." Pp. 308–22 (chapter 20) in *Latinos/as in the United States: Changing the Face of América*, edited by Havidán Rodríguez, Rogelio Sáenz, and Cecilia Menjívar. New York: Springer.

Gopinath, Gayatri, 2005. *Impossible Desires: Queer Diasporas and South Asian Public Cultures*. Durham, NC: Duke University Press.

Granhag, Pär Anders, Leif A. Strömwall, and Maria Hartwig. 2005. "Granting Asylum or Not? Migration Board Personnel's Beliefs about Deception." *Journal of Ethnic and Migration Studies* 31(1): 29–50.

Guenette, Louise. 2000. "Touting Tourism." *Business Mexico* 10(3): 42–47.

Gutiérrez, David G. 1995. *Walls and Mirrors: Mexican Americans, Mexican Immigrants, and the Politics of Ethnicity*. Berkeley: University of California Press.

Gutmann, Matthew C. 1996. *The Meanings of Macho: Being a Man in Mexico City*. Berkeley: University of California Press.

Guzmán, Manolo. 1997. "'Pa' La Escuelita con Mucho Cuida'o y por la Orillita': A Journey through the Contested Terrains of the Nation and Sexual Orientation." Pp. 209–28 in *Puerto Rican Jam*, edited by Ramón Grosfoguel and Frances Negrón-Muntaner. Minneapolis: University of Minnesota Press.

———. 2006. *Gay Hegemony/Latino Homosexualities*. New York: Routledge.

Hall, C. Michael. 1994a. "Gender and Economic Interests in Tourism Prostitution: The Nature, Development, and Implications of Sex Tourism in South-East Asia." Pp. 142–63 in *Tourism: A Gender Analysis*, edited by Vivian Kinnaird and Derek Hall. New York: Wiley.

———. 1994b. *Tourism in the Pacific Rim: Development, Impacts, and Markets*. New York: Halsted Press.

Hammonds, Evelynn. 1994. "Black (W)holes and the Geometry of Black Female Sexuality." *Differences: A Journal of Feminist Cultural Studies* 6(2/3): 126–45.

Haour-Knipe, Mary, ed. 1996. *Crossing Borders: Migration, Ethnicity, and AIDS*. London: Taylor & Francis.

Haour-Knipe Mary, and Richard Rector, eds. 1996. *Crossing Borders: Migration, Ethnicity, and AIDS*. London: Taylor & Francis.

Haraway, Donna. 1988. "Situated Knowledges: The Science Question in Feminism and the Privilege of Partial Perspective." *Feminist Studies* 14(3): 575–99.

Harding, Sandra. 1986. *The Science Question in Feminism*. Ithaca, NY: Cornell University Press.

———. 1991. *Whose Science? Whose Knowledge? Thinking from Women's Lives*. Ithaca, NY: Cornell University Press.

———, ed. 2003. *The Feminist Standpoint Theory Reader: Intellectual and Political Controversies*. New York: Routledge.

Harris, Laura Alexandra. 1996. "Queer Black Feminism: The Pleasure Principle." *Feminist Review* 54: 3–30.

Hartsock, Nancy. 1983. *Money, Sex, and Power: Toward a Feminist Historical Materialism*. New York: Longman.

———. 1996. "Theoretical Bases for Coalition Building: An Assessment of Postmodernism." Pp. 256–74 in *Feminism and Social Change: Bridging Theory and Practice*, ed. Heidi Gottfried. Urbana: University of Illinois Press.

Harvard Law Review (HLR). 1990. *Sexual Orientation and the Law*. Cambridge, MA: Harvard University Press.

Harvey, David. 1990. *The Condition of Postmodernity: An Enquiry into the Origins of Cultural Change*. London: Blackwell.

Hearn, Jeff, and David L. Collinson. 1994. "Theorizing Unities and Differences between Men and between Masculinities." Pp. 97–118 in *Theorizing Masculinities*, edited by Harry Brod and Michael Kaufman. Thousand Oaks, CA: Sage.

Hennessy, Rosemary. 1993. *Materialist Feminism and the Politics of Discourse*. New York: Routledge.

———. 2000. *Profit and Pleasure: Sexual Identities in Late Capitalism*. New York: Routledge

Hennessy, Rosemary, and Chrys Ingraham, eds. 1997. *Materialist Feminism: A Reader in Class, Difference, and Women's Lives*. New York: Routledge.

Herdt, Gilbert H. 1994 [1981]. *Guardians of the Flute: Idioms of Masculinity*. New York: McGraw-Hill.

———. 1997. *Sexual Cultures and Migration in the Era of AIDS: Anthropological and Demographic Perspectives*. Oxford, UK: Clarendon Press.

Hernández-Montiel, Geovanni v. Immigration and Naturalization Service (INS). 2000. 225 F.3d 1084 (9th Cir. 2000). Argued August 24, 2000 (http://www.ca9.uscourts.gov/ca9/ newopinions.nsf/3184F875F26B8B85882569520075 7AB9/$file/9870582.pdf?openelement). Retrieved: October 21, 2007.

Hirsch, Jennifer S. 2003. *A Courtship after Marriage: Sexuality and Love in Mexican Transnational Families*. Berkeley: University of California Press.

Holcomb, Briavel, and Michael Luongo. 1996. "Gay Tourism in the United States." *Annals of Tourism Research* 23(3): 711–13.

Hondagneu-Sotelo, Pierrette. 1994. *Gendered Transitions: Mexican Experiences of Immigration*. Los Angeles: University of California Press.

———, ed. 2003. *Gender and U.S. Immigration: Contemporary Trends*. Berkeley: University of California Press.

Hondagneu-Sotelo, Pierette, and Michael Messner. 1994. "Gender Displays and Men's Power: 'The New Man' and the Mexican Immigrant Man." Pp. 200–218 in *Theorizing Masculinities*, edited by Harry Brod and Michael Kaufman. Thousand Oaks, CA: Sage.

Hood, Kathryn E., P. Draper, L. Crockett, and A. C. Petersen. 1987. "The Ontogeny and Phylogeny of Sex Differences in Development: A Biopsychosocial Synthesis." Pp. 49–77 in *Current Conceptions of Sex Roles and Sex Typing: Theory and Research*, edited by D. Bruce Carter. New York: Praeger.

hooks, bell. 1990. *Yearning: Race, Gender, and Cultural Politics*. Boston: South End Press.

Howe, Cymene, Suzanna Zaraysky, and Lois Lorentzen. 2008. "Transgender Sex Workers and Sexual Transmigration between Guadalajara and San Francisco." *Latin American Perspectives* 158 (Jan.): 31–50.

Human Rights Watch/Immigration Equality. 2006. *United States: Family, Unvalued: Discrimination, Denial, and the Fate of Binational Same-Sex Couples under U.S. Law*. New York: Human Rights Watch/Immigration Equality.

Humphreys, Laud. 1970. *Tearoom Trade: Impersonal Sex in Public Places.* New York: Aldine.

Huntington, Samuel P. 2004. *Who Are We? The Challenge to America's National Identity.* New York: Simon & Schuster.

Hurtado, Aida, Patricia Gurin, and Timothy Peng. 1994. "Social Identities: A Framework for Studying the Adaptations of Immigrants and Ethnics: The Adaptations of Mexicans in the United States." *Social Problems* 41(1): 129–51.

Hussain, Mark, and Athar Hussain. 1984. *Michel Foucault.* New York: Macmillan.

Immigration Equality. 2006. "Annual Report" (http://www. immigrationequality.org/uploadedfiles/2006%20Annual%20Report.pdf).

Immigration Equality: Lesbian and Gay Immigration Rights Task Force. 1995. *Immigration Equality: Lesbian and Gay Immigration Rights Task Force.* Informational Pamphlet. New York: Immigration Equality.

Immigration and Naturalization Service. 1975. *Extension Training Program, Lesson 5.3.* Washington, DC: Government Printing Office.

———. 1987. *Extension Training Program, Lesson 3.2.* Washington, DC: Government Printing Office.

———. 1997. *Quick Check Guide for Entry to the United States of America.* Washington, DC: Government Printing Office.

———. 1999. "History of the United States INS Asylum Officer Corps and Sources of Authority for Asylum Adjudication." Washington, DC: Immigration and Naturalization Services (http://www.ailc.com/services/asylum/history.htm). Retrieved: November 21, 2007.

———. 2000. "Early Immigrant Inspection along the U.S./Mexican Border." Washington, DC: Immigration and Naturalization Services (http://.uscis.gov/portal/site/uscis). Retrieved: November 21, 2007.

Ingram, Gordon Brent. 1997. "Marginality and the Landscapes of Erotic Alien(n)nation." Pp. 27–53 in *Queers in Space: Communities, Public Places, Sites of Resistance*, edited by Gordon Brent Ingram, Anne-Marie Bouthillette, and Yolanda Retter. Seattle: Bay Press.

Ingram, Gordon Brent, Anne-Marie Bouthillette, and Yolanda Retter. 1997. *Queers in Space: Communities, Public Places, Sites of Resistance.* Seattle: Bay Press.

Irwin, Robert McKee. 2003. *Mexican Masculinities.* Minneapolis: University of Minnesota Press.

Jagose, Annamarie. 1996. *Queer Theory: An Introduction.* New York: New York University Press.

Jameson, Fredric. 1992. *Postmodernism; or, The Cultural Logic of Late Capitalism.* Chapel Hill, NC: Duke University Press.

Johnston, Lynda. 2005. *Queering Tourism: Paradoxical Performances of Gay Pride Parades.* New York: Routledge.

Jones, Kathleen B. 1988. "On Authority; or, Why Women Are Not Entitled to Speak." Pp. 119–33 in *Feminism and Foucault: Reflections on Resistance*, edited by I. Diamond and L. Quinby. Boston: Northeastern University Press.

———. 1990. "Citizenship in a Woman-Friendly Polity." *Signs: Journal of Women in Culture and Society* 15(4): 781–812.

———. 1994. "Identity, Action, Locale: Thinking about Citizenship, Civic Action, and Feminism." *Social Politics* 1(3): 256–70.

Joseph, Miranda. 2002a. "The Discourse of Global/Localization." Pp. 71–99 in *Queer Globalizations: Citizenship and the Afterlife of Colonialism*, edited by Arnaldo Cruz-Malavé and Martin F. Manalansan IV. New York: New York University Press.

———. 2002b. "Family Affairs: The Discourse of Global/Localization." Pp. 71–99 in *Queer Globalizations: Citizenship and the Afterlife of Colonialism*, edited by Arnaldo Cruz-Malave and Martin F. Manalansan IV. New York: New York University Press.

Kearney, Michael. 1991. "Borders and Boundaries of State and Self at the End of Empire." *Journal of Historical Sociology* 4(1): 52–74.

Keen, Lisa. 1995. *Washington Blade*. March 24 (http://www.qrd.org/ world/immigration/). Retrieved: November 24, 2007.

Kimmel, Michael S., and Michael A. Messner. 1995. "Introduction." Pp. viii–xxiii in *Men's Lives*, edited by M. S. Kimmel and M. A. Messner. Boston: Allyn and Bacon.

King, Dave. 2003. "Gender Migration: A Sociological Analysis (or the Leaving of Liverpool)." *Sexualities* 6(2): 173–94.

King, Katie. 1994. *Theory in Its Feminist Travels: Conversations in U.S. Women's Movements*. Bloomington: Indiana University Press.

———. 2002. "'There Are No Lesbians Here': Lesbianisms, Feminisms, and Global Gay Formations." Pp. 33–48 in *Queer Globalizations: Citizenship and the Afterlife of Colonialism*, edited by Arnaldo Cruz-Malave and Martin F. Manalansan IV. New York: New York University Press.

King, Rosemary. 2000. "Border Crossings in the Mexican-American War." *Bilingual Review* 25(1): 63–86.

Kingston, Maxine Hong. 1990. *China Men*. New York: Vintage Books.

Kinsey, A. C., W. Pomeroy, and C. Martin. 1948. *Sexual Behavior in the Human Male*. Philadelphia: Saunders.

Klein, Julie Thompson. 1996. *Crossing Boundaries: Knowledge, Disciplinarities, and Interdisciplinarities*. Charlottesville: University Press of Virginia.

Kleinberg, Seymour. 1989. "The New Masculinity of Gay Men, and Beyond." Pp. 101–14 in *Men's Lives*, edited by Michael Kimmel and Michael Messner. Boston: Allyn and Bacon.

Kulick, Don. 1998. *Travesti: Sex, Gender, and Culture among Brazilian Transgendered Prostitutes*. Chicago: University of Chicago Press.

La Fountain-Stokes, Larry. 1999. "1989 and the History of a Queer Puerto Rican Century." Pp. 197–215 in *Chicano/Latino Homoerotic Identities*, edited by David William Foster. New York: Garland.

Lambda Legal Defense and Education Fund (LLDEF). 1995. Handout. "Basic Immigration Law Concepts."

Lancaster, Roger N. 1992. *Life Is Hard: Machismo, Danger, and the Intimacy of Power in Nicaragua*. Berkeley: University of California Press.

———. 2005. "Tolerance and Intolerance in Sexual Cultures in Latin America." Pp. 255–76 in *Passing Lines: Sexuality and Immigration*, edited by Brad Epps, Keja Valens, and Bill Johnson Gonzáles. Cambridge, MA: Harvard University Press.

Leap, William L., and Tom Boellstorff, eds. 2004. *Speaking in Queer Tongues*. Urbana: University of Illinois Press.

Levine, Martin P. 1979. "Gay Ghetto." *Journal of Homosexuality* 4(4): 363–77.

Lewis, Oscar. 1959. *Five Families: Mexican Case Studies in the Culture of Poverty*. New York: Basic Books.

Limón, José. 1994. *Dancing with the Devil: Society and Cultural Poetics in Mexican-American South Texas*. Madison: University of Wisconsin Press.

Lipsitz, George. 1998. *The Possessive Investment in Whiteness: How White People Profit from Identity Politics*. Philadelphia: Temple University Press.

Luibhéid, Eithne. 1994. "Identity, Action, Locale: Thinking about Citizenship, Civic Action, and Feminism." *Social Politics* 1(3): 256–70.

———. 1998. "'Looking Like a Lesbian': The Organization of Sexual Monitoring at the United States-Mexican Border." *Journal of the History of Sexuality* 8(3): 477–506.

———. 2002. *Entry Denied: Controlling Sexuality at the Border*. Minneapolis: University of Minnesota Press.

———. 2005. "Heteronormativity, Responsibility, and Neo-liberal Governance in U.S. Immigration Control." Pp. 69–104 in *Passing Lines: Sexuality and Immigration*. Cambridge, MA: Harvard University Press.

Luibhéid, Eithne, and Lionel Cantú, eds. 2005. *Queer Migrations: Sexuality, U.S. Citizenship, and Border Crossing*. Minneapolis: University of Minnesota Press.

Luibhéid, Eithne, and Sasah Khokha. 2001. "Building Alliances between Immigrant Rights and Queer Movements." Pp. 77–90 in *Forging Radical Alliances across Difference: Coalition Politics for the New Millennium*, edited by Jill M. Bystydzienski and Steven P. Schacht. Boulder, CO: Rowman and Littlefield.

Lumsden, Ian G. 1991. *Homosexuality, Society, and the State in Mexico*. México: Solediciones, Colectivo Sol.

———. 1996. *Machos, Maricones, and Gays: Cuba and Homosexuality*. Philadelphia: Temple University Press.

Luongo, Michael Theodore. 2007. *Gay Travels in the Muslim World*. Philadelphia: Harworth.

———, ed. 2004. *Between the Palms: A Collection of Gay Travel Erotica*. Philadelphia: Harworth.

MacCannell, Dean. 1999 [1976]. *The Tourist: A New Theory of the Leisure Class*. Berkeley: University of California Press.

Madsen Camacho, Michelle E. 2000. "The Politics of Progress: Constructing Paradise in Huatulco, Oaxaca." Ph.D. dissertation, University of California, Irvine.

Mahler, Sarah J., and Patricia R. Pessar. 2006. "Gender Matters: Ethnographers Bring Gender from the Periphery toward the Core of Migration Studies." *International Migration Review* 40(1): 27–63.

Manalasan, Martin F. 2000. "Diasporic Deviants/Divas: How Filipino Gay Transmigrants 'Play with the Work.'" Pp. 183–203 in *Queer Diasporas*. Durham, NC: Duke University Press.

———. 2003. *Global Divas: Filipino Gay Men in the Diaspora*. Durham, NC: Duke University Press.

———. 2006. "Queer Intersections: Sexuality and Gender in Migration Studies." *International Migration Review* 40(1): 224–49.

Manalasan, Martin F., and Arnaldo Cruz-Malavé, eds. 2002. *Queer Globalizations: Citizenship and the Afterlife of Colonialism*. New York: New York University Press.

Markwell, Kevin, and Gordon Waitt. 2006. *Gay Tourism: Culture and Context*. New York: Routledge.

Marshall, T. H. 1964 [1950]. *Class, Citizenship, and Social Development: Essays by T. H. Marshall*. Garden City, NY: Doubleday.

Martin, Biddy. 1988. "Feminism, Criticism, and Foucault." Pp. 3–20 in *Feminism and Foucault: Reflections on Resistance*, edited by Irene Diamond and Lee Quinby. Boston: Northeastern University Press.

Massad, Joseph. 2002. "Re-Orienting Desire: the Gay International and the Arab World." *Public Culture* 14:361–85.

Massey, Doreen B. 1994. *Space, Place, and Gender*. Minneapolis: University of Minnesota Press.

Massey, Douglas S., Joaquin Arango, Graeme Hugo, Ali Kouaouci, Adela Pellegrino, and J. Edward Taylor. 1993. "Theories of International Migration: Review and Appraisal." *Population and Development Review* 19(3): 431–67.

Massey, Douglas S., and Kristin Espinosa. 1995. "What's Driving Mexico-U.S. Migration? A Theoretical, Empirical, and Policy Analysis." Unpublished paper.

McIntosh, Mary. 1968. "The Homosexual Role." *Social Problems* 16(69): 182–92.

———. 1993. "Queer Theory and the War of the Sexes." Pp. 30–52 in *Activating Theory: Lesbian, Gay, Bisexual Politics*, edited by Joseph Bristow and Angelia R. Wilson. London: Lawrence and Wishart.

McLelland, Mark, and Romit Dasgupta, eds. 2005. *Genders, Transgenders, and Sexualities in Japan*. New York: Routledge.

McWilliams, Carey. 1948. *North from Mexico: The Spanish-Speaking People of the United States*. New York: Praeger.

Mead, Margaret. 1935. *Sex and Temperament in Three Primitive Societies*. New York: McGraw-Hill.

Miles, Lesley. 1993. "Women, AIDS, and Power in Heterosexual Sex: A Discourse Analysis." *Women's Studies International Forum* 16(5): 497–511.

Miller, Alice M. 2005. "Gay Enough: Some Tensions in Seeking the Grant of Asylum and Protecting Global Sexual Diversity." Pp. 137–88 in *Passing Lines: Sexuality and Immigration*, edited by Brad Epps, Keja Valens, and Bill Johnson González. Cambridge, MA: Harvard University Press.

Mirandé, Alfredo. 1997. *Hombres y Machos: Masculinity and Latino Culture*. Boulder, CO: Westview Press.

Mogorevejo, Norma. 2000. *Un Amor Que Se Atrevió A Decir Su Nombre* [A Love That Dare Not Speak Its Name]. México: CDAHL.

———. 2005. "Immigration, Self-Exile, and Sexual Dissidence," Pp. 411–24 in *Passing Lines: Sexuality and Immigration*, edited by Brad Epps, Keja Valens, and Bill Johnson González. Cambridge, MA: Harvard University Press.

Mohanty, Chandra Talpede. 1991a. "Cartographies of Struggle." Pp. 1–50 in *Third World Women and the Politics of Feminism*, edited by Chandra Talpede Mohanty, Ann Russo, and Lourdes Torres. Bloomington: Indiana University Press.

———. 1991b. "Under Western Eyes: Feminist Scholarship in Colonial Discourse." Pp. 51–30 in *Third World Women and the Politics of Feminism*, edited by Chandra Talpede Mohanty, Ann Russo, and Lourdes Torres. Bloomington: Indiana University Press.

Mohanty, Chandra, Ann Russo, and Lourdes Torres. 1991. *Third World Women and the Politics of Feminism*. Bloomington: Indiana University Press.

Moore, Joan, and Harry Pachon. 1985. *Hispanics in the United States*. Englewood Cliffs, NJ: Prentice-Hall.

Moraga, Cherríe. 1981. Introduction. Pp. xiii–xix in *This Bridge Called My Back: Writings by Radical Women of Color*, edited by Cherríe Moraga and Gloria Anzaldúa. Watertown, MA: Persephone Press.

Morton, Donald, ed. 1996. *The Material Queer*. Boulder, CO: Westview Press.

Mouffe, Chantal. 1992. "Feminism, Citizenship, and Radical Democratic Politics." Pp. 369–84 in *Feminists Theorize the Political*, edited by Judith Butler and Joan W. Scott. New York: Routledge.

Moya, Paula M. L. 1997. "Postmodernism, 'Realism,' and the Politics of Identity: Cherríe Moraga and Chicana Feminism." Pp. 125–50 in *Feminist Genealogies, Colonial Legacies, Democratic Futures*, edited by M. Jacqui Alexander and Chandra Talpede Mohanty. New York: Routledge.

Mukherjea, Ananya, and Salvador Vidal-Ortiz. 2006. "Studying HIV Risk in Vulnerable Communities: Methodological and Reporting Shortcomings in the Young Men's Study in New York City." *Qualitative Report* (on-line journal) 11(2).

Muñoz, José Esteban. 1999. *Disidentifications: Queers of Color and the Performance of Politics*. Minneapolis: University of Minnesota Press.

Murray, Steven O. 1995. *Latin American Male Homosexualities*. Albuquerque: University of New Mexico Press.

———. 1996. *American Gay*. Chicago: University of Chicago Press.

Murray, Steven O., and Wayne R. Dynes. 1995. "Hispanic Homosexuals: A Spanish Lexicon." Pp. 180–92 in *Latin American Male Homosexualities*, edited by Stephen O. Murray. Albuquerque: University of New Mexico Press.

Nagel, Joane. 2003. *Race, Ethnicity, and Sexuality: Intimate Intersections, Forbidden Frontiers*. New York: Oxford University Press.

Nakano Glenn, Evelyn. 2004. *Unequal Freedom: How Race and Gender Shaped American Citizenship and Labor*. Cambridge, MA: Harvard University Press.

Napholz, Linda. 1994. "Dysphoria among Hispanic Working Women: A Research Note." *Hispanic Journal of Behavioral Sciences* 16: 500–509.

Naples, Nancy A. 1994. "Contradictions in Agrarian Ideology: Restructuring Gender, Race-Ethnicity, and Class." *Rural Sociology* 59(1): 110–35.

———. 1996. "Feminist Revisiting of the 'Insider/Outsider' Debate: The 'Outsider Phenomenon' in Rural Iowa." *Qualitative Sociology* 19(1): 83–106.

———. 2003. *Feminism and Method: Ethnography, Discourse Analysis, and Activist Research*. New York: Routledge.

———. Forthcoming. "Policing the Borders in the Heartland." In *International Migration and Human Rights: The Global Repercussions of U.S. Policy*, edited by Samuel Martínez. Berkeley: University of California Press.

Nash, June, and Helen I. Safa, eds. 1986. *Women and Change in Latin America: New Directions in Sex and Class*. South Hadley, MA: Bergin & Garvey.

Nelson, Barbara. 1984. "Women's Poverty and Women's Citizenship: Some Political Consequences of Economic Marginality." *Signs: Journal of Women in Culture and Society* 19(2): 209–31.

Nolan, Mary Lee, and Sideny Nolan. 1988. "The Evolution of Tourism in Twentieth-Century Mexico." *Journal of the West* 27(4): 14–26.

Orloff, Ann Shola. 1993. "Gender and the Social Rights of Citizenship: The Comparative Analysis of Gender Relations and Welfare States." *American Sociological Review* 58: 303–28.

O'Rourke, David. K. 1998. "Our War with Mexico: Rereading Guadalupe Hidalgo." *Commonweal* 125(5): 8–9.

Oxnam, G. Bromley. 1970 [1920]. *The Mexican in Los Angeles: Los Angeles City Survey*. San Francisco: R and E Research Associates.

Pateman, Carol. 1988. *The Sexual Contract*. Stanford, CA: Stanford University Press.

———. 1992. "Equality, Difference, Subordination: The Politics of Motherhood and Women's Citizenship." Pp. 17–31 in *Beyond Equality and Difference: Citizenship, Feminist Politics, and Female Subjectivity*, edited by Gisela Bock and Susan James. New York: Routledge.

Paternostro, Silvana. 1998. *In The Land of God and Man: Confronting Our Sexual Culture*. New York: Dutton.

Patton, Cindy. 2002. "Stealth Bombers of Desire: The Globalization of 'Alterity' in Emerging Democracies." Pp. 195–218 in *Queer Globalizations: Citizenship and the Afterlife of Colonialism*, edited by Arnaldo Ctuz-Malavé and Martin F. Manalansan IV. New York: New York University Press.

Patton, Cindy, and Benigno Sánchez-Eppler, eds. 2000. *Queer Diasporas*. Durham, NC: Duke University Press.

Paur, Jasbir Kaur. 2002. Queer Tourism: Geographies of Globalization. Special issue of GLQ: A Journal of Lesbian and Gay Studies 8(1): 1–2.

Pedraza, Silvia. 1991. "Women and Migration: The Social Consequences of Gender." *Annual Review of Sociology* 17: 303–26.

Pellegrini, Ann. 2002. "Consuming Lifestyle: Commodity Capitalism and Transformations in Gay Identity." Pp. 134–48 in *Queer Globalizations: Citizenship and the Afterlife of Colonialism*, edited by Arnaldo Cruz-Malave and Martin F. Manalansan IV. New York: New York University Press.

Peña, Manuel. 1991. "Class, Gender, and Machismo: The 'Treacherous-Woman' Folklore of Mexican Male Workers." *Gender & Society* 5(1): 30–46.

Peña, Susana. 2004. *Pájaration* and Transculturation: Language and Meaning in Miami's Cuban American Gay Worlds." Pp. 231–50 in *Speaking in Queer Tongues*, edited by William L. Leap and Tom Boellsorff. Urbana: University of Illinois Press.

———. 2005. "Mariel and Cuban American Gay Male Experience and Representation." Pp. 125–45 in *Queer Migrations: Sexuality, U.S. Citizenship, and Border Crossings*, edited by Eithne Luibhéid and Lionel Cantú, Jr. Minneapolis: University of Minnesota Press.

———. 2007a. "Latina/o Sexualities in Motion." In *Final Report to the Ford Foundation by the Latina/o Sexualities Research Agenda Project Board*. New York: Ford Foundation.

———. 2007b. "'Obvious Gays' and the State Gaze: Cuban Gay Visibility and U.S. Immigration Policy during the 1980 Mariel Boatlift." *Journal of the History of Sexuality* 16(3): 482–514.

Phelan, Shane. 2001. *Sexual Strangers: Gays, Lesbians, and Dilemmas of Citizenship*. Philadelphia: Temple University Press.

Piore, Michael J. 1979. *Birds of Passage: Migrant Labor in Industrial Societies*. Cambridge, UK: Cambridge University Press.

Pleck, Joseph. 1981. *The Myth of Masculinity*. Cambridge, MA: MIT Press.

———. 1993. "Are 'Family-Supportive' Employer Policies Relevant to Men?" Pp. 217–37 in *Men, Work, and Family,* edited by Jane C. Hood. Newbury Park, CA: Sage.

Portes, Alejandro. 1996. *Immigrant America: A Portrait.* 2d ed. Berkeley: University of California Press.

———, ed. 1995. *The Economic Sociology of Immigration: Essays on Networks, Ethnicity, and Entrepreneurship.* New York: Russell Sage Foundation.

Portes, Alejandro, and Jozsef Borocz. 1989. "Contemporary Immigration: Theoretical Perspectives on Its Determinants and Modes of Incorporation." *International Migration Review* 23: 606–30.

Portes, Alejandro, and Rubén G. Rumbaut. 1990. *Immigrant America: A Portrait.* Berkeley: University of California Press.

———. 1996. *Immigrant American: A Portrait.* 2d ed. Berkeley: University of California Press.

Portes, Alejandro, and Alex Stepick. 1993. *City on the Edge: The Transformation of Miami.* Berkeley: University of California Press.

Prieur, Annick. 1998. *Mema's House, Mexico City: On Transvestites, Queens, and Machos.* Chicago: University of Chicago Press.

———. 1990. *The World Labour Market: A History of Migration.* London: Zed.

Pronger, Brian. 1990. "Gay Jocks: A Phenomenology of Gay Men in Athletics." Pp. 141–52 in *Sport, Men, and the Gender Order,* edited by Michael A. Messner and Don F. Sabo. Champaign, IL: Human Kinetics.

Prus, Robert. 1996. *Symbolic Interaction and Ethnographic Research: Intersubjectivity and the Study of Human Lived Experience.* Albany: State University of New York.

Queer Immigration (QI). 1995. "Alla Pitcherskaia vs. U.S. Board of Immigration Appeals." *Queer Resource Directory.* [No specific date retrieved available, resource directory not online as of this printing.] (See http://www.qrd.org/www/world/ immigration/index.html.)

Quiroga, José. 2000. *Tropics of Desire: Interventions from Queer Latino America.* New York: New York University Press.

Rabin, Joan S. 1987. "Two-paycheck Families: Psychological Responses to Social Change." Pp. 193–210 in *Current Conceptions of Sex Roles and Sex Typing: Theory and Research,* edited by D. Bruce Carter. New York: Praeger.

Rafael Alarcón, Jorge Durand, and Humberto Gonzalez. 1987. *Return to Aztlán: The Social Process of International Migration from Western Mexico.* Berkeley: University of California Press.

Ramos, Juanita, ed. *Companeras: Latina Lesbians.* New York: Latina Lesbian History Project.

Randazzo, Timothy. 2005. "Social and Legal Barriers: Sexual Orientation and Asylum in the United States." Pp. 30–60 in *Queer Migrations: Sexuality, U.S. Citizenship, and Border Crossing,* edited by Eithne Luibhéid and Lionel Cantú. Minneapolis: University of Minnesota Press.

Redding, Andrew A. 1995. "Perspective Series: Mexico: Democracy and Human Rights." Washington, DC: U.S. Department Of Justice.

———. 1998. *Mexico: Treatment of Homosexuals.* Washington, DC: U.S. Department of Justice.

Reddy, Chandan. 1998. "Home, Houses, Nonidentity: Paris Is Burning." Pp. 355–79 in *Burning Down the House: Recycling Domesticity,* edited by Rosemary Marangoly George. Boulder, CO: Westview Press.

Reiss, Albert J. Jr. 1961. "The Social Integration of Queers and Peers." *Social Problems* 9: 102–20.

Rhode, Deborah, ed. 1990. *Theoretical Perspectives on Sexual Difference.* New Haven, CT: Yale University Press.

Robertson, Roland. 1990. "Mapping the Global Condition: Globalization as the Central Concept." *Theory, Culture & Society* 7: 15–30.

Robinson, William I. 1992. "The Global Economy and the Latino Populations in the U.S.: A World Systems Approach." *Critical Sociology* 19(2): 29–59.

Rodríguez, Juana María. 2003. *Queer Latinidad: Identity Practices, Discursive Spaces.* New York: New York University Press.

Romero, Héctor Manuel. 1986. "Nada es indiferente al turismo." P. 142 in *Enciclopedia Mexicano del Turismo: Temática socioeconómica de turismo* [The Encyclopedia of Mexican Tourism: The Socioeconomic Subject of Tourism], Vol. 3. Mexico, DF: Editorial LIMUSA. (Author's translation.)

Roopnarine, Jaipaul L., and Nina S. Mounts. 1987. "Current Theoretical Issues in Sex Roles and Sex Typing." Pp. 7–31 in *Current Conceptions of Sex Roles and Sex Typing: Theory and Research*, edited by D. Bruce Carter. New York: Praeger.

Rosaldo, Renato. 1997. "Cultural Citizenship, Inequality, and Multiculturalism." Pp. 27–38 in *Latino Cultural Citizenship*, edited by William C. V. Flores and Rina Benmayor. Boston: Beacon Press.

Roscoe, Bill, and Stephen O. Murray, eds. 1998. *Boy-Wives and Female Husbands: Studies in African Homosexualities.* New York: St. Martin's Press.

Rose, Gillian. 1993. *Feminism and Geography: The Limits of Geographical Knowledge.* Minneapolis: University of Minnesota Press.

Rosenbloom, Rachel. 1995. *Unspoken Rules: Sexual Orientation and Women's Human Rights.* New York: Continuum International Publishing Group.

Rostow, Ann. 2005. "Mexican Gay Man Gets U.S. Asylum." Gay.com, August 15 (http://www.gay.com/news/article. html?2005/08/15/5). Retrieved: February 23, 2008.

Rotundo, E. Anthony. 1994. *American Manhood: Transformations in Masculinity from the Revolution to the Modern Era.* New York: Basic Books.

Rubenstein, William B. 1993. *Lesbians, Gay Men, and the Law.* New York: Norton.

Rubin, Gayle. 1992 [1984]. "Thinking Sex: Notes for a Radical Theory of the Politics of Sexuality." Pp. 3–44 in *The Lesbian and Gay Studies Reader*, edited by Henry Abelove, Michéle Aina Barale, and David M. Halperin. New York: Routledge.

Said, Edward W. 1978. *Orientalism*. New York: Pantheon Books.

Saldaña, Delia H. 1994. "Acculturative Stress: Minority Status and Distress." *Hispanic Journal of Behavioral Sciences* 16: 116–28.

Salgado de Snyder, V. Nelly, Richard C. Cervantes, and Amado M. Padilla. 1990. "Gender and Ethnic Differences in Psychosocial Stress among Hispanics." *Sex Roles* 22: 441–53.

Sánchez-Crispín, Álvaro, and Álvaro Lopez-Lopez. 1997. "Gay Male Places of Mexico City." Pp. 197–212 in *Queers in Space: Communities, Public Places, Sites of Resistance*, edited by Gordon Brent Ingram, Anne-Marie Bouthillette, and Yolanda Retter. Seattle: Bay Press.

Sandoval, Chela. 2002. "Dissident Globalizations, Emancipatory Methods, Social-Erotics." Pp. 20–32 in *Queer Globalizations: Citizenship and the Afterlife of Colonialism*, edited by Arnaldo Cruz-Malavé and Martin F. Manalansan IV. New York: New York University Press.

Sarvasy, Wendy. 1994. "From Man and Philanthropic Service to Feminist Social Citizenship." *Social Politics* 1(3): 306–25.

Sarvasy, Wendy, and Birte Siim. 1994. "Gender, Transitions to Democracy, and Citizenship." *Social Politics* 1(3): 249–55.

Sassen, Saskia. 1988. *The Mobility of Labor and Capital*. Cambridge, UK: Cambridge University Press.

———. 1991. *The Global City*. Princeton, NJ: Princeton University Press.

Sassen-Koob, Saskia. 1982. "Recomposition and Peripheralization at the Core." Pp. 88–100 in *The New Nomads*, edited by Marlene Dixon and Susanne Jonas. San Francisco: Synthesis.

Schaefer, Claudia. 1996. *Danger Zones: Homosexuality, National Identity, and Mexican Culture*. Tucson: University of Arizona Press.

Schrag, Philip G. 2000. *A Well-Founded Fear: The Congressional Battle to Save Political Asylum in America*. New York: Routledge.

Scott, Joan W. 1992. "Experience." Pp. 22–40 in *Feminists Theorize the Political*, edited by Judith Butler and Joan W. Scott. New York: Routledge.

Scott, John. 1995. *Sociological Theory: Contemporary Debates*. Aldershot, UK: Edward Elger.

Sears, Clare. 2008. "All That Glitters: Trans-ing California's Gold Rush Migration." *GLQ: A Journal of Lesbian and Gay Studies* 14(2–3): 383–402.

Sedgwick, Eve K. 1990. *Epistemology of the Closet*. Los Angeles: University of California Press.

Seidman, Steven. 2002. *Beyond the Closet: The Transformation of Gay and Lesbian Life*. New York: Routledge.

———, ed. 1996. *Queer Theory/Sociology*. Cambridge, MA: Blackwell.

Selden, Raman, and Peter Widdowson. 1993. *A Reader's Guide to Contemporary Literary Theory*. Lexington: University Press of Kentucky.

Shah, Nayan. 2001. *Contagious Divides: Epidemics and Race in San Francisco's Chinatown.* Berkeley: University of California Press, 2001.

Shelton, Beth Anne, and Daphne John. 1993. "Ethnicity, Race, and Difference: A Comparison of White, Black, and Hispanic Men's Household Labor Time." Pp. 131–50 in *Men, Work, and Family,* edited by Jane C. Hood. Newbury Park, CA: Sage.

Shotter, John. 1993. *Psychology and Citizenship: Identity and Belonging.* London: Sage.

Singer, Bennett L., and David Deschamps. 1994. *Gay and Lesbian Stats: A Pocket guide of Facts and Figures.* New York: New Press.

Skocpol, Theda. 1992. *Protecting Soldiers and Mothers: The Political Origins of Social Policy in the United States.* Cambridge, MA: Harvard University Press.

Smith, Dorothy E. 1987. *The Everyday World as Problematic: A Feminist Sociology.* Boston: Northeastern University Press.

———. 1990a. *The Conceptual Practices of Power: A Feminist Sociology of Knowledge.* Toronto: University of Toronto Press.

———. 1990b. *Texts, Facts, and Femininity: Exploring the Relations of Ruling.* London: Routledge.

———. 1998. *Writing the Social World.* Toronto: University of Toronto Press.

Smith, Joan, Immanuel Wallerstein, Maria del Carmen, and Mark Beittel, eds. 1992. *Creating and Transforming Households: The Constraints of the World-Economy.* Cambridge, MA: University Press.

Smith, Michael Peter, and Matte Bakker. *Citizenship across Borders: The Political Transnationalism of El Migrante.* Ithaca, NY: Cornell University Press.

Smith, Paul Julian, and Emilie L. Bergmann. 1995. "Introduction." Pp. 1–14 in *¿Entiedes? Queer Readings, Hispanic Writings,* edited by Emilie L. Bergmann and Paul Julian Smith. Durham, NC: Duke University Press.

Soja, Edward W. 1989. *Postmodern Geographies: The Reassertion of Space in Critical Social Theory.* London: Verso.

———. 1996. *Thirdspace: Journeys to Los Angeles and Other Real-and-Imagined Places.* Cambridge, MA: Blackwell.

Somerville, Siobhan B. 2005. "Sexual Aliens and the Racialized State: A Queer Reading of the 1952 U.S. Immigration and Nationality Act." Pp. 75–91 in *Queer Migrations: Sexuality, U.S. Citizenship, and Border Crossings,* edited by Eithne Luibhéid and Lionel Cantú, Jr. Minneapolis: University of Minnesota Press.

Soysal, Yasemin Nuhoglu. 1994. *Migrants and Postnational Membership in Europe.* Chicago: University of Chicago Press.

Stark, Oded. 1991. *The Migration of Labor.* Cambridge, MA: Blackwell.

State of California, Department of Finance. 1996a. *Race/Ethnic Population Estimates: Components of Change by Race, 1990–1995.* Sacramento: State of California (http:// dof.ca.gov.html/Demograp/race-eth.htm).

————. 1996b. *Legal Immigration to California by County: Federal Fiscal year (FFY) 1990–1995*. Sacramento: State of California (http://www.dof.ca.gov. html/ Demograp/entyimm.htm).

Stavans, Ilan. 1995. *The Hispanic Condition: Reflections on Culture and Identity in America*. New York: HarperCollins.

Strongman, Roberto. 2002. "Syncretic Religion and Dissident Sexuality." In *Queer Globalizations: Citizenship and the Afterlife of Colonialism*, edited by A. Cruz-Malavé and M. F. Manalansan. New York: New York University Press.

Suárez-Orozco, Marcelo M. 2005. "Everything You Ever Wanted to Know about Immigration but Were Afraid to Ask." Pp. 51–67 in *Passing Lines: Sexuality and Immigration*, edited by Brad Epps, Keja Valens, and Bill Johnson González. Cambridge, MA: Harvard University Press.

————, ed. 1999. *Crossings: Mexican Immigration in Interdisciplinary Perspectives*. Cambridge, MA: Harvard University Press.

Suárez-Orozco, Marcelo M., and Mariela Páez, eds. 2002. *Latinos: Remaking America*. Berkeley: University of California Press.

Subero, Gustavo. 2008. "Fear of the Trannies: On Filmic Phobia and Transvestism in the New Latin American Cinema." *Latin American Research Review* 43(2): 159–79.

Taylor, Clark L. 1995. "Legends, Syncretism, and Continuing Echoes of Homosexuality from Pre-Columbian and Colonial México." Pp. 80–99 in *Latin American Male Homosexualities*, edited by Stephen O. Murray. Albuquerque: University of New Mexico Press.

Tomlinson, J. 1999. *Globalization and Culture*. Chicago: University of Chicago Press.

Torpey, John. 1998. "Coming and Going: On the State Monopolization of the Legitimate Means of Movement." Working Paper, Center for the Study of Democracy, University of California, Irvine.

Trevino, Joseph, and Patrick J. McDonnell. 1999. "More Seek Asylum to Flee Anti-Gay Persecution." *Los Angeles Times*, March 13, B1.

Troiden, Richard R. 1988. *Gay and Lesbian Identity: A Sociological Analysis*. Dix Hills, NY: General Hall.

Truong, Thanh-Dam. 1990. *Sex, Money, and Morality: Prostitution and Tourism in Southeast Asia*. Atlantic Highlands, NJ: Zed.

Turner, William B. 2000. *A Genealogy of Queer Theory*. Philadelphia: Temple University Press.

Tyler, Forrest B., Sandra L. Tyler, Anthony Tommasello, and Yuxin Zhang. 1992. "Psychosocial Characteristics of Marginal Immigrant Latino Youth." *Youth & Society* 24: 92–115.

U.S. Census Bureau. 1992. *Poverty in the United States: 1991*. Current Population Reports, Consumer.

———. 1993a. *1990 Census of Population: Persons of Hispanic Origin in the United States*. 1990 CP-3-3: 153–90.

———. 1993b. *Hispanic Americans Today*. Current Population Reports, Population Characteristics, P23–183. Washington, DC: U.S. Government Printing Office.

———. 1994. *The Hispanic Population in the United States, 1993*. Current Population Reports, Population Characteristics, P20475. Washington, DC: U.S. Government Printing Office.

———. 2001. *2000 Characteristics of Population and Housing*. Profiles of General Demographic Characteristics, 2000. Washington, DC: U.S. Government Printing Office.

———. 2004. *Hispanic and Asian Americans Increasing Faster Than Overall Population*. Washington, DC: U.S. Department of Commerce.

U.S. Census Bureau News. 2008. *U.S. Hispanic Population Surpasses 45 Million, Now 15 Percent of Total*. Washington, DC: U.S. Department of Commerce.

U.S. Immigration and Naturalization Service, Statistical Yearbook of the Immigration and Naturalization Service. 1995. Washington, DC: Government Printing Office.

Valentine, David. 2003. "I Went to Bed with My Own Kind Once: The Erasure of Desire in the Name of Identity." *Language & Communication* 23: 123–38.

———. 2007. *Imagining Transgender: An Ethnography of a Category*. Durham, NC: Duke University Press.

Valocchi, Stephen. 2005. "Not Yet Queer Enough: The Lessons of Queer Theory for the Sociology of Gender and Sexuality." *Gender & Society* 19(6): 750–70.

Vidal-Ortiz, Salvador. 2004. "On Being a White Person of Color: Using Autoethnography to Understand Puerto Ricans' Racialization." *Qualitative Sociology* 27(2): 179–203.

———. 2005. "Sexuality and Gender in Santería: LGBT Identities at the Crossroads of Religious Practices and Beliefs." Pp. 115–37 in *Gay Religion*, edited by Scott Thumma and Edward R. Gray. Walnut Creek, CA: AltaMira Press.

Vila, Pablo. 2000. *Crossing Borders, Reinforcing Borders: Social Categories, Metaphors, and Narrative Identities on the U.S.-Mexico Border*. Austin: University of Texas Press.

———. 2003. "The Limits of American Border Theory." Pp. 306–41 in *Ethnography at the Border*, ed. Pablo Vila. Minneapolis: University of Minnesota Press.

———. 2005. *Border Identifications: Narratives of Religion, Gender, and Class on the U.S.-Mexico Border*. Austin: University of Texas Press.

———, ed. 2003. *Ethnography at the Border*. Minneapolis: University of Minnesota Press.

Wakeford, Nina. 2002. "New Technologies and 'Cyber-queer' Research." Pp. 115–44 in *Handbook of Lesbian and Gay Studies*, edited by Diane Richardson and Steve Seidman. London: Sage.

Wallerstein, Immanuel. 1974. *The Modern World System I: Capitalist Agriculture and the Origins of the European World-Economy in the Sixteenth Century.* San Diego, CA: Academic Press.

———. 1991. *Geopolitics and Geoculture: Essays on the Changing World-System.* Cambridge, MA: Harvard University Press.

———, ed. 1980. *Studies of the Modern World-System.* New York: Academic Press.

Warner, Michael. 1993. *Fear of a Queer Planet: Queer Politics and Social Theory.* Minneapolis: University of Minnesota Press.

Warren, Jenifer. 1994. "Asylum OK'd on Basis of Homosexuality (U.S. Immigration and Naturalization Service Grants Asylum to Gay Mexican Man)." *Los Angeles Times*, March 25, A3.

Weeks, Jeffrey. 1977. *Coming Out: Homosexual Politics in Britain from the Nineteenth Century to the Present.* London: Quartet.

———. 1993. *Sexuality and Its Discontents: Meanings, Myths, and Modern Sexualities.* London: Routledge.

Wen, Patricia, and Frank Phillops. 2006. "Bishops to Oppose Adoption by Gays: Exemption Bid Seen from Antibias Laws." *Boston Globe*, February 1 (http://www.boston.com/news/local/articles/2006/02/16/bishops_to_oppose_adoption_by_gays). Retrieved: June 11, 2008.

Weston, Kath. 1991. *Families We Choose: Lesbians, Gays, Kinship.* New York: Columbia University Press.

Williams, Norma. 1990. *The Mexican American Family: Tradition and Change.* Dix Hills, NY: General Hall.

———. 1993. "Elderly Mexican American Men: Work and Family Patterns." Pp. 68–86 in *Men, Work, and Family,* edited by Jane C. Hood. Newbury Park, CA: Sage.

Wilson, Carter. 1995. *Hidden in the Blood: A Personal Investigation of AIDS in the Yucatán.* New York: Columbia University Press.

Windle, Michael S. 1987. "Measurement Issues in Sex Roles and Sex Typing." In *Current Conceptions of Sex Roles and Sex Typing: Theory and Research,* edited by D. Bruce Carter. New York: Praeger.

Wockner, Rex. 1997a. "Guadalajara Mayor Seemingly Bans Gays." International News #156, April 23 (http://www.qrd/world/ wockner/news.briefs/156-04.23.97). Retrieved: November 21, 2007.

———. 1997b. "Crowds Cheer March on Tijuana Strip" (http://.qrd.org/qrd/world/wockner/baja.news/crowds.cheer.tijuana.pride.march-07.06.97). Retrieved: November 21, 2007.

Wood, Charles, H. 1982. "Equilibrium and Historical Structural Perspectives on Migration." *International Migration Review* 16(2): 298–319.

Wright, Timothy. 2005. "Gay Organizations, NGOs, and the Globalization of Sexual Identity: The Case of Bolivia." Pp. 279–94 in *Same-sex Cultures and Sexualities: An Anthropological Reader,* edited by Jennifer Robertson. Cambridge, MA: Blackwell.

Yamamoto, Ryoko. 2007. "Crossing Boundaries: Legality and the Power of the State in Unauthorized Migration." *Sociology Compass* 1(1): 95–110.

Yans-McLaughlin, ed. 1990. *Immigration Reconsidered: History, Sociology, and Politics.* New York: Oxford University Press.

Yarbro-Bejarano, Yvonne. 1997. "Crossing the Border with Chabela Vargas: A Chicana Femme's Tribute." Pp. 33–43 in *Sex and Sexuality in Latin America,* edited by Daniel Balderston and Donna J. Guy. New York: New York University Press.

Young, Robert J.C. 1995. *Colonial Desire: Hybridity in Theory, Culture and Race.* New York: Routledge.

Yuval-Davis, Nira. 1991. "The Citizenship Debate: Women, Ethnic Processes, and the State." *Feminist Review* 39: 58–68.

Zavella, Patricia. 1997. "Playing with Fire': The Gendered Construction of Chicana/Mexicana Sexuality." Pp. 394–409 in the *Gender/Sexuality Reader,* edited by Roger N. Lancaster and Micaela Di Leonardo. London: Routledge.

———. 2003. "Talking Sex: Chicanas and Mexicanas Theorize about Silences and Sexual Pleasures." Pp. 228–53 in *A Critical Reader: Chicana Feminism,* edited by Gabriella F. Arrenondo, Aida Hurtado, Norma Klahn, Olga Najera-Ramirez, and Patricia Zavella. Durham, NC: Duke University Press.

Zavella, Patricia, and Xóchitl Castañeda. 2005. "Sexuality and Risks: Gendered Discourses about Virginity and Disease among Young Women of Mexican Origin." *Latino Studies* 3(2): 226–38.

Index

About the Editors

NANCY A. NAPLES is Professor of Women's Studies and Sociology at the University of Connecticut. She is the author of *Feminism and Method: Ethnography, Discourse Analysis, and Activist Research* and *Grassroots Warriors: Activist Mothering, Community Work, and the War on Poverty.* The latter book was a finalist for the C. Wright Mills Award, Society for the Study of Social Problems (1999). Her edited books include *Community Activism and Feminist Politics: Organizing across Race, Class, and Gender* (Routledge, 1998); *Teaching Feminist Activism: Strategies from the Field,* coedited with Karen Bojar (Routledge, 2002); and *Women's Activism and Globalization: Linking Local Struggles and Transnational Politics,* coedited with Manisha Desai (Routledge, 2002). Her next book, *Restructuring the Heartland: Racialization and the Social Regulation of Citizenship,* investigates the link between global economic change and community-based social restructuring. Her research has been published in numerous journals, including *Journal of Latino/a-Latin American Studies; Signs: Journal of Women in Culture and Society; National Women's Studies Association Journal; Women & Politics; Social Politics;* and *Feminist Economics.*

SALVADOR VIDAL-ORTIZ is Assistant Professor of Sociology at American University. His 2005 dissertation, "'Sexuality' and 'Gender' in Santería: Towards a Queer of-Color Critique in the Study of Religion," received the 2006 Paul Monette-Roger Horowitz Dissertation Prize, awarded by the Center for Lesbian and Gay Studies of the City University of New York. He has published over a dozen essays, articles, and book chapters on race and ethnic studies, Puerto Rican/Latino studies, transsexuality and transgender studies, and gender and sexuality. He is currently preparing a book manuscript tentatively titled "An Instrument of the *Orishas*: Racialized Sexual Minorities in *Santería.*"